Country Locator for Volume 6

ITALY, MALTA, AND SAN MARINO

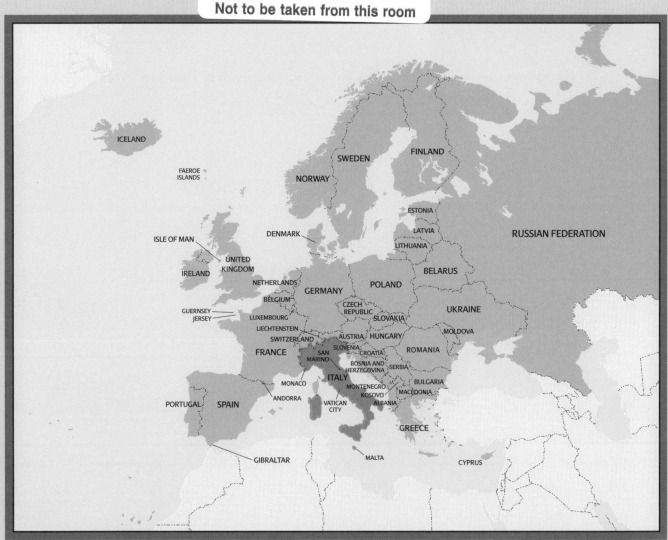

The following countries, dependencies, and states are covered in the thirteen-volume encyclopedia *World and Its Peoples: Europe*. Detailed discussion of the following can be found in the volumes indicated in parentheses.

EUROPE

6

ITALY, MALTA, AND SAN MARINO

Marshall Cavendish
Reference
New York

SET CONSULTANTS
Jeremy Black, Department of History, School of Humanities and Social Sciences, University of Exeter, England

Pat Morris, formerly School of Biological Sciences, Royal Holloway, University of London, Egham, England

John Harrington, Department of Geography, Kansas State University, Manhattan, Kansas

Ceri Peach, School of Geography, University of Oxford, England

John Rennie Short, Department of Geography and Public Policy, University of Maryland, Baltimore

VOLUME CONSULTANTS
Anna Bull, Professor of Italian History and Politics, Department of European Studies and Modern Languages, University of Bath, England

Ciro Paoletti, Associazione Studi Storici e Militari, Ostia-Rome/State University, La Sapienza, Rome, Italy

Henry Frendo, Institute of Maltese Studies, University of Malta, Msida

WRITERS
Rachel Bean, Church Stretton, Shropshire, England

Stefano Bruno, Dipartimento Meccanica, University of Calabria, Cosenza, Italy

Helen Doe, Centre for Maritime Historical Studies, University of Exeter, England

Michelle Felton, School of Geographical Sciences, University of Bristol, England

Henry Frendo, Institute of Maltese Studies, University of Malta, Msida

Eva Garau, Italian Section, Department of European Studies and Modern Languages, University of Bath, England

Gregory Hanlon, Department of History, Faculty of Arts and Social Sciences, Dalhousie University, Halifax, Nova Scotia, Canada

John Haywood, History Department, Lancaster University, England

John Plowright, Master of the Scholars, Repton School, Derby, England

John Swift, Division of History and Geography, Faculty of Education, University of Cumbria, Carlisle, England

For **MARSHALL CAVENDISH**
Publisher: Paul Bernabeo
Project Editor: Stephanie Driver
Production Manager: Alan Tsai
Indexer: Cynthia Crippen, AEIOU, Inc.

For **BROWN REFERENCE GROUP**
Consultant Editor: Clive Carpenter
Deputy Editors: Graham Bateman, Derek Hall, Peter Lewis, Briony Ryles
Cartography: Encompass Graphics Ltd
Picture Research: Martin Anderson, Andrew Webb
Managing Editor: Tim Harris

For **A GOOD THING, INC.**
Page Production: Howard Petlack

Website: www.marshallcavendish.us

This publication represents the opinions and views of the authors based on personal experience, knowledge, and research. The information in this book serves as a general guide only. The authors and publisher have used their best efforts in preparing this book and disclaim liability rising directly and indirectly from the use and application of this book.

Other Marshall Cavendish Offices:
Marshall Cavendish Ltd. 5th Floor, 32-38 Saffron Hill, London EC1N 8 FH, UK • Marshall Cavendish International (Asia) Private Limited, 1 New Industrial Road, Singapore 536196 • Marshall Cavendish International (Thailand) Co Ltd. 253 Asoke, 12th Flr, Sukhumvit 21 Road, Klongtoey Nua, Wattana, Bangkok 10110, Thailand • Marshall Cavendish (Malaysia) Sdn Bhd, Times Subang, Lot 46, Subang Hi-Tech Industrial Park, Batu Tiga, 40000 Shah Alam, Selangor Darul Ehsan, Malaysia

Marshall Cavendish is a trademark of Times Publishing Limited

All websites were available and accurate when this book was sent to press.

Library of Congress Cataloging-in-Publication Data

World and its peoples. Europe.
   p. cm.
   Includes bibliographical references and index.
   ISBN 978-0-7614-7883-6 (set : alk. paper) -- ISBN 978-0-7614-7884-3 (v. 1 : alk. paper) -- ISBN 978-0-7614-7887-4 (v. 2 : alk. paper) -- ISBN 978-0-7614-7889-8 (v. 3 : alk. paper) -- ISBN 978-0-7614-7890-4 (v. 4 : alk. paper) -- ISBN 978-0-7614-7892-8 (v. 5 : alk. paper) -- ISBN 978-0-7614-7893-5 (v. 6 : alk. paper) -- ISBN 978-0-7614-7894-2 (v. 7 : alk. paper) -- ISBN 978-0-7614-7896-6 (v. 8 : alk. paper) -- ISBN 978-0-7614-7897-3 (v. 9 : alk. paper) -- ISBN 978-0-7614-7900-0 (v. 10 : alk. paper) -- ISBN 978-0-7614-7902-4 (v. 11 : alk. paper) -- ISBN 978-0-7614-7903-1 (v. 12 : alk. paper) -- ISBN 978-0-7614-7904-8 (v. 13 : alk. paper)
   1. Europe--Geography--Encyclopedias. 2. Europe--Civilization--Encyclopedias. 3. Europe--History--Encyclopedias. I. Marshall Cavendish Corporation. II. Title: Europe.
   D900.W67 2009
   940.03--dc22
                                                    2009004321

12 11 10 09 1 2 3 4 5

Printed in Malaysia

Front cover: David Fraser/Danita Delimont; **Shutterstock**: Denis Babenko (bl), Alexey Arkhipov (br).
dreamstime: Daniel Budiman 802, Javarman 808, W.kaveney 822; **iStockphoto**: Kermarrec Aurelien 820, Anne Clark 814, Michael O Fiachra 824, Gaspare Messina 741, Lidian Neeleman 805, David Pullicino 734; **photos.com**: 743, 745, 752, 755, 758, 764, 767, 768, 774, 778, 788, 789, 800, 804, 844, 849, 858; **Robert Hunt Library**: 792, 796, 811; **Shutterstock**: 727, 728, Cornel Achierei 829, 848, Albo 813, Georgios Alexandris 763, Arly 747, Alexey Arkhipov 834, Danilo Ascione 830, Diego Barucco 732, Claudio Bertoloni 735, Ivan Cholakov 729, Vladimir Daragan 721, Drimi 815, Gasper Furman 816, Gertjan Hooijer 838, jbor 812, Pavel K 854, Jonathan Larsen 832, Cecilia Lim H M 842, Alexander Maksimenko 840, 847, William Attard McCarthy 846, Ana Menéndez 831, Clara Natoli 749, Mikhail Nekrasov 852, 853, nhtg 806, Knud Nielson 733, ollirg 836, Thomas M Perkins 807, Pierdelune 825, Kenneth V Pilon 817, Julia R. 738, Natallia Rasadka 737, M Rohana 839, Bruce Shippee 766, Perov Stanislav 833, Manuela Szymaniak 739, Milan Vasicek 859, Asier Villafranca 726, Tomasz Wieja 809, witchcraft 803; **Wikimedia Commons**: 762, Daderot 753, Dagos 790, Giovanni Dall'Orto 779, Generale Lee 756.

CONTENTS

Geography and Climate

The Italian peninsula is one of three major European landmasses that jut southward into the Mediterranean Sea. Italy includes many islands in the Mediterranean, including the large islands of Sardinia and Sicily. Farther south, the islands of Malta form a separate nation, and within the peninsula are two microstates, San Marino and the Vatican City (or the Holy See).

THE TIBER RIVER

Flowing through Rome, the Italian national capital, the Tiber River (in Italian, Tevere) is the third-longest river in Italy, some 252 miles (405 km) long. The waterway rises on Mount Fumaiolo in the border district between the Tuscan and Emilian Apennines. In its upper reaches, the Tiber flows through gorges, and in its middle course approaching Rome the river runs through a wide valley. South of Rome, the course becomes braided (has more than one channel), with the Fiumicino running north of the main distributary, the Fiumara. The Tiber enters the Tyrrhenian Sea through a delta near Ostia. Since Roman times, the mouth of the river has advanced some 2 miles (3 km), leaving the port of Ostia Antica inland. A strong northward current along the coast prevents the delta from forming more rapidly.

With a basin covering some 6,950 square miles (about 18,000 sq. km), the Tiber drains much of central western Italy. The waterway was important for navigation in Roman times, but progressive silting impeded passage for ships; although the river is still navigable for small craft as far inland as Rome, it is no longer of commercial significance. The Tiber was once prone to flooding, but the construction of high stone embankments in the late nineteenth century has since protected Rome and its environs from flooding.

THE PO RIVER

Italy's longest waterway, the Po River flows from the Cottian Alps eastward across northern Italy to the Adriatic Sea, a distance of 405 miles (652 km). The waterway drains the large Padan (or Padanian) Plain, which covers an area of some 27,100 square miles (nearly 70,200 sq. km). The fertile plain is one of Italy's most important agricultural regions and is also the main center of industry and population.

The Po descends from the Cottian Alps over rapids, tumbling toward the Piedmont lowlands. West of the city of Turin, the waterway suddenly veers northward to flow through the city, beyond which it receives the Dora Riparia tributary. Passing north of the foot of the Monferrato uplands, the Po flows out onto the plain, where it begins a meandering course. This middle section of the waterway is characterized by many bends and oxbow lakes, cut-off stretches of water that were once meanders of the main river.

This section of the Po has changed its course many times over centuries; the river marked the boundary between Lombardy to the north and Emilia Romagna to the south, and the boundary lines follow the historic rather than the present-day course of the river. The principal tributaries of the Po flow from the Alps southward to join the waterway along its north bank. From west to east, they include the Ticino, Adda, Oglio, and Mincio rivers. The tributaries that flow northward from the Apennines to join the Po along its south bank are much shorter and have a lesser volume of water and a considerable seasonal variation in flow. Although the waterway is navigable as far inland as Pavia, south of Milan, only small vessels can navigate its winding course, and the Po is of little commercial importance in modern times.

In the east, the Po enters the Adriatic Sea through a delta, which is formed from silt carried by the waterway. The delta, which has five main distributaries and many smaller channels, is extending outward by around 200 acres (some 80 hectares) a year. The principal distributary, the Po della Pila, has the greatest volume and is the only navigable channel in the delta. Immediately north of the delta, the Adige River enters the Adriatic.

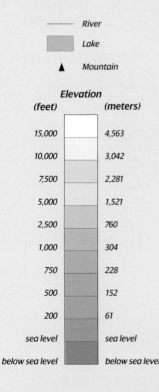

——	River	
▮	Lake	
▲	Mountain	

Elevation

(feet)	(meters)
15,000	4,563
10,000	3,042
7,500	2,281
5,000	1,521
2,500	760
1,000	304
750	228
500	152
200	61
sea level	sea level
below sea level	below sea level

SWITZERLAND

AUSTRIA

A L P S

Monte Bianco
de Courmayeur
15,616 ft

Monte
Rosa
15,203 ft

Lake
Maggiore

South
Tirol

Rhaetian
Alps

Dolomites

Adige

Julian Alps

SLOVENIA

Graian Alps

A L P S

Lake
Como

Lombardy

Lake
Iseo

Kras
Plateau

46°

Dora Riparia

Lake
Garda

Veneto

Cottian Alps

Piedmont

Ticino

Adda

Oglio

Mincio

Po

Po

Maira

Po Valley

Adige

Po
Delta

Gulf of
Venice

CROATIA

Liguria

Ligurian Apennines

Emilia Romagna

Reno

A P E N N I N E S

Maritime Alps

Gulf of
Genoa

Riviera di
Levante

FRANCE

44°

Riviera di Ponente

Tuscan Apennines

Rubicon

44°

SAN MARINO

MONACO

8°

Arno

Umbrian Apennines

Marche

Chienti

Adriatic
Sea

Ligurian
Sea

Capraia

Tuscany

Lake
Trasimeno

14°

Elba

Pianosa

Lake
Bolsena

Tiber

Abruzzi

Corsica
(FRANCE)

Montecristo

Giglio

Lake
Bracciano

Abruzzi Apennines

Tremiti

16°

42°

42°

VATICAN CITY

Lazio

Testa del
Gargano

Strait of Bonifacio

Caprera

Liri

Fortore

Molise

Asinara

8°

Ponza
Islands

Gulf of
Gaeta

Campanian Apennines

Volturno

Campania

Puglia

Mount Vesuvius
4,203 ft

18°

Sardinia

Ischia

Bradano

Salentina Peninsula

Tirso

Capri

Gulf of
Salerno

Lucanian Apennines

Basilicata

40°

Tyrrhenian
Sea

Cilento
Mountains

40°

San Pietro

Campidano
Plain

Gulf of
Taranto

Cape Santa
Maria di Léuca

18°

Sant'Antioco

Crati

Calabria

Strait of Otranto

Cape Teulada

Calabrian
Apennines

Cape Rizzuto

8°

Ustica

Lipari
Islands

Stromboli

Ionian
Sea

Strait of Messina

Egadi Islands

38°

Mount Etna
10,924 ft

38°

16°

Sicily

M e d i t e r r a n e a n

Salso

Strait of Sicily

Pantelleria

N

TUNISIA

Cape Passero

S e a

50   100 miles

36°

Gozo   Comino

36°

80   160 km

Pelagie
Islands

Malta

MALTA

Lampedusa

14°

The Land of Italy, Malta, and San Marino

Until the mid-nineteenth century, Italy was a geographical area rather than a country. The various regions had been separate countries or under the rule of outside powers, and the cultural and other differences that evolved over centuries reflect geographical and climatic differences. As a result, Italy has great diversity.

Italy comprises a long, relatively narrow peninsula, which, with the large southern island of Sicily, almost divides the Mediterranean basin in two. It is not by accident that Italy or Italian states have, at various times in history, dominated the Mediterranean. As well as the Italian Peninsula and Sicily, Italy also includes the island of Sardinia, other much smaller islands, an extensive lowland to the north of the peninsula, and the great arc of the Alps, which form a natural boundary between Italy and surrounding countries. The peninsula ends in the shape of a boot (the southern end is popularly referred to in Italian as *Lo Stivale*, meaning "the boot"), with the region of Calabria as the "toe" and Puglia as the "heel." The region includes three other small countries: the archipelago of Malta to the south of Sicily; the small republic of San Marino, enclaved in the Apennine Mountains of peninsular Italy; and the headquarters of the Roman Catholic Church, the Vatican City State, which is a tiny enclave within Rome, the Italian national capital. The Vatican is the world's smallest independent country.

From the Alpine crest in the north to the tip of Sicily in the south is a total distance of some 810 miles (1,300 km). Much of the nation is upland—around 35 percent is classified as mountainous and another 41 percent as hills. Lowland is restricted to the North Italian Plain and a series of discontinuous coastal plains in the Italian Peninsula, including the Tavoliere Plain in Puglia. Most of the Italian Peninsula comprises the Apennine Mountains, which run north-south from the Alps in the northwest region of Liguria to Calabria in the far south.

History, geography, climate, culture, and economics divide Italy into different regions, but a basic division into the north, central Italy, the south, and the islands is commonly recognized. The south and the islands are economically less developed than the rest of the country. Together, the south and the islands are called the Mezzogiorno (an Italian word meaning "midday," referring to the midday sun); by convention, the Mezzogiorno comprises the regions of Calabria, Basilicata, Puglia, Molise, Abruzzi, Campania, Sardinia, and Sicily. Northern Italy is the principal center of population, commerce, and industry in the country. Northern Italy is normally understood to mean the regions of Valle d'Aosta, Piedmont, Liguria, Lombardy, Trentino–Alto Adige/Südtirol, Venetia, Emilia Romagna, and Friuli–Venezia Giulia. A distinction is often made between the northwest—Valle d'Aosta, Piedmont, Liguria, Lombardy—and the northeast, the other regions of northern Italy. Central Italy comprises the regions of Marche, Umbria, Lazio, and Tuscany.

Combining geographical, cultural, economic, and traditional divisions, the following broad regions can be recognized: the Italian Alps; the North Italian Plain and northeast lowlands; central Italy; the peninsular Mezzogiorno; Sicily; and Sardinia.

THE ITALIAN ALPS

The Alps form a barrier between Italy and the rest of Europe, stretching in an arc from the Ligurian coast in northwest Italy through the Ligurian Alps and the Cottian and Graian Alps along the border with France. The Alpine chain then swings eastward, along the Swiss frontier, forming the Rhaetian Alps. To the east, the Dolomites, south of the Austrian border, are part of the Italian Alps, which end in the Julian Alps at the Slovene frontier.

The Ligurian Alps run east-west along the coast of Liguria, reaching a height of 8,698 feet (2,651 m). In the east, a relatively small gap, the Colle di Cadibona, separates the Ligurian Alps from the Apennines. The mountains run along the rocky coast, with only a few small areas of lowland. Along the center-east section of the Ligurian coast is Genoa, Italy's largest port, with transportation links inland through the Giovi Pass with the industrial regions of Piedmont and Lombardy, which lie north of the mountains. West along the Ligurian coast is the Italian Riviera, with several resorts, including San Remo and Imperia, in a region with a mild Mediterranean climate. The Ligurian Alps end in the west at the Col de Tende, north and west from which stretch the Maritime and Cottian Alps.

Lake Como was formed by an obstruction across a deep glaciated valley, which gives it narrow but long dimensions.

The Alpine chain in its western part includes the highest mountain peaks of western Europe, including Monte Rosa (Dufourspitze) at 15,203 feet (4,634 m) and Mont Blanc, at 15,771 feet (4,807 m). The highest point in Italy is a secondary peak of Mont Blanc (whose principal summit is in France), Monte Bianco de Courmayeur, at 15,616 feet (4,760 m). This section of the Italian Alps contains a number of hydroelectric power facilities, which provide power for the industries of Piedmont. It also contains Italy's smallest region, French-speaking Valle d'Aosta.

The central Alps form a high barrier that is broken by a small number of passes (including the Brenner Pass in the east), which are major routes between northern and Mediterranean Europe. Beyond the Brenner Pass, the Eastern Alps stretch as far as the lower Julian Alps and include the Dolomites, a high region of limestone peaks with 40 glaciers. The Dolomites are a major tourist region for skiing as well as summer vacations at resorts such as Cortina d'Ampezzo. The Adige Valley, running north toward the Brenner Pass, includes the major cities in the region, Bolzano and Trento. The upper Adige region, known as the South Tirol or Südtirol, is German-speaking.

Around the southern rim of the Alps are foothills that rise to around 8,200 feet (some 2,500 m) and descend to the North Italian Plain. In the east, limestone is widespread, and a karst landscape, an eroded limestone terrain characterized by caves and subterranean streams, has been formed. Where the foothills meet the plain south of the Central Alps is a string of lakes that formed in deeply eroded valleys. The shores of these lakes—from west to east, Lakes Maggiore, Lugano, Como, Iseo, and Garda—are lined by popular resorts.

THE NORTH ITALIAN PLAIN AND NORTHEAST LOWLANDS

Stretching from near Turin in the west to the Adriatic Sea in the east, the North Italian Plain occupies around 12 percent of the total land area of Italy. The Po River runs west to east through the center of the plain and is joined by major tributaries flowing from the Alps along its northern bank. The waterway gives its name to the lowland, which is also known as the Padan Plain or the Po Valley. Formed from alluvium eroded from the uplands, the plain is one of the most fertile regions—and also the most heavily populated—in Italy. Physically, the plain has several different terrains, including terraces in the west and northwest, where clay ridges alternate with gravels and sands—this section is the least productive part of the North Italian Plain. To the south and east, more fertile soils support pastures for cattle and farmland that produces grapes, cereals (corn and wheat), sugar beets, and fruits. In the east, toward the Adriatic, more boggy areas surround Venice.

The western part of the plain is the Piedmont (literally, "mountain foot") Plain around Turin, a large industrial city whose metropolitan area was home to 1,702,000 people in 2008. Turin, the capital of the region of Piedmont (the region around Italy was unified in 1861), is the center of the Italian automobile industry. Lowland Piedmont is an important wine producer, with vineyards

A hilltop town, characteristic of Tuscany, where settlements were built to take advantage of strong natural defenses.

lining south-facing slopes, for example the Asti Hills. The relatively low Monferrato Hills, east of Turin, are intensely cultivated, while the fertile lowlands are used to grow wheat, rice under irrigation, fruits, and vegetables, and to raise cattle. The Alpine foothills of Piedmont are an important dairying area. Piedmont lies along important routes that pass through Alpine passes, such as the Simplon Pass, to the north on the way to France and Switzerland.

To the east of Piedmont and north of the Po is Lombardy, the most populous region in Italy. With a 2008 population of 9,632,000, Lombardy is home to 16 percent of Italy's people. In the north, Lombardy contains a section of the Alps and the Alpine foothills, but central and southern Lombardy form the Lombard Plain. The plain is dotted with cities that were important in medieval times, such as Brescia and Bergamo (both near the southern edge of the foothills), and that now share in the industrial development of Milan, the regional capital of Lombardy. Milan, whose metropolitan area was home to almost 3 million people in 2008, is a major route hub and the commercial, financial, and industrial capital of Italy, with automobile, iron and steel, textile and clothing, and machinery industries. Milan lies in the upper plains of Lombardy (which grow fruit trees and mulberries) and is surrounded by a ring of satellite towns. The lower plains of Lombardy, to the south in the region along the Po River, is one of the most important farming areas in Italy, growing corn, wheat, rice (under irrigation), and sugar beets as well as a variety of fodder crops. The lower plains are heavily populated, with settlements tending to be on gravels, which are poorer soil, and away from possible flooding.

East again, and still north of the Po, is the extensive lowland of Venetia. The region is characterized by small farms that are often worked only on a part-time basis. The main crops are corn, vegetables, fruits, sugar beets, and tobacco. Along the coast, the large Venetian Lagoon, the largest coastal wetland in the Mediterranean basin, covers an area of some 212 square miles (550 sq. km) behind dunes. The lagoon formed when the sea level rose, flooding the coastal plain. The city of Venice, which in modern times is a major tourist center, grew on islands in the lagoon.

South of Venice, the Po enters the Adriatic in a delta; north of the lagoon, the lowland continues through Friuli. Northern Friuli lies in the Alps and Alpine foothills, while southern Friuli is a plain divided by waterways running from the mountains to the Adriatic. The plain is commonly divided into the High Friulian Plain, a farming region that grows corn, grapes, and sugar beets, and the coastal Low Friulian Plain, a cattle-raising region that is marshy in places. Friuli lies on an east-west routeway to the city of Trieste, an industrial center and major port, which developed as the principal port for much of central Europe when it was part of the Austro-Hungarian Empire before World War I (1914–1918). Since becoming Italian, the port has partly declined, owing to the loss of its hinterland.

The Po River meanders and has, over centuries, constantly changed its course. South of the Po is Emilia Romagna, the north of which is part of the large alluvial North Italian Plain. Emilia Romagna forms a triangle, with its base along the Adriatic coast. The lowland narrows toward the west between the Po and the foothills of the Apennines. The region is divided by strong lines formed by the main east-west highway and parallel railroad, which follows an ancient Roman route, along the border between the plain and the lowest part of the Apennine foothills. This route is marked by a straight line of cities across the region, from the coast, Rimini, Forli, Bologna, Modena, Reggio nell'Emilia, Parma, and Piacenza on the Po River. These cities include historic former capitals of small states that once existed in the region. In modern times, they are industrial centers with food processing, automobile construction, ceramics, and other industries. North of these cities, the farms of the fertile plain grow wheat, corn, tomatoes, vegetables, and grapes and raise dairy cattle and pigs. Emilia Romagna is famous for its wine, including Lambrusco, and the region is characterized by many agricultural and other cooperatives. A series of beach resorts lines the Adriatic coast, while the south of the region contains part of the Emilian and Tuscan Apennines.

CENTRAL ITALY

Forming a spine through the Italian Peninsula, the Apennines occupy the greater part of central Italy. In the north, the mountains are largely limestone and sandstone, while in the southern part of central Italy, limestone predominates. In the northwest, in the Apuan Alps, there is marble, including the famous white marble of Massa and Carrara, still commercially worked. Along either side of the main Apennine ridge, which is around 120 miles (some 190 km) wide in central Italy, are the sub-Apennines, lower uplands that run parallel. In the west, the valleys of the Arno River in Tuscany and the Tiber River in Lazio run between the Apennines and sub-Apennines. The combined Apennine and sub-Apennine belt is so broad through central Italy that lowlands are restricted and, particularly in the west, there are rocky headlands along the coast. Although high ground also reaches the Adriatic coast, there are some stretches of coastal plain.

Tuscany, in the west, is mountainous in the Apennines and hilly through most of the rest of the region, except in the Arno Valley. Much of the Tuscan hill country is gentle and undulating with fields bordered by cypresses, and plains stretch along the coastal areas of southern Tuscany. Hills occupy some two-thirds of the region, which is dotted by characteristic small hill towns; the towns are often walled and include medieval defensive towers, for example San Gimignano. South-facing slopes are covered by vineyards that produce wines such as Chianti. In the hills, cattle are raised, including the local Chianina variety, and the region also has extensive olive groves. The historic city of Florence, along the Arno, is a transportation, educational, and tourist center and is dominated by service industries. Along the coast, the cities of Livorno, which has petrochemical facilities, and Piombino, which has a steel industry, are ports, while the inland city of Prato makes textiles. The Maremma, a former marsh near the southern coast, has been reclaimed. Tourism is important throughout the region, not only in Florence but also in such cities as Siena and Pisa.

Inland, Umbria is largely mountainous in the east, descending through hill country to the north-south Tiber Valley through the center. The northern part of the Tiber Valley contains Lake Trasimeno near Perugia, the regional capital, while the western part of the region is hilly. The Valnerina, in the center-south, is a reclaimed lake and marsh region that forms an agricultural region. Umbria is sparsely populated and is known as the "green heart of Italy" because it is well-watered.

Through passes in the Umbrian Apennines is the region of Marche, along the Adriatic coast. The Apennine crest forms the region's western border, and short, fast-flowing rivers flow to the narrow coastal plain and the sea. The greater part of the region's population lives along the coast; inland, transportation links are circuitous and relatively poor. Some inland settlements occupy defensive locations, for example the tiny republic of San Marino along the northern border of Marche. The soil of Marche is relatively unproductive.

Lazio, the southwestern part of central Italy, lies mainly in the sub-Apennine hills with only a small portion of the Apennines in the east. The landscape of Lazio's coastline, with

The picturesque coastline of the Amalfi Peninsula in southern Italy.

pines and extensive grasslands, gives way to a more hilly and intensely cultivated countryside inland. In the hills of northern Lazio, Lakes Bracciano and Bolsena fill the craters of extinct volcanoes. The southern coastal areas contain former marshes, the Pontine Marshes, which—along with the northern Maremme and the central Campagna di Roma marshes—were drained in the early twentieth century. The reclaimed areas were then populated and new towns (such as Latina) were established; a flourishing agriculture now grows fruits and vegetables, wheat, and corn and raises dairy cattle. The region focuses on Rome, the Italian national capital, which had a population of 3,402,000 in the metropolitan area in 2008. Rome is a major center of service industries and has a large tourist sector, based both on the sites of ancient Rome and on pilgrimage associated with the Vatican. Rome's industries have spread to the towns south of the capital. Inland, the foothills are fertile, and sunny slopes are lined with vineyards and olive groves.

The natural harbor of Messina in Sicily was first settled in the eighth century BCE.

THE MEZZOGIORNO

Southern Italy is divided by the main ridges of the Apennines. The sub-Apennines run parallel to the Apennines in the south, often reaching the coast, where lowland is greatly restricted. The only major lowlands are around Naples and in Puglia in the southeast. The south is characterized by low precipitation and hot summers, when drought and heat give the grass an arid appearance, contrasting with the colors of the Mediterranean flowers, shrubs, and trees. Rivers and lakes are relatively few on the Adriatic side of the Mezzogiorno, while the Tyrrhenian side is generally less arid. Southern Italy is still the most rural area of the country, and small villages are traditionally isolated. Everywhere, settlement is concentrated along or near the coast.

The south is less developed than northern Italy, often with poorer soils, and is sparsely populated in many areas. The Mezzogiorno has traditionally been a region of emigration, and much of the workforce for the industrial development of the north in the 1950s and 1960s came from the south. Farming is widespread, despite the terrain and a land-holding system under which (until the 1950s when a land reform program began) much of the land was held in large estates and rented to sharecroppers, farmers who paid part of the crop as rent. There have been efforts to develop the infrastructure and industries of the south through a state fund called the Casa per il Mezzogiorno, which led to the establishment of facilities such as steelworks at Taranto in Puglia.

The most densely populated part of the Mezzogiorno is Campania, the region around Naples. Much of Campania is mountainous, including the Neapolitan Apennines, in the east, and the Cilento Mountains. Inland, the only significant lowland is the basin of Benevento. Lowlands north of Naples and south of Sorrento are fertile, and volcanic soils are widespread. Fertile slopes—including those of Mount Vesuvius, an active volcano—are intensively cultivated, often with three crops: one on the ground beneath fruit trees, with grapes grown between the trees. Crops include grapes, early vegetables, flowers, peaches, apricots, tobacco, and citrus fruits. A network of satellite towns surrounds Naples, a major port, which has a wide range of industries. In 2008, the Naples metropolitan area had a population of 2,229,000, and the Naples area, with food processing, metallurgy, chemicals, textiles, and decorative arts, is the only important center of industry in the Mezzogiorno. To the south, tourism is important in the resorts of the Sorrento Peninsula and on the islands of Capri and Ischia.

In eastern Campania, there are few natural routes through the Apennines; on both sides of the Italian Peninsula, transportation links are largely north-south. In the eastern Mezzogiorno, the regions of Abruzzi and Molise contrast with heavily-populated Campania. Three rugged ridges of the Apennines stretch north-south through Abruzzi, reaching 9,560 feet (2,914 m) at Gran Sasso. Much of the interior is deforested and is pasture for sheep, which are brought to the lowlands in winter. Small basins between Apennine ridges are farmed, and rivers provide irrigation water along the coast, where wheat, olives, and fruits are grown. The larger towns, such as Pescara, are along the coast; the region's inaccessibility has, in part, been reduced by an expressway from the west coast to Pescara.

RIVERS OF ITALY

River	Length in miles	Length in km
Po	405	652
Adige	255	410
Tiber	252	405
Adda	194	312
Oglio	175	282
Ticino *	154	248
Arno	150	241

* Not all the course of this waterway flows through the region.

Molise, to the south, is a small region. Like Abruzzi, it is mountainous in the west, with hills covering most of the rest of the region. A narrow coastal strip and the Volturno Valley form Molise's lowlands, which occupy less than one-tenth of its area. Much of the interior is pastureland, while wheat is grown in the lowlands. There is little industry.

Puglia, the southeastern region of the Mezzogiorno, is, at its nearest point, only about 60 miles (100 km) from Albania across the Strait of Otranto. The region mostly comprises low plateaus and coastal plains. Northern Puglia includes the Tavoliere Plain, the largest lowland in Italy apart from the North Italian Plain. The Gargano Promontory in the north is a limestone upland, south and west of which is a limestone plateau, the Puglia Tableland. To the south is the lower Murge Plateau, while the far south, the Salento Peninsula, is a rocky lowland containing the Lecce and other plains. Because of a lack of surface water, an aqueduct system was constructed early in the twentieth century, bringing water from the Apennines. Much of the region is farmed, and the Tavoliere Plain is known as the "granary of Italy," growing wheat, oats, and barley. Elsewhere in Puglia, olives, fruits (including figs and grapes), and vegetables grow, while the Lecce Plain grows tobacco. Rubble walls, olive trees, and small white farmhouses characterize the landscape of Puglia. The cities of Bari and Taranto are important commercial ports, and, in modern times, the Salento Peninsula has become a popular tourist destination.

East of Puglia, Basilicata—an almost landlocked region largely covered in forests and rugged peaks in the west and hills and valleys in the east—is sparsely populated. There is a narrow coastal plain along the Gulf of Taranto. A largely agricultural region, Basilicata raises sheep, goats, and cattle in the uplands and grows wheat, olives, and grapes in the lowlands. In modern times, horticulture has expanded, but there is little industry.

Calabria, the narrow "toe" of Italy, is a rugged granite peninsula that is linked to the main Apennine ridge by the massif of Mount Pollino. The region also contains the separate La Sila massif in the center, south of which the peninsula narrows before broadening into the Calabrian Apennines, which end in the south at the Aspromonte Massif. The Strait of Messina, a two-mile- (3 km) wide narrows, separates Calabria from Sicily. The region has poor soils and is extensively forested, with cereal and olive cultivation restricted to the lower river valleys. There are few cities; the largest, Reggio di Calabria, is a ferry port linking the mainland with Sicily.

SICILY

Triangular in shape, Sicily is mountainous, apart from the Plain of Catania, west of the city of Catania, along the east coast. The fertile plain is at the foot of Mount Etna, an almost constantly active volcano, which rises to 10,924 feet (3,330 m). Northern Sicily contains the Nébrodi and other mountains, running east-west parallel to the coast. Offshore, the Eolian or Lipari Islands are small islands that include active and dormant volcanoes. Palermo (the island's capital), along a bay in the northwest, is the most populous city on Sicily. Southern Sicily is the most arid area in Italy. Where soils and water supplies allow, cereals, olives, almonds, citrus fruits, and vegetables are grown. Most of the interior is deforested and is used as pasture. Oil and natural gas from off the south coast have spurred some industry, including oil refining and chemicals, but Sicily is relatively underdeveloped industrially.

SARDINIA

Rising to 6,017 feet (1,834 m), Sardinia has a mountainous granitic core. The interior is covered by Mediterranean scrubland (maquis) and is used for pasture for sheep and goats. Inland, many areas are depopulated, and most of the population is concentrated along the coast, around Cagliari (the island's capital and main ferry port in the south) and modern beach resorts along the northeast coast, the Costa Smeralda. The island is relatively well-watered, with fast-flowing rivers. Cereals, grapes, and olives grow in the lowlands, and cork is commercially produced from the cork oak. Small fishing ports line the indented, rocky coast.

S. BRUNO

Malta

The Maltese archipelago, an independent nation-state since 1964, is located about 56 miles (90 km) south of Sicily, in the center of the Mediterranean basin. The archipelago comprises three inhabited islands—from east to west, Malta (the largest), Comino (the smallest), and Gozo—as well as four uninhabited islets. The islands appear as low, terraced hills emerging from the sea, with cliffs and jagged coastlines alternating with natural bays. At 816 feet (249 m), the highest point is along Dingli Cliffs, on Malta.

The landscape is bare, all the forests having been felled in ancient times. There is no surface water, and water supply has long been a problem for the islanders, who now pump water from water tables and implement careful water conservation measures. Eastern Malta is densely populated, with almost one-half of the nation's population concentrated in an agglomeration around Valletta, the national capital, and its large sheltered natural harbor. Apart from its climate and location, Malta has almost no resources. Farming is restricted by poor soils and lack of water and is small scale and largely part-time, with an emphasis on horticulture. Industry, formerly associated with the harbor and ship servicing and repair, has diversified, with textiles, pharmaceuticals, and computer parts among the industries that have been attracted to industrial parks. However, the economy depends upon tourism, largely from Great Britain, the former colonial power.

Geology of Italy, Malta, and San Marino

Italy is geologically young, owing its formation to an orogeny (mountain-building period) that lasted until some 15 million years ago. Subsequently, volcanism, glaciation, and erosion have shaped the land.

Earth's lithosphere (outer layer) is made of around 15 main plates (tectonic plates), which move across the semimolten layer beneath. Italy was created as a result of the collision between two tectonic plates. From around 100 million years ago, during the Cretaceous period (142 to 65 million years ago), the African plate moved northward to collide with the larger Eurasian plate. The collision and subsequent shortening and compression of the crust created the two major mountain chains of Italy, and volcanism and earthquakes associated with tectonic movement continue to the present time.

THE ALPINE OROGENY

The Alpine orogeny started when the African plate moved toward the Eurasian plate, slowly closing the Tethys Sea, which lay between them. As the plates converged, rock formations between them, from the floor of the Tethys Sea, were severely deformed and forced to rise. At the same time, sedimentary rocks (rocks laid down in layers) in the basin between the plates were metamorphosed (changed by heat or pressure). The compression was accompanied by thrust faulting, in which large areas of compressed, uplifted rock broke away and then slid over the plate.

Geologically, the Alpine chain consists of two main parts, defined by the age and type of the rocks that form the mountains. The northern section of the Alpine chain is made of crystalline Ediacaran (600 to 545 million years ago) and older schists; these rocks are part of the older crystalline bedrock against which the sedimentaries were folded. The southern part of the Alps is mostly made of younger dolomites (sedimentary carbonate rocks) and other calcareous rocks (rocks made wholly or partly of calcite).

The orogeny was complex, and the Mediterranean Sea, which now lies between Africa and Europe, does not form the boundary between the plates, which lies to the north. The materials laid down and later compressed between the plates, overlapped in what is now the Apennine mountain chain, which rotated counterclockwise from the western end of the Alps to its current geographical position.

The uplift of folded material formed two mountain chains: the Alps, along the northern continental border of the African plate, and the Apennines, which form the backbone of the Italian Peninsula and end in northern Sicily. The highest point of the uplifted material is Mont Blanc, at 15,771 feet (4,807 m), which is in France but just across the border from Italy. In Italy, a secondary peak of Mont Blanc, Monte Bianco de Courmayeur, reaches 15,616 feet (4,760 m).

MARINE RETREAT

In the last 35 million years, the sea retreated, exposing lowlands in northern Italy. Former gulfs now form the North Italian Plain, which stretches from the region of Turin in the west to beyond Venice in the east. Subsequently, renewed compression forced up what are now the islands of Sardinia and Corsica to the east and, as the fragment of plate on which they stood moved eastward, pressure brought the Apennine mountain chain above sea level.

By around 25 million years ago, the Alps, the Apennines, northern Sicily, Sardinia, and the ancestor of the North Italian Plain were above sea level. Subsequently, small sections of plate (microplates) were moved in a complex series of sometimes overlapping movements to create the skeleton of the current shape of the Italian Peninsula. Material eroded from the uplands was deposited in shallow coastal areas to create most of the limited coastal plains of the Italian Peninsula.

The Mediterranean Sea had not, however, attained its present shape. Plate movement and compression raised mountains in the western part of the basin, isolating the Mediterranean from the Atlantic Ocean, some 6 million years ago. Consequently, the level of the landlocked sea became progressively lower through strong evaporation, and many sedimentary saline rocks were formed. Around 5 million years ago, further movement and erosion to the west opened up the Strait of Gibraltar, and the Mediterranean Sea was again linked to the Atlantic Ocean. An inflow of water from the Atlantic covered the newly formed saline sediments, and the Mediterranean gradually took its present shape.

ALPINE GLACIATION

Climatic changes, before around 650,000 years ago, led to the most recent ice age, when northern Europe was covered by ice and massive glaciers formed on the Alps. Ice moved down the mountains under the force of gravity, acting as a powerful erosional agent. Rock surfaces were smoothed, and deep U-shaped valleys were cut by glaciers. In places, hanging valleys, where smaller tributary glaciers cut less deeply than the main glacier, were eroded. Rocks were plucked from valley floors and sides and then were used by glaciers to abrade surfaces, wearing them away. Glaciers began in rounded basins, called cirques, on mountainsides, and, above the glaciers, freezing and seasonal melting opened up cracks in rocks to produce the jagged frost-shattered peaks that are typical of the high Alps in Italy.

*Mount Etna is the largest active volcano in Europe and erupts
frequently.*

Material carried away in the ice was transported by glaciers
to their snouts, where it was deposited as moraine. Moraines
now block lower Alpine valleys in northern Italy, holding back
lakes, such as Lake Como, in deep basins that were scoured out
by glaciers. The ice also carried great quantities of sediment to
the Po Valley of northern Italy, where soil carried from the north
now forms the most fertile land in the nation.

THE APENNINES

The Apennines and Alps meet in Liguria, the coastal region of
northwest Italy. There are notable differences in the geological
compositions of the two chains. The Apennines consist mostly of
Mesozoic (248 to 65 million years ago) and Cenozoic (since 65
million years ago) beds. These are mainly friable (easily broken)
rocks, such as those made from calcareous and clay minerals.
However, the Apuan Alps of northern Tuscany contain marble,
including the famous white marble of Massa and Carrara, while
the Calabrian Apennines in the far south of peninsular Italy are
granitic. Along the western (Tyrrhenian) side of the Apennines,
there are secondary chains and evidence of the volcanism that
accompanied the orogeny, including extinct volcanic cones.

The rocks of the Apennine chain are easily eroded by rain

and wind. As a result, Apennine slopes are unstable and are
subject to landslides. Along the coasts, calanques—deep valleys
between limestone, usually with one end submerged by the
sea—are formed. In modern times, massive deforestation has
increased the susceptibility of the Apennines to erosion.

SICILY AND SARDINIA

The northern part of Sicily belongs to the Eurasian plate (and is
part of the Apennine chain), while the southern part of the
island is part of an African microplate called Iblea. The Iblea
microplate is sliding under the Eurasian plate, creating upland
as material along the plate edge folds. At the same time, molten
material wells up faults along the edge of the microplate, at the
surface forming volcanoes, such as Vulcano and Stromboli in the
Lipari Islands and Mount Etna in eastern Sicily. Earthquakes are
also associated with the faults. Sicily is famous for its rock salt as
well as sulfur and gypsum, which were formed due to the deposit
of saline material, carbonates, and sulphates, when the
shrinking Mediterranean Sea was isolated from the Atlantic
Ocean and the sea level lowered because of evaporation.

Sardinia, along with Corsica and the Spanish Balearic
Islands, was part of a microplate, which some 30 million years
ago began to rotate counterclockwise under pressure, owing to
the compression of the African plate against the Eurasian plate.
Eventually, the movement of the microplate brought Sardinia to

its present position, and the pressure it exerted contributed to the uplift of the Apennines. The rocks that form Sardinia are crystalline and are considerably older than most in Italy, with much of the island formed from Paleozoic (545 to 248 million years ago) rocks that were uplifted from the Tethys Sea.

VOLCANISM AND EARTHQUAKES

The Alpine orogeny was accompanied by considerable volcanic activity, particularly in the central region between the Eurasian and Africa plates—that is, the region now occupied by Italy. Compression and folding brought heavy faulting, and magma welled up these faults. Magma spews onto the surface as lava, forming volcanoes.

Italy has within its borders three active volcanoes and many dormant ones, while other submerged cones are under the sea to the south and southwest of the Italian Peninsula. There are three main volcanic clusters: in Campania; in northeastern Sicily and the adjoining Tyrrhenian Sea; and some 60 miles (around 100 km) south of Sicily, around the small island of Pantelleria.

The name *volcano* was first given to an island in the Sicilian Lipari (or Eolian) archipelago, Vulcano (last active in 1888–1890). In ancient times, locals identified the top of the mountain with the forge of Vulcan, the blacksmith of the gods. The archipelago contains another volcanic island, Stromboli, which is almost continuously active. It was explosive in mid-2008, but lava has not flowed since 2002.

Mount Etna rises 10,924 feet (3,330 m) above the Sicilian city of Catania and is the largest active volcano in Europe. Its eruptions are slow and are constantly monitored, mostly coming from secondary craters. One of the most active volcanoes in the world, Etna is almost continuously active. In the twenty-first century, Etna violently erupted in 2001 (when the town of Zafferana was threatened by lava), in 2002–2003 (when the eruption was large enough to be recorded from space), and in 2007.

The city of Naples is dominated by Vesuvius (4,203 feet or 1,281 m), a quiescent but unpredictable volcano, which completely destroyed the Roman towns of Pompeii and Herculaneum in the most famous eruption of the Classical age in 79 CE. Vesuvius last erupted in 1944, but not in a pyroclastic ash eruption, the type that caused so many fatalities in the first century CE. Vesuvius is constantly monitored for signs of activity; it is estimated that, in the event of a hot ash cloud eruption, up to 600,000 people would have to be evacuated from the vicinity of the volcano. Elsewhere in Campania, the volcanoes of Monte Nuovo and Ischia have been extinct since 1538 and 1301, respectively. However, minor volcanic activities occur around Naples, where there are thermal springs. There are similar springs throughout the Apennine chain, where long extinct volcanic calderas (basin-shaped craters) gradually filled with water to become lakes.

There are also submarine volcanoes, including vents around Pantelleria, the ephemeral island of Giulia Ferdinando, and Mount Marsili, which lies beneath the Tyrrhenian Sea. Mount Marsili, Europe's largest underwater volcano, is active.

The Geology of Malta

The Maltese archipelago is relatively young and is the result of complex interactions between Eurasian and African plates since the Triassic (248 to 206 million years ago) period. Malta was part of a land connection between Africa and Sicily, but subsequently the sea level rose, tectonic activity broke microplates in the zone of compression between Africa and Eurasia, and the islands were separated from the continents. The oldest rocks known in Malta, coralline limestone, date to only 33 to 30 million years ago. The archipelago, which emerged from the sea about 10 million years ago, is made entirely of sedimentary marine rocks structured in a few layers: upper coralline limestone, greensands, blue clay, Globigerina limestone (named for a genera of plankton), and lower coralline limestone.

There is near constant movement along the many fault lines associated with the Alpine orogeny. Earthquakes have been an ever-present factor in Italian history, and while the Alpine zone and Sardinia are relatively stable, the Apennine chain still suffers rapid rock movements far below the surface. In the twentieth century, southern and central Italy suffered several disastrous earthquakes. In 1908, at Reggio di Calabria and Messina, some 100,000 people were killed, and much of both cities was destroyed. In 1980, an earthquake centered in Irpinia (Campania) resulted in 2,914 deaths and damage over 10,000 square miles (26,000 sq. km). Seismic activity is most frequent in Campania, Friuli (in the northeast), Calabria and eastern Sicily (particularly the area surrounding the Strait of Messina), and Molise. In 2009, more than 290 people died in an earthquake in and near L'Aquila.

S. BRUNO

Marble is quarried in the mountains near Carrara, Tuscany.

Climate of Italy, Malta, and San Marino

The climate of Italy and of its small neighbors, San Marino and Malta, is mostly Mediterranean with warm, dry, summers and cool winters. There are many local climatic variations shaped by the terrain.

Italy consists of mountainous terrain in the north; to the south, an extensive plain and a long, narrow, mainly upland peninsula tends northwest or southeast and is surrounded by the Mediterranean Sea. Extending from 37°N through 45°N, Italy includes Sicily, a large island situated at the southern tip of the Italian Peninsula, and Sardinia, an island off the west coast of the peninsula. The region includes varied landscape, different terrains, and diverse local climate zones over a relatively small area. The main influences on the climate are the prevailing westerly winds, the mountainous terrain, and a number of characteristic regional winds.

PREVAILING WINDS AND HIGH PRESSURE SYSTEMS

The climate of the region is a broad Mediterranean type with dry, warm summers that, toward the south, tend to drought. Winters are cool and humid, and few areas experience frost. Rainfall mainly comes during the winter months but may accompany thunderstorms in summer, spring, or the fall.

At the latitudes of central Europe, the prevailing westerly winds blow across the North Atlantic Ocean to bring moist, maritime air to the continent. This air is relatively cool in summer and relatively warm in winter, compared to the temperature of the large continental landmass of Europe, which heats up and cools down more rapidly than the ocean. Average temperatures, both in summer and winter in Italy, tend to be moderated by this maritime air; as a result, extremes of hot and cold are rare, particularly along the coasts. Cold continental air in winter from northern Europe only occasionally reaches Italy.

The North Atlantic Oscillation (NAO) is a global atmospheric air pattern that also influences the climate of the region. The NAO is a characteristic pattern of atmospheric pressure in which low pressure over the Azores, an island group in the North Atlantic, is associated with high pressure over Iceland; this is called a negative NAO index. Conversely, an area of high pressure over the Azores results in low pressure over Iceland; this is called a positive NAO index. A negative NAO index means that the prevailing westerly winds have shifted southward toward southern Europe, including Italy. Consequently, there are more storms and heavier rainfall in Italy, particularly during the winter and spring. Conversely, a positive NAO index means that the westerly winds are farther north, so that southern Europe, including Italy, is drier than normal. The NAO pattern tends to remain fixed for several years, for example as a negative NAO index, before changing to the other pattern (a positive NAO index) for the next few years.

REGIONAL AND LOCAL WINDS

Characteristic regional winds such as the sirocco, bora, mistral, and *tramontana* winds and local *föhn* winds also help shape the weather but on a shorter-term basis. The sirocco is a hot wind that comes from the hot, dry deserts of North Africa and moves northward across the Mediterranean to Italy. As it crosses the sea, it picks up some moisture. The sirocco can blow in summer and the fall and causes high temperatures over most of the Italian Peninsula, especially in the south (the Mezzogiorno). In the fall, the sirocco is frequently followed by thunderstorms and heavy rain.

The *tramontana* is a cold, dry wind that blows south or southwest from and across the mountains of the Apennines, which cover most of central Italy. The bora is a strong, cold gusty wind from the north that can blow during winter into northeastern Italy, over Trieste, the region of Friuli–Venezia Giulia, and the northern Adriatic Sea southward as far as Rimini. The mistral is a cold, dry northwesterly wind that can blow across Sardinia. It brings clear weather and is most common in winter and spring.

A *föhn* wind is a local wind that can occur on the opposite side of a mountain range or ridge to the prevailing wind. It brings rapid warming and can cause local temperatures to rise by up to 36°F (20°C) or more within hours.

REGIONAL CLIMATES

The climate of Italy is mostly a Mediterranean type, but it varies in terms of rainfall and temperature patterns, with generally warmer summer and winter temperatures in the Mezzogiorno and, usually,

Malta has a very dry climate and an almost total lack of surface water.

more precipitation in the highlands and along the east (Adriatic) coast than along the west (Ligurian and Tyrrhenian) coasts. The region can be divided into four main climatic-geographic zones: the Italian Alpine region, the North Italian Plain, the interior Apennine mountain region, and the coastal regions (including the islands of Sicily, Sardinia, and Malta).

THE ITALIAN ALPS

The Italian Alps form the most northerly part of Italy, bordering with France, Switzerland, Austria, and Slovenia. This mountainous region contains peaks—the highest of which are over 10,000 feet (3,000 m)—divided by deep, glaciated valleys. Aspect is important in the mountains; south- and west-facing slopes are sunnier and warmer than north- and east-facing slopes. Some north-facing slopes are permanently in shadow, never receiving direct sunlight. The Alpine region has a characteristic local wind, the *föhn*, which can blow from the north over the mountaintops and suddenly raise temperatures and lower the humidity. The *föhn* can often cause rapid snowmelt in winter and the spring and may bring avalanches.

Precipitation over the mountains is generally heavy, with the heaviest rainfall in the summer, when there are frequent thunderstorms. Bolzano, at an elevation of 790 feet (241 m) in the region of Trentino–Alto Adige/Südtirol, is typical of the region, with an average maximum temperature of 84°F (29°C) in July and an average maximum temperature of 42°F (6°C) in January. Average temperatures are colder at higher altitudes.

To the south of the Alpine region are several large lakes, including Lakes Como, Maggiore, Lugano, and Garda, which modify the climate. Along the shores, the climate is the mildest and sunniest in the Alpine region. Average daily sunshine over the lakes is, generally, from three to four hours in winter and up to nine hours in summer.

THE NORTH ITALIAN PLAIN

The North Italian Plain (or Po Valley) is an extensive flat, low-lying agricultural region covering much of northern Italy, from Turin in the west to Trieste in the east. The climate is characterized by hot, sunny summers with occasional thunderstorms and rainfall, and cool winters with frequent fog, frost, and snow. Average daily sunshine totals range from two to three hours in winter to as many as nine hours in summer. In the eastern part of this region, around Trieste and along the northern Adriatic coast, there is a characteristic wind called the bora, which is a cold wind originating in central Europe. The bora can affect northeastern Italy in winter, noticeably lowering temperatures within hours.

Central within the North Italian Plain, Milan has a climate typical of this region, with average maximum monthly temperatures in January of 41°F (5°C) and minimum temperatures of 32°F (0°C). Average maximum temperatures in July are 84°F (29°C), and minimum temperatures are 68°F (20°C)

Saint Mark's Square is the lowest point in Venice, which makes it prone to flooding during high tides.

in the same month. Total annual rainfall is approximately 40 inches (102 cm). Precipitation falls throughout the year, with a peak in October and November; the driest month is January. Summers are sunny with an average of nine hours of clear sunshine per day, while winters are typically cloudy with just two hours of sunshine per day.

THE APENNINE REGION AND MEDITERRANEAN COASTS

From Genoa in the north to Brindisi in the south, the long Apennine mountain range runs through the middle of the Italian Peninsula and contains peaks that reach to over 5,500 feet (some 1,800 m). The climate of both the Apennine uplands and coastal region is a Mediterranean climate, with mild winters and hot, dry summers, but the climate is modified by local landscape, with average temperatures being lower in the mountains. Summers last longer in the south than farther north and have constant sunny conditions. The fall, winter, and spring over the mountains are characterized by much more variable weather with frequent clouds.

The Italian Peninsula has long western and eastern coastlines, along which conditions vary according to local terrain, aspect, and other factors. Those regions facing moist prevailing winds have more rainfall than those on the opposite side of uplands. There are many localized rain shadows, areas where rainfall is reduced because of protection from prevailing, rain-bearing winds. In winter, the northeastern coastline, north of Pescara, may be occasionally affected by cold bora winds, which come from central Europe southward into the region. The sunniest parts of the Mezzogiorno are the islands of Sicily and Sardinia and the mainland region of Puglia, which can experience up to 11 hours of direct sun in summer.

Venice is typical of the northern coasts, with an annual rainfall of 32 inches (81 cm) falling throughout the year. Average July maximum temperatures are 81°F (27°C) and average January maximum temperatures are 52°F (11°C). Brindisi, in Puglia, is typical of the Mezzogiorno, with July maximum temperatures of

83°F (28°C) and an annual rainfall of just 22 inches (64 cm), with almost no rain in the summer months.

MALTA

Malta consists of two main small low-lying islands and a number of islets, situated centrally in the Mediterranean. Malta has a Mediterranean climate with warm, dry summers and mild, wet winters, and occasional fog from November though March. Average annual precipitation, of around 22 inches (56 cm), falls almost entirely between October and April. Typical average July maximum temperatures are 86°F (30°C), and January minimum temperatures are 49°F (9°C).

CLIMATE HAZARDS

Through northern and central Italy, there are occasional river floods after heavy rainfall, especially in the fall. Occasional regional-scale summer droughts and water shortages can severely affect agriculture. Summer heat waves can occur across Italy, with increased heat-related illnesses, such as heatstroke.

Avalanches are a hazard in the Alps, where snow accumulates on slopes of between 30° and 45°—snow will not accumulate in any quantity on steeper slopes. A sudden rise in temperature can melt and loosen snow, while vibrations or a loud noise can dislodge it. Avalanches most often occur in spring, when snow from the mountains, in the areas known as "starting zones," melts. During fighting in the Alpine valleys

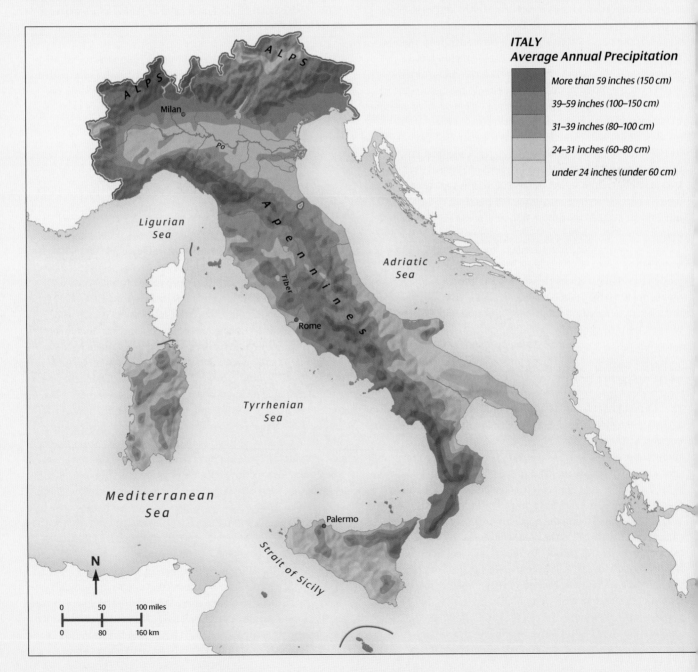

ITALY
Average Annual Precipitation

- More than 59 inches (150 cm)
- 39–59 inches (100–150 cm)
- 31–39 inches (80–100 cm)
- 24–31 inches (60–80 cm)
- under 24 inches (under 60 cm)

Snow in the Dolomites mountain range.

during World War I (1914–1918), some 50,000 Italian and Austrian troops were killed by avalanches, mainly triggered by gunfire.

Climate-related diseases carried by insects in Italy, including mosquito-borne malaria and tick-borne encephalitis, are beginning to increase with climate change. Although officially free of malaria since 1970, several cases of malaria have been reported in the early twenty-first century, mostly in Venice. Milder winters allow mosquitoes and other insects a longer breeding season and more opportunity to develop and transmit disease. Early in the twenty-first century in Campania, in southern Italy, there was an increase in visceral leishmaniasis, a serious disease transmitted by sand flies.

CLIMATE CHANGE

Global climate change is resulting in warmer average temperatures over Europe, and temperature rises are expected to be considerable over Italy, with an increase in average temperatures of approximately 6.5°F to 8°F (3.5°C to 4.5°C) from 1990 through 2080. The Alps are expected to be most affected by increasing temperatures, with shorter periods of snow cover, melting glaciers, and migration of local ecosystems up the mountain slopes.

Rainfall patterns are expected to change, with decreased summer rainfall in Italy and most of southern Europe. This trend is likely to lead to more frequent droughts and water shortages in summer, particularly in the driest areas, and some dry areas in the Mezzogiorno may be at risk of becoming small deserts.

Average sea levels are also expected to rise, and the low-lying area around the city of Venice is particularly sensitive to flooding from rising sea levels. Venice is already increasingly vulnerable to flooding, because of the gradual erosion of its foundations and unusually high tides caused by global warming. At the start of the twentieth century, parts of Venice were flooded, on average, around five times a year. In modern times, the danger of flooding has increased by more than threefold. Saint Mark's Square, the lowest part of the city, is now

frequently flooded. In 1998, a major engineering project that would have included the erection of large metal barriers to prevent abnormally high tides from entering the city was abandoned in favor of the much cheaper option of dredging canals and raising the level of streets.

M. FELTON

CLIMATE

MILAN, ITALY

45°37'N 08°43'E Height above sea level 767 feet (234 m)

	J	F	M	A	M	J	J	A	S	O	N	D
					Mean maximum							
(°F)	41	46	55	64	73	81	84	82	75	63	50	43
(°C)	5	8	13	18	23	27	29	28	24	17	10	6
					Mean minimum							
(°F)	32	36	43	50	57	63	68	66	61	52	43	36
(°C)	0	2	6	10	14	17	20	19	16	11	6	2
					Precipitation							
(in.)	1.7	2.4	3.0	3.7	3.0	4.6	2.5	3.6	2.7	4.9	4.8	3.0
(cm)	4.4	6.0	7.7	9.4	7.6	11.8	6.4	9.1	6.9	12.5	12.2	7.7

PALERMO, ITALY

38°10'N 13°05'E Height above sea level 65 feet (20 m)

	J	F	M	A	M	J	J	A	S	O	N	D
					Mean maximum							
(°F)	61	61	63	68	75	81	86	86	82	77	70	64
(°C)	16	16	17	20	24	27	30	30	28	25	21	18
					Mean minimum							
(°F)	46	46	48	52	57	64	70	70	66	61	54	50
(°C)	8	8	9	11	14	18	21	21	19	16	12	10
					Precipitation							
(in.)	2.8	1.7	2.0	1.9	0.7	0.4	0.1	0.7	1.6	3.0	2.8	2.4
(cm)	7.1	4.3	5.0	4.9	1.9	0.9	0.2	1.8	4.1	7.7	7.1	6.2

ROME, ITALY

41°48'N 12°15'E Height above sea level 16 feet (5 m)

	J	F	M	A	M	J	J	A	S	O	N	D
					Mean maximum							
(°F)	52	55	59	66	73	82	86	86	79	72	61	55
(°C)	11	13	15	19	23	28	30	30	26	22	16	13
					Mean minimum							
(°F)	41	41	45	50	55	63	68	68	63	55	48	43
(°C)	5	5	7	10	13	17	20	20	17	13	9	6
					Precipitation							
(in.)	2.8	2.4	2.2	2.0	1.8	1.5	0.6	0.8	2.5	3.9	5.1	3.7
(cm)	7.1	6.2	5.7	5.1	4.6	3.7	1.5	2.1	6.3	9.9	12.9	9.3

Flora and Fauna of Italy, Malta, and San Marino

Italy and its small neighbors have a great diversity of habitats within a relatively small area. The flora and fauna are extremely varied with remarkable differences between adjoining valleys and uplands.

From the Alpine summits of northern Italy, through the Po Valley and into the Apennine uplands that run north-south for nearly 700 miles (around 1,100 km), to the Mediterranean islands that surround the Italian Peninsula, there is great diversity of plants and animals, including some species that are endemic (found nowhere else) to the region. Italy, despite its high density of population and more than three thousand years of intensive urbanization and agriculture, still has notable plant and animal biodiversity. The plant life comprises some 6,700 species, while the region's fauna includes one-third of all animal species living in Europe. Less than one-fifth of Italian territory is forested, and a substantial portion of wooded areas are within national parks or other preserves, protected by legislation.

THE SEA

The Adriatic, Tyrrhenian, and Ligurian seas surrounding Italy are home to about 500 different species of fish, mollusks, crustaceans, and invertebrates—these represent more than 80 percent of the animal species presently in the Mediterranean basin. Relatively common species include swordfish, white sharks, and tuna, as well as a variety of corals and sponges and many invertebrates, such as jellyfish. Localized pollution, fishing practices that destroy coral, and overfishing have damaged some marine habitats and brought about a reduction in the numbers of fish.

PRINCIPAL HABITATS

Within Italy, Alpine and Mediterranean flora and fauna are often found in adjoining areas, sometimes even at the same latitude. There are many different local vegetational zones, but three broad types can be recognized: Alpine, the northern lowland or Po Valley, and the Mediterranean region. The Alpine habitats are confined to the high mountain ranges and valleys that form Italy's border regions with France, Switzerland, Austria, and Slovenia. To the south, the broad northern Italian lowland, the Po Valley, forms a distinct environment. Much of this region was once covered by deciduous woodland, now mostly cleared. The third region, which covers the Apennines, central and southern Italy, Sicily, Sardinia, and the smaller Italian islands, is considerably larger than the other two broad regions combined. This Mediterranean peninsular and insular region was also once partly forested; in modern times, woodland remains only in some upland districts.

ALPINE HABITATS

The Alpine habitats of northern Italy are very different from the stereotype of Italy as a warm, Mediterranean country. The climate is characterized by low winter temperatures and high summer rainfall. In the Alps, mountain flora is found above around 6,560 feet (some 2,000 m). The Alpine forests contain coniferous species: firs and pines, including the Norwegian spruce. At lower altitudes, there are larches, ash, and yew; above the coniferous forests are shrubs such as (introduced) rhododendrons (which are increasingly widespread in places, seriously damaging native species), dwarf junipers, and willows. Higher again, Alpine flower meadows are dotted, in season, with primroses, glacial buttercups, gentians, Alpine crocuses, Alpine pansies, and the characteristic edelweiss. Just below the perennial glaciers, mosses and lichens are almost the only species able to survive.

A mouflon wild sheep in Sardinia.

A farm in Tuscany with characteristic cypress trees.

To live in the Alpine habitat, animals must adapt, hibernate, or change the color of their fur or plumage in winter to make them more difficult for predators to find. The region is home to small mammals, like marmots, blue hares, and Alpine rabbits. Larger mammals include ibexes, chamois, and roe deer. Mammalian predators include lynxes and small populations of brown bears and wolves. Avian predators include the golden eagle, falcons, kites, buzzards, and eagle-owls. Other birds include various species of grouse. The lower reaches of the mountains are also home to many insects, including a variety of butterflies and some dragonflies, such as the gold-ringed dragonfly.

THE PO VALLEY

Descending from the Alps, beech woods give way to some remaining stands of cork oaks and laurels before, southward from Lakes Como, Maggiore, and Garda, the Po Valley begins. This broad lowland, the most fertile region of Italy, is the most changed habitat in the Italian Peninsula. Almost nothing remains of its former covering of deciduous woodland. Centuries of farming and other human activity have turned this region into one of cultivation and human settlement. However, some patches of natural habitat remain in marshes and boggy land that are home to rushes, grasses, pondweed, and water lilies and populations of frogs and other amphibians, snakes, small freshwater crustaceans, and fish. The most common tree throughout the region is the poplar, except on isolated higher clay

or sandy pockets, where pines grow amid heathers. Human activities have reduced the number of animals, although small animals, such as foxes, rabbits, stoats, and hedgehogs, and some deer remain.

MEDITERRANEAN PENINSULAR AND INSULAR HABITATS

The mild Mediterranean climate, with hot, dry summers and rainy winters, is a favorable environment for many animals and plants. There is great variety of habitat in a countryside characterized by hills and mountains, which end abruptly in cliffs at the sea, and the coastal zones in peninsular and insular Italy are sometimes the only areas that can be classified as plains.

Dense Mediterranean maquis, made up of deciduous and evergreen endemic species, is now very sparse. Intensive deforestation, which started in Roman times and continued until the twentieth century, caused the maquis to degrade into poorer vegetation in places. Where woods survive, the most common tree is holm oak in inland regions. In some parts of the south, such as the Calabrian Apennines, patches of native forest, containing oaks (truffle and oriental), ash, and poplars, have survived.

Most of the coastal hills of the south and interiors of both Sicily and Sardinia have a rocky, bare appearance. Patches of carob forest remain on Sardinia, but most has been cleared and has been replaced by tough grasses. In Calabria, beech woods are still relatively widespread, while parts of Abruzzi have pine and fir forests. Puglia, Sicily, and Sardinia have little tree cover, and much of interior Sardinia supports myrtle.

As in the Alps, the trees of the region are clearly stratified. At around 1,000 feet (some 300 m), Mediterranean species are replaced by ilex and oaks and, at slightly higher altitudes, by chestnuts. Above around 2,300 feet (some 700 m), beech and conifers become the main trees. The Gran Sasso peaks in Abruzzi rise above 7,550 feet (some 2,300 m), above which vegetation resembling that of Alpine meadows grows.

Dominant species in coastal areas are mainly shrubs, which include aromatic plants like rosemary, thyme, mastic, broom, and myrtle, as well as ferns and diverse herbs and grasses. Trees in the coastal Mediterranean districts include wild almonds, oleanders, wild olives, various species of oak, carobs, and Aleppo pines. Most of these species are evergreens and have a generous, colorful covering of flowers in spring and summer. Forest floors

are home to a wide variety of plants in the understory, including wild raspberries, anemones, belladonna, various lilies, and orchids. Some valleys contain some specimens of the rare Loricato pine. In Sicily, there are communities of papyrus, a tall aquatic plant with small green-stalked flowers, once used to make paper. Throughout the coastal regions and limited lowlands, introduced species, such as palms, lemons, oranges, cedars, and eucalyptus have spread, flourishing in the warm Mediterranean climate.

In the coastal regions, birds include cormorants, Corsican and royal seagulls, ravens, swallows, and magpies. Other birds include Pellegrino hawks and many species of crows. There are also many insects, amphibians, and small mammals, including rabbits, mice, and rats. At higher levels, larger animals have

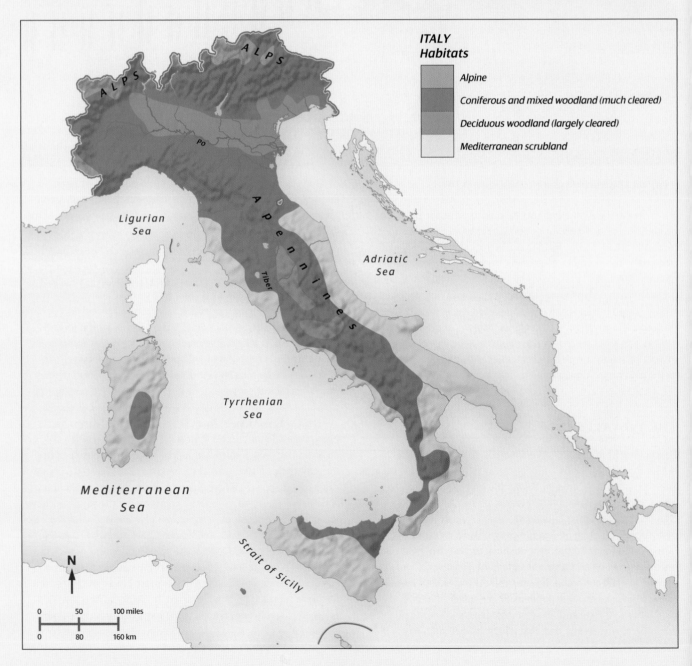

ITALY
Habitats

Alpine

Coniferous and mixed woodland (much cleared)

Deciduous woodland (largely cleared)

Mediterranean scrubland

survived, including a few brown bears, deer, wild boar, small populations of wolves, wild cats, gray squirrels, foxes, and chamois. Sardinia is one of the few places in Europe where an endemic wild sheep (the mouflon) has survived. Through the region, woodpeckers, rock pipits, pigeons, and Alpine accentors live in wooded and semi-wooded areas. There are also many migratory visitors. Lowlands with sufficient water have populations of amphibians such as newts and frogs, including some rare species, while drier areas are home to snakes and lizards, which often bask on house and garden walls.

PRESERVES

Italy has 22 national parks, covering about 5 percent of the nation's total surface area. The Abruzzi and Gran Paradiso national parks were established in 1922, followed by Circeo,

A traditional Sicilian swordfish fishing boat. The Mediterranean swordfish, once common, is now much reduced as a result of overfishing.

Flora and Fauna of Malta

Malta is largely deforested, the result of exploitation for shipbuilding and domestic fuel. As a result, the surviving animals and plants have had to adapt to a new environment. Nevertheless, Malta is surprisingly biodiverse, and some important endemic plants and animals are relics from before the last ice age, without close relatives anywhere else in the world.

Malta has no remaining natural forests (except for one small wood). There is some cultivated forest of holm oak and Aleppo pine as well as some small stands of carob trees. A major forestation project around the Torri l-Ahmar preserve along the northern coast is in progress. Maquis, which occupies some of the noncultivated areas, includes Mediterranean species like mastic, olive, carob, myrtle, acanthus, heather, and Maltese spurge, while wild Maltese thyme adds its distinctive scent to the rocky limestone countryside. Citrus trees, grapes, and olives flourish, but some areas have been degraded to steppe, with eroded soil and low, tough grasses. Endemic species, like Maltese fleabane, Maltese sea-lavender, and Maltese rock centaury, the protected national plant (also known as *widnet il-bahari*), grows in patches in dry, poor soil.

Maltese animals include typical Mediterranean species of small mammals, marine birds, insects, and marine fish (the islands have no natural freshwater lakes or rivers). The blue rock thrush is Malta's protected national bird. Two species of seagulls breed along some cliffs. The interior of Malta and the smaller island of Gozo are home to populations of lizards, hedgehogs, weasels, rabbits, and bats. Turtles visit some coastal areas, but their once teeming breeding grounds at Ramla l-Hamra, on Gozo, are long gone. Environmental protection has become an electoral issue in Malta. Shooting migratory birds in spring has long been a Maltese tradition. For the first time in 2008, this hunting activity was prohibited.

south of Rome, and Stelvio, in the eastern Alps, in the mid-1930s. The Calabrian national parks of Sila and Aspromonte were founded in 1968–1969. Smaller natural preserves and protected areas are widespread across Italy.

Endangered species are carefully protected, and some of these animals have a particular importance for Italian history and traditions. One of the most ancient symbols of Rome was the wolf: according to legend, Rome was founded by twins, Romulus and Remus, who had been abandoned and were subsequently raised by a she-wolf. The Italian wolf population now numbers between 1,000 and 1,200 and, although the animals are protected, some farmers shoot wolves, which, they claim, take too many lambs. Lynxes are becoming rare, while the Marsican brown bear lives only in Abruzzi, where its population was estimated to be between 40 and 50 early in the twenty-first century.

Marine protected areas have been established in various locations where fishing is then strictly prohibited. The total protected sea surface amounts to 743 square miles (1,925 sq. km), including some species-rich Sicilian and Sardinian bays. Mediterranean monk seals, an endangered endemic species, sometimes appear along Sardinian and Tuscan coasts. This seal, the world's rarest pinniped (the order of aquatic mammals that includes seals, sea lions, and the walrus), is one of the most critically endangered mammals on Earth and is thought to number no more than 500 individuals. Only two viable Mediterranean monk seal colonies survive: one in the Greek Aegean, the other along the coast of the Western Sahara.

S. BRUNO

History and Movement of Peoples

Italy before the Rise of Rome

Pre-Roman Italy was a region of considerable cultural, ethnic, and linguistic diversity. A number of different peoples—Etruscans, Ligurians, Sicels, Italics, Messapians, and Greeks—dominated different parts of the region.

By around the middle of the first millennium BCE, Italy was home to eight ethnic groups. The Etruscans, Ligurians, and Sicels (Sicilians) are all believed to be descendants of the original modern human population of the region, who migrated into Italy between 30,000 and 40,000 years ago. They had adopted farming around 5000 BCE, bronze technology by 2000 BCE, and iron technology around 900 BCE. Etruscans, Ligurians, and Sicels spoke languages that are unrelated to any modern European languages. The Italics, Messapians, Gauls, and Greeks all spoke Indo-European languages and migrated to Italy at different times between 1100 and 500 BCE. There were also small colonies of Phoenicians, originally from western Asia, in Sicily and Sardinia.

THE ETRUSCANS

As the founders of the first civilization of western Europe, the Etruscans were the most influential people of pre-Roman Italy. The immediate precursor of the Etruscan civilization was the early Iron Age Villanova culture (c. 900–700 BCE) of Etruria (approximately modern Tuscany). This culture developed from local Urnfield cultures, late Bronze Age cultures that take their name from their custom of cremation and placing the ashes in urns. Like the Urnfield cultures, the Villanova culture showed influences from central Europe.

Etruria had fertile farmland, abundant deposits of copper and iron ores, and, along the coast, good natural harbors, which led the Etruscans to become maritime traders. By 500 BCE, the Etruscans had expanded northward into the Po River Valley and founded several colonies along the coast of Campania, south of Rome.

The Etruscans lived in independent city-states, each ruled by a king. The cities were members of a loose confederation called the Etruscan League, which was organized for mutual defense. Through their trading activities, Etruscans came into close contact with Greek colonies in southern Italy. The Etruscans were generally hostile to the Greeks, regarding them as commercial competitors. However, this did not prevent the Etruscans from taking a keen interest in Greek culture and, by the sixth century BCE, their civilization had become Hellenized. The Etruscans are known to have had a highly literate culture,

but few of their writings have survived, and those that have survived have defied complete translation. The Romans were hostile to the Etruscans and presented them in an unfavorable light in their own writings.

Most of what we know about the lives and values of the Etruscans comes from their cemeteries. Many Etruscan burial places were formally planned like towns. Tombs were cut directly into bedrock, decorated with wall paintings of feasting and entertainment, and richly furnished. Etruscan funeral rites, where two slaves were forced to fight to the death, became the basis of the Roman gladiatorial tradition. Skilled bridge builders and engineers, the Etruscans were pioneers in the use of the arch.

LIGURIANS, SEA PEOPLE, AND SICELS

The Ligurians were a tribal people who lived around the Gulf of Genoa and had colonies in Corsica and Sardinia. Sardinia was also home to other peoples who built circular stone towers, called *nuraghe*, for defense against pirates. It is thought that these peoples may have included the Shardana, one of the "Sea Peoples" who raided Egypt and the eastern Mediterranean region in the thirteenth century BCE.

The Sicels of Sicily were divided into two groups, the Siculi in the east and the Sicani in the west. By the sixth century BCE, the Sicels had lost control of the Sicilian coast to Greek and Phoenician colonists, and they eventually became Hellenized in culture and language. The most impressive surviving monument of the Sicels is the vast necropolis (city of the dead) at Pantalica, where thousands of tombs were cut into sheer cliff faces.

MAGNA GRAECIA

From the eighth century BCE, Greeks settled coastal Sicily and southern Italy, establishing colonies in the region that became known as Magna Graecia (literally, "Great Greece"). It is thought that population pressure or crop failures may have acted as a spur to this outward migration from western and southern Greece. Throughout Magna Graecia, Hellenistic culture had a

This terracotta sarcophagus, from the sixth century BCE, is from the Etruscan necropolis in Cerveteri.

lasting impact, and the Greeks brought with them not only their culture but their religion and alphabet, which became the source of the Etruscan alphabet. Greek cities flourished throughout the Magna Graecia region, including Syracuse (modern Siracusa) and Akragras (Agrigento) in Sicily, and Capua and Neapolis (Naples) on the Italian Peninsula.

THE ITALICS

The Italics were probably the most numerous and widespread ethnic group of pre-Roman Italy. They were divided into several main groups: the Veneti, who lived in the far northeast, and the Umbrians, Sabines, Apulians, Latins, Samnites, Lucanians, and Bruttians, who lived in central and southern Italy. With the exception of the Latins, the Italics were tribal peoples in the sixth century BCE. The Latins were organized in small city-states, the largest of which was Rome. Latins had a strong sense of common identity, sharing a language (Latin) and religion, as well as the myth that they were all descendants of Latinus, the father-in-law of the Trojan hero Aeneas. Like the Etruscan city-states, Latin cities were organized in a defensive league. Members of the league shared rights of residence and trade with one another. Latin culture

was strongly influenced by both the Etruscans and the Greeks. The Latin (or Roman) alphabet, now the world's most widely used, was derived from the Etruscan alphabet (which was itself derived from the Greek alphabet).

MESSAPIANS AND GAULS

The Messapians, who lived along the coasts of Puglia, in southern Italy, were an Illyrian people who had migrated across the Adriatic Sea from the Balkans. They were distantly related to the Albanians. By about 500 BCE, the Messapians were organized in a confederation of city-states and had developed a literate culture under Greek influence.

The most recent immigrants to Italy were the Gauls, a Celtic people from central Europe. One Celtic people, the Insubres, had occupied the western part of the Po River Valley as early as 1000 BCE, but the main Gaulish migration did not take place until around 400 BCE, when they occupied most of Italy north of the Apennine mountains. The area of Gaulish settlement became known as Cisalpine Gaul. The Insubres became the first Celtic people to develop a literate culture when they adopted a version of the Etruscan alphabet in the sixth century BCE.

J. HAYWOOD

The Roman Kingdom and Republic

Ancient Rome was initially a kingdom but, in 509 BCE, the Romans overthrew their monarchy. Under the republic, Rome became a great imperial power.

According to legend, Rome was founded in 753 BCE by twin brothers, Romulus and Remus. The brothers quarreled over which of them should be king of the city. Romulus killed Remus and named the city Rome for himself. Actually, settlement on the site of Rome dates back to around 1000 BCE.

THE KINGDOM OF ROME

Most historians now regard Romulus as an entirely legendary figure. However, his supposed successor, Numa Pompilius (reigned c. 713–673 BCE), was probably a real person. Rome benefited from its position at the lowest bridging point of the Tiber River and easy access to the sea, becoming a prosperous commercial center by 600 BCE. Rome's growth was also aided by its willingness to extend citizenship (usually a jealously restricted privilege in the ancient Mediterranean world) to immigrants who accepted its values. This ability to assimilate new populations was critical to Rome's later success as an imperial power. In 509 BCE, the last king of Rome, Tarquin the Proud (reigned 535–509 BCE), was overthrown by an aristocratic revolution. The republic cannot have become firmly established until after around 474 BCE, however, when the Etruscans withdrew from the region.

THE EARLY REPUBLIC

Under the republic, leadership passed to the Senate, an assembly of the principal male citizens. The Senate was dominated by the heads of the patrician families, who claimed to be descended from the senators appointed by Romulus to advise him. To prevent any one family from dominating the republic, the Senate established a system in which two men (women did not have political rights), the consuls, shared regal powers. One of the dominant themes of the republican period of Roman history (509–27 BCE) was the struggle between the patricians, who wished to maintain their monopoly on power, and the plebeians (non-aristocratic citizens), who wanted greater political influence.

Consuls were elected by the citizen assembly, but voting was by class and was structured so that the richer classes could always outvote the numerically larger poorer classes. To defend their interests, the plebeians created their own popular assembly and elected their own officers, the tribunes. To protect them from attack by the patricians, the plebeians declared the tribunes to be sacred. The plebeians also used "secession," a form of mass civil disobedience, in their struggle with the patricians. The first success of the plebeians came in 451–449 BCE, when they forced the publication of a written law code, the Twelve Tables, which became the foundation of Roman law. This code still forms the basis of law in many countries today. Further concessions made plebeians eligible for election to magistracies, increased the number of plebeians appointed as senators, and gave decisions of the popular assembly the force of law. Despite this, the Roman republic remained essentially an aristocratic oligarchy.

TERRITORIAL EXPANSION

In 396 BCE, the Romans conquered the nearby Etruscan city of Veii, almost doubling its territory. Then, in 387 BCE, Rome was sacked by an invading army of Celtic Gauls, who had recently occupied the Po Valley. The Gauls also attacked the Etruscans and occupied many of their cities. Rome quickly recovered from the sack, but the Etruscans were permanently weakened by their territorial losses. In 338 BCE, Rome conquered its Latin neighbors and incorporated them into the Roman state, giving them full Roman citizenship.

Over the next 60 years, Rome steadily expanded its control to all of peninsular Italy, ending with the capture of the Greek city of Taranto in 272 BCE. The most serious opposition came from the Samnites, with whom the Romans fought three wars (343–341 BCE, 327–304 BCE, and 298–290 BCE). Conquered communities were granted half-citizenship, which gave them most of the rights of Roman citizens but not the right to vote. In time, as these communities became more Romanized, they were offered full citizenship. Colonies of Roman citizens were planted in conquered territory to encourage the process of Romanization. In this way, the diverse Italian peoples were assimilated. By 68 BCE, the entire free-born population of Italy had become Roman citizens.

THE PUNIC WARS

In 264 BCE, a dispute over spheres of influence in Sicily with the North African city of Carthage—which had been founded and settled by Phoenicians from western Asia—led to the outbreak of the First Punic War (264–241 BCE). Rome's eventual victory brought it control of Carthaginian colonies in Sicily, Sardinia, and Corsica. These territories were administered by governors and became the first provinces of the Roman Empire. In 225 BCE, the Romans brought all of modern Italy under their control when they conquered Cisalpine Gaul, in the Po Valley.

A new dispute with Carthage broke out in 218 BCE, this time over Spain, where the Carthaginians had established a new empire, leading to the outbreak of the Second Punic War (218–202 BCE). Carthaginian general Hannibal (247–182 BCE) invaded Italy, hoping that Rome's Italian subjects would rebel. However, most remained loyal to Rome, and the war ended with Rome taking over Carthage's empire in Spain. Carthage was itself conquered in the Third Punic War (149–146 BCE).

EMPIRE AND POLITICAL CRISES

During the Second Punic War, King Philip V (reigned 221–179 BCE) of Macedon (northern Greece) allied with Carthage. In 211 BCE, the Romans sent an army to Greece in retaliation. By 146 BCE, Macedon and Greece were under Roman control. Greek influence on Roman civilization greatly increased as a result. In 133 BCE, the last king of Pergamum in Anatolia (modern Turkey) willed his kingdom to the Roman Empire. Rome was now the dominant power of the Mediterranean world.

Rome's transition from city-state to empire put the republican constitution under increasing strain. The politically influential patrician class benefited disproportionately from the plundered wealth that flooded into Italy, widening social divisions. Bribery and corruption became common in government. The rich used their war profits to build up large landed estates called *latifundia*, worked by cheap labor from the newly conquered provinces. Unable to compete, citizen farmers fell into debt, lost their land, and migrated to Rome to join the ranks of the urban poor. Because only landowners could serve in the army, the strength of the Roman army was compromised; constant wars also placed great political power in the hands of generals.

The tribune Tiberius Gracchus (168–133 BCE) and his brother Gaius (c. 159–121 BCE) attempted to force land reform, but both were murdered by mobs in the pay of the patricians. An invasion by two German tribes, the Cimbri and Teutones, in 113–101 BCE prompted the consul Gaius Marius (157–86 BCE) to abolish the property qualification for military service and create the professional legionary army that became the mainstay of Roman power for the next 500 years. Rome's problems continued with a rebellion by the Italian cities in 91–89 BCE, slave revolts in southern Italy and Sicily in 73–71 BCE, and increasingly violent competition for power among the Roman elite. None of this inhibited the further growth of the empire, however. Politicians such as Crassus (Marcus Licinius Crassus; 115–53 BCE), Pompey (Gnaeus Pompeius Magnus; 106–48 BCE) and Julius Caesar (102–44 BCE) saw conquests as a way to win prestige, wealth, and a loyal following of legionaries to help them pursue their ambitions. Pompey conquered Anatolia, Syria, and Palestine in 67–62 BCE.

A marble bust (c. 50 BCE) of Julius Caesar (100–44 BCE) in the Vatican Museum.

Caesar conquered Gaul in 58–52 BCE. Crassus, however, was killed trying to conquer Parthia in 53 BCE.

Competition between Pompey and Caesar led to civil war in 49–46 BCE, which finally destroyed the republic. Caesar, the victor, declared himself dictator for life and began to introduce a wide range of reforms aimed at improving conditions for the poor. He was popular with the underprivileged, but the senatorial class resented its loss of power and suspected that he planned to restore the monarchy. On March 15, 44 BCE, Caesar was stabbed to death in the Senate, sparking a new civil war.

J. HAYWOOD

The Early Roman Emperors

After the fall of the republic, stability was restored to the Roman world by the introduction of imperial rule by Augustus (Octavian; 63 BCE–14 CE; reigned 27 BCE–14 CE). The first five emperors, the Julio-Claudian emperors, were related.

The civil war that followed the assassination of Roman dictator Julius Caesar (102–44 BCE) was won by his nephew and adopted son, Octavian, after he defeated his rival Mark Antony (83–30 BCE) at the naval battle of Actium in 31 BCE. The members of the Senate (the assembly of the principal male citizens of Rome) and their families hoped that Octavian would restore the republic but feared that he would rule as a military dictator like Caesar. Among the rest of the Roman population, there was little enthusiasm for the restoration of the republic, which had become discredited in its eyes by its corruption and violence. Octavian's solution was to introduce a new form of government that was in reality a thinly disguised absolute monarchy.

In 27 BCE, Octavian took a new name, Augustus ("revered one"), and adopted the title princeps ("first citizen"); his successors preferred the title imperator ("commander"), from which the word *emperor* comes. Two consuls continued to be elected from among the senators, but they had little power. Under the republic, the consuls had been the highest elected officials of the state, the joint heads of government, who had ruled together. The Senate also still met under the empire, but its role became purely advisory.

AUGUSTUS

Augustus embellished Rome with fine buildings and set up a police force and fire brigade. He won over the people with doles of cash and grain and free public entertainment. Augustus made great efforts to build an efficient government that could command the respect and loyalty of Roman citizens and people in the provinces alike. Anticorruption measures cleaned up government in Italy and the provinces. A cult of the emperor as a divine figure was promoted to give the provinces a focus of loyalty. Augustus kept the army out of politics by keeping it busy establishing a defendable frontier for the empire, far from Rome.

Under Augustus, the empire was extended northward to the Danube River. Egypt was annexed, and independent kingdoms in Mauretania (northern modern Algeria and Morocco), Thrace (northeast Greece), and Anatolia (modern Turkey) were reduced to tributary status. Augustus's attempt to conquer Germany was a failure, however, and he advised his successors against further territorial expansion. Despite this, the empire continued to expand for another century.

TIBERIUS

Augustus was succeeded by his stepson, Tiberius (42 BCE–37 CE; reigned 14–37 CE). An able soldier and administrator, Tiberius also had an insecure and suspicious nature. After the death (possibly by poisoning) of his son Drusus (13 BCE–23 CE) in 23 CE, Tiberius retreated to his private villa on the island of Capri. In his absence, rumors about his supposedly depraved private life flourished at Rome. Tiberius made extensive use of the treason laws, which forbade disrespect to the emperor, to curb free speech and destroy his enemies. An atmosphere of terror pervaded the aristocracy during the emperor's later years, and few mourned his death in 37 CE.

CALIGULA AND CLAUDIUS

It soon became apparent that the successor of Tiberius, his grandnephew Gaius (12–41 CE; reigned 37–41 CE), better known by his nickname Caligula, was incapable of ruling. Violent, unpredictable, and convinced that he was a god, Caligula alienated the Senate by appointing his horse as consul. In 41 CE, he was murdered by an officer of the praetorian guard (the imperial bodyguard). After the murder of Caligula, the Senate talked about restoring the republic, but the praetorians forced it to recognize Caligula's uncle, Claudius (10 BCE–54 CE; reigned 41–54 CE) as emperor. The episode exposed two serious weaknesses in the imperial regime: that there was no constitutional way to depose a bad emperor, and that emperors needed the support of the army to retain power.

Claudius's position at the beginning of his reign was weak because he had no links with the army. To win popularity with the legions, he began the Roman conquest of Britain in 43 CE. The project was never completed, and the far north (the greater part of modern Scotland) always remained independent. Claudius took great interest in the provinces, encouraging provincials to take Roman citizenship and making them eligible to join the Senate. He was also an able administrator, but his promotion of freed slaves to positions of power antagonized the aristocracy.

NERO

In 54 CE, Claudius was poisoned by his wife, Agrippina (15–59 CE), to secure the succession of Nero (37–68 CE; reigned 54–68 CE), her son by a previous marriage. Unstable, Nero murdered

The Colosseum in Rome was built by Emperor Vespasian (reigned 69–79 CE).

his mother; his wives; his tutor, the philosopher Seneca the Younger (4 BCE–65 CE); and his half-brother, Britannicus (41–55 CE), the son of Claudius. His reign descended into arbitrary tyranny. Searching for a scapegoat after a disastrous fire that destroyed much of Rome in 64 CE, Nero began the first persecution of Christians.

Nero's downfall was ultimately caused by his neglect of the army. In 68 CE, a rebellion broke out in the army in Gaul and Spain. When the praetorian guards joined the rebellion, Nero fled from Rome and committed suicide. His death brought to an end the Julio-Claudian dynasty.

The turbulent political life of Rome under the dynasty had affected only the senatorial elite. The governmental institutions introduced by Augustus were strong enough to function smoothly irrespective of the personal qualities of the emperors, providing the great mass of Roman citizens and provincials with peace and prosperity.

UNREST AND THE FLAVIAN EMPERORS

The death of Nero was followed by a year of civil war, known as the Year of Four Emperors, after the four rivals for power. The eventual victor was Vespasian (9–79 CE; reigned 69–79), commander of the army in Palestine and a member of the Flavian family. A popular and unpretentious ruler, Vespasian, who was of relatively humble origins, restored stability, and the throne passed peacefully in turn to his sons, Titus (39–81 CE; reigned 79–81 CE) and Domitian (51–96 CE; reigned 81–96 CE). Domitian was a fine soldier and administrator, but his autocratic rule made him unpopular. After a conspiracy against him was discovered in 87 CE, he launched a reign of terror against the senatorial class, who lived in constant fear of denunciation by informers and execution on trumped-up treason charges. In 96 CE, Domitian was murdered by members of his personal staff.

J.HAYWOOD

The Nervo-Trajanic, Antonine, and Illyrian Emperors

The age of the Nervo-Trajanic and Antonine emperors (96–192 CE) is generally considered to be the golden age of the Roman Empire. By its end, however, the empire was facing serious internal and external problems that brought it to the brink of collapse in the third century CE.

Following the assassination of Emperor Domitian (51–96 CE; reigned 81–96 CE), the elderly senator Nerva (c. 30–98 CE; reigned 96–98 CE) was chosen as emperor. Although short, Nerva's reign began a century of peace and prosperity for the Roman Empire. Aware that his lack of military experience gave him little appeal to the army, Nerva adopted as his son and successor Trajan (53–117 CE; reigned 98–117), an experienced general with a distinguished career defending the Rhine frontier. When Nerva fell ill and died shortly after, Trajan's succession was unopposed.

TRAJAN

Trajan had been born in Spain and was the first emperor to come from the provinces. This was a sign of the widening of Roman identity under the empire. Many provincials had become wealthy serving the empire and had become Romanized in their way of life, language, and culture. They saw themselves as being as Roman as anyone born in Rome or Italy. Thanks to the peace and security provided by the Roman Empire, many provinces were now more prosperous than Italy. Italian agriculture suffered because it was cheaper to ship grain in bulk from Egypt and North Africa to Rome than it was to cart it from the surrounding countryside, and Italy's importance within the empire diminished accordingly.

Trajan was a strong and competent ruler: he was remembered by later generations as the "good emperor." His domestic policies supported agricultural improvements, extended the road system, and increased welfare for the poor. At Ostia, the port of Rome, he built a new harbor, and he also constructed new markets in the city itself. Trajan's foreign policy was aggressive, and it was during his reign that the Roman Empire reached its greatest extent following the conquest of Dacia (modern Romania), Armenia, and Mesopotamia (modern Iraq), which had been part of the Parthian Empire. Like Nerva, Trajan adopted his chosen successor, his nephew Hadrian (76–138 CE; reigned 117–138 CE), as his son, so ensuring a smooth transition of power on his death.

HADRIAN

Hadrian, who like Trajan was born in Spain, believed that the empire had become overextended. He withdrew from most of Trajan's conquests in the east and devoted considerable attention to fortifying the frontiers of the empire. A cultured Hellenist, Hadrian spent around half of his reign traveling within the empire for which he sought strong defenses. On his journeys, the emperor inspected the legions and ordered the construction of stone walls in Britain and North Africa and mostly wooden fortifications between the Rhine and Danube rivers to secure the limits of the empire.

A great patron of the arts, Hadrian constructed a lavish villa at Tivoli, near Rome; the gardens partly remain as the best-surviving example of a Roman garden and sacred landscape. He admired Greek learning, wrote poetry, was interested in architecture, and founded cities and temples. In Greece, he completed the construction of the Athenian temple to Zeus (the Greek equivalent of Jupiter) on a monumental scale and even revised the ancient constitution of the city of Athens. In Palestine, Hadrian's decision to construct a temple to Jupiter on the site of the Jewish Second Temple and to ban circumcision led to a major Jewish revolt. The rebellion was put down with ferocity; many Jews were killed, cities destroyed, and the population of Judaea dispersed. Hadrian determined to root out Judaism, and he even renamed Judaea as Syria Palaestina and its capital, Jerusalem as Aelia Capitolina, forbidding Jews from entering the city. Although the last years of his reign were marked by intrigue and growing unpopularity, Hadrian succeeded in leaving a stable, efficiently run empire and, in many ways, came to be seen as a model for later imperial rulers.

THE LATER TRAJAN EMPERORS

Like Trajan, Hadrian chose his successor, Antoninus Pius (86–161 CE; reigned 138–161 CE) by adoption. Antoninus Pius, in turn, adopted his son-in-law, the philosopher Marcus Aurelius (121–180 CE; reigned as coruler 161–169 CE; sole ruler 169–180

The ruins of Hadrian's Villa (Villa Adriana) remain as a large archaeological complex and garden in Tivoli, near Rome.

CE), as his adopted heir. Marcus Aurelius chose Lucius Verus (130–169 CE; reigned 161–169 CE), Hadrian's original choice as heir, to be a coruler.

The adoptive system was finally abandoned, with disastrous results, by Marcus Aurelius, who allowed his incompetent and megalomaniacal son Commodus (161–192 CE; reigned 180–192 CE) to succeed him. Commodus believed himself to be Hercules, the mythical hero and son of the god Jupiter. Commodus abandoned his father's campaign against the Germans, who later ravaged the Rhine borderlands.

THE PERIOD OF ANARCHY

After Commodus was murdered, strangled by a wrestler, in 192 CE, a civil war broke out between rival emperors. The eventual winner, Septimius Severus (146–211 CE; reigned 193–211 CE), a North African, was an able soldier but he failed to restore stable dynastic rule. His son and successor, Marcus Aurelius Antoninus I, better known by his nickname Caracalla (188–217 CE; reigned 211–217 CE), was another tyrant whose reign ended with his murder. Caracalla's one memorable achievement was to extend Roman citizenship to all free inhabitants of the empire in 212 CE.

After Caracalla, emperors came and went in rapid succession for the next 50 years. Dynastic instability was exacerbated by new threats to the empire's frontiers from the Germanic peoples to the north and the Persians in the east. In conditions of nearly constant warfare, the army came to dominate the political life of the empire. Any emperor who was not a good soldier was very quickly overthrown. Rival emperors, promoted by different legions, fought one another for power, while leaving the frontiers open to invasion. In the 260s CE, Gaul, Britain, and Spain (in the west), and Syria, Palestine, and Egypt (in the east) temporarily seceded from Rome under Roman rulers who won local support from the legions by organizing defenses against the invaders. At the same time, Dacia was permanently lost to the Germans.

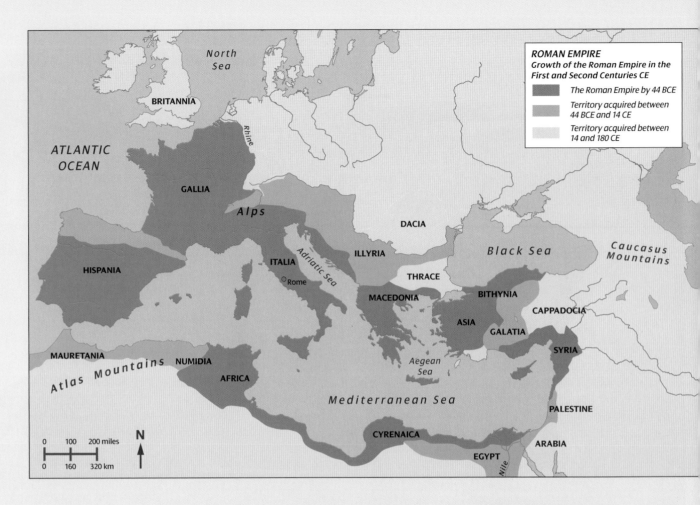

ROMAN EMPIRE
Growth of the Roman Empire in the First and Second Centuries CE

- The Roman Empire by 44 BCE
- Territory acquired between 44 BCE and 14 CE
- Territory acquired between 14 and 180 CE

Emperors were constantly vulnerable to attempted coups. Of the 26 emperors who ruled between 235 CE and 284 CE, all but one died by violence. The efforts of the emperors to buy the loyalty of their troops led them to debase the coinage to raise extra money, but this simply added inflation to the empire's problems. Trade and urban life declined, and recurrent epidemics caused the population to decrease, creating a labor shortage both for the military and for agriculture.

Protected by the Alps and its distance from the frontiers of the empire, Italy did not suffer as badly from invasions as many other provinces, but Milan was attacked by Germanic tribes in 259 CE, and, in 271 CE, a Germanic force penetrated almost to Rome before withdrawing. Politically, Italy's importance in the empire declined still further, however. Most of the emperors who ruled in the third century CE were Illyrian soldiers from the western Balkans, which was the major recruiting ground of the Roman army. Constant wars kept the emperors in the field, and few of them ever visited Rome.

THE ILLYRIAN EMPERORS

The first steps toward the empire's recovery were taken by Emperor Gallienus (218–268 CE; reigned 259–268 CE), who created a more flexible and mobile army by breaking up the

legions into smaller units and increasing the numbers of cavalry. This move also reduced the strength of individual legions as centers of discontent and rebellion. Gallienus was followed by a succession of able, if short-lived, Illyrian emperors who gradually restored the territorial integrity of the empire and secured its frontiers.

Probus (232–282 CE; reigned 276–282 CE) took great interest in farming, and he allowed Franks and other Germanic peoples into frontier regions of the empire to settle unpopulated regions. This immigration and settlement policy had the inadvertent consequence of bringing future enemies of the Roman Empire within its borders. Probus also embarked on military campaigns, adopting the principle that the legions should not be allowed to become idle in case their lack of pressing duty in conquest might prompt them to turn against the emperor.

The internal stability of the empire showed no signs of improving, however. After Emperor Carus (c. 230–283 CE; reigned 282–283 CE) was murdered in 283 CE, another civil war broke out over the succession. The winner, Diocletian (245–313 CE; reigned 284–305 CE), may have seemed at first to be simply another Illyrian soldier, soon to be overthrown and murdered in a coup, but his reign was destined to be one of the most important in Roman history.

J. HAYWOOD

The Collegiate Emperors and the Fall of the Western Roman Empire

Reforms by the emperor Diocletian (245–313 CE; reigned 284–305 CE) saved the Roman Empire from collapse at the end of the third century CE, but the empire was unable to resist a new wave Germanic invasions that began at the end of the fourth century CE.

Diocletian introduced many reforms intended to restore economic confidence, bring inflation under control, defend the frontiers, and address labor shortages. He reformed the army and recodified the legal system. In 303 CE, he also began one of the fiercest persecutions of Christians.

THE COLLEGIATE EMPIRE

Diocletian's most important reform was to introduce a collegiate system to the imperial office in an attempt to restore political stability. Diocletian recognized that the empire was too large, and the problems facing it too complex, for it to be efficiently ruled by one person. He therefore divided the empire into two halves. He ruled the east from Nicomedia in Anatolia, while he appointed a colleague, Maximian (c. 250–305; reigned 286–305 CE), to rule the west (which included Italy). Rome was too far from the frontiers to be convenient, so Maximian moved his capital to Milan. Each emperor, or Augustus, was supported by a junior emperor with the title of Caesar. Diocletian's idea was that on the death or retirement of the Augustus, the Caesar would take his place and then appoint another Caesar as heir apparent. The system was intended to secure smooth successions and ensure that the Augustus already had extensive experience of government.

Diocletian's system was only partly successful. In 305 CE, Diocletian and Maximian abdicated in favor of their Caesars, Galerius (c. 260–311 CE; reigned 305–311 CE) and Constantius (250–306 CE; reigned 305–306 CE). Diocletian retired to his palace at Spalatum (modern Split in Croatia) and played no further part in politics. He died in bed of old age, in 313 CE, the first emperor to die a natural death for one hundred years.

THE EASTERN AND WESTERN EMPIRES

Diocletian's division of the empire into eastern and western halves became normal over the next century, and the Roman Empire was permanently divided after 395 CE. The collegiate system did not survive, however. Diocletian had not counted on the ambitions of Maximian's son Maxentius (c. 278–312; reigned in the west 306–312 CE), and Constantius's son Constantine (c. 272–337; reigned as Constantine I from 306 CE, undisputed in the west 312–324 CE, and in a reunited empire 324–337 CE). The army supported the hereditary principle, so when Constantius died in Britain in 306 CE, the army there immediately declared Constantine Augustus. Meanwhile, Maxentius had also declared himself Augustus, and a new and complex round of civil wars broke out.

By 324 CE, Constantine had eliminated all his rivals and reunited the empire under his sole rule. Constantine believed that the Christian God had helped him win a victory over his rival Maxentius in 312 CE. In gratitude, Constantine issued the Edict of Milan (313 CE), which legalized Christianity and ended years of intermittent persecution by the emperors. Constantine also built many churches, including the first basilica of Saint Peter on the Vatican Hill and the first cathedral of Saint John Lateran in Rome. The bishops of Rome (the popes) used the city's prestige to reinforce leadership of the entire Christian church. Although this was never to be universally accepted, Rome emerged as the major center of Christianity, compensating for its loss of political status after Constantine founded a completely new capital for the empire at Constantinople (modern Istanbul) in 324 CE.

GERMANIC INVASIONS

Throughout the fourth century CE, Germanic tribes maintained constant pressure on the empire's northern frontiers. The situation became critical in the 370s CE, after the Huns invaded eastern Europe, conquering some Germanic tribes and forcing others to flee. One group of refugees, the Visigoths, was admitted to the empire in 376 CE and allowed to settle in the Balkans. The Romans subsequently treated the Visigoths badly, who then rebelled. In 378 CE, Visigoths defeated and killed the eastern emperor Valens (c. 328–378; reigned 364–378 CE) at the battle of Adrianople (modern Edirne, Turkey). The Visigoths were pacified in 382 CE, but rebelled again under their new king, Alaric (reigned 395–410 CE) in 395 CE. In 401 CE, Alaric invaded Italy but was driven out. In 408 CE, Alaric invaded Italy a second time and laid siege to Rome, hoping to force the western

Diocletian's Palace is near modern-day Split in Croatia.

emperor, Honorius (384–423 CE; reigned 395–423 CE), to negotiate with him. Safe in the new western capital at Ravenna, along the Adriatic coast of Italy, Honorius refused; in August 410 CE, Alaric captured and sacked Rome. Honorius still refused to negotiate. Alaric died a few months later, and the Visigoths moved on, finally settling in Gaul.

THE LAST WESTERN EMPEROR

The situation in the Western Roman Empire continued to deteriorate through the fifth century CE. By the 470s CE, Germanic tribes had occupied all of the western empire except Italy. While the Germanic invasions had caused massive economic dislocation and urban decline in the rest of the western empire, Italy had remained relatively unscathed. The most serious invasion was in 452 CE, when Attila (406–453; reigned 434–435) and the Huns ravaged the Po River Valley. In 455 CE, Rome was sacked again, this time by the Vandals, who

had seized North Africa. After Alaric's invasion in 410 CE, the city of Rome rapidly declined, its population falling from around one million in 410 CE to fewer than 50,000 by around 550 CE. The city was saved from complete decay by its historical prestige and growing popularity as a pilgrimage destination. Other Italian cities, including the new capital, Ravenna, flourished. The Roman administration continued to function smoothly, and most of the fabric of Roman life and culture remained intact. The Roman emperors of the west had become politically irrelevant, however. They were the puppets of their generals, to be made and disposed of at will.

In 476 CE, Odoacer (or Odovacar; 435–493 CE), a Germanic mercenary in Roman service, overthrew the last powerless western emperor, Romulus Augustulus (c. 461 or 463–after 476 CE; reigned 475–476 CE), and became ruler of Italy. Although this event is popularly regarded as marking the fall of the Roman Empire, the eastern half of the empire survived until 1453, becoming known as the Byzantine Empire.

J. HAYWOOD

The Ostrogoths and the Lombards

After the deposition of the last Roman emperor of the west in 476 CE, Italy came under the control of a succession of Germanic rulers.

When Odoacer (or Odovacar; 435–493 CE), a Germanic mercenary in Roman service, overthrew the last western emperor in 476 CE, he sent ambassadors to the emperor of the Eastern (or Byzantine) Roman Empire, Zeno (reigned 474–491 CE), offering to rule Italy as imperial viceroy. Zeno accepted Odoacer's offer, and, as a result, Italy remained legally a part of the Eastern Roman Empire, not an independent kingdom. Odoacer maintained the Roman administration and, for most of the population of Italy, life continued unchanged.

THE OSTROGOTHIC KINGDOM

The Eastern Roman Empire was less exposed to Germanic invasion than the west, but it had been forced to allow the Ostrogoths to settle on its territory in the Balkans. In 488 CE, Zeno saw an opportunity to get rid of his unwanted Ostrogothic neighbors. He offered the king of the Ostrogoths, Theodoric (454–526 CE; reigned 471–526 CE), a commission to overthrow Odoacer and rule Italy until the emperor could claim sovereignty in person. Accepting the offer, Theodoric invaded Italy in 489 CE and, in 493 CE, he captured Ravenna, which was the capital of the Western Roman Empire, and executed Odoacer. Although Theodoric used the title of king, as had Odoacer, he officially ruled Italy as an imperial viceroy. Like Odoacer, Theodoric relied on Roman bureaucrats to run his government, although only Goths were allowed to serve in his army.

Theodoric maintained a legal separation between the Ostrogoths (who numbered only around 40,000) and the Italian population. Each lived by separate law codes, and intermarriage was forbidden. The Ostrogoths were Arians, a form of Christianity that the Italian Catholics regarded as heretical; consequently, each people had their own churches and bishops. Theodoric provided Italy with peace and prosperity, but he failed

The Mausoleum of Theodoric (454–526 CE; reigned 471–526 CE) is located just outside Ravenna, Italy. It was built by Theodoric in 520 CE as his future tomb. The mausoleum is now a UNESCO World Heritage Site.

to provide a strong male heir and, after his death, the kingdom passed to a succession of weak rulers.

THE LOMBARDS

Between 535 and 554 CE, Italy was reconquered by the Eastern Roman Empire. Ostrogothic resistance was stiff, and the country was left devastated. The Italian economy collapsed, and urban life declined. In 568 CE, another Germanic people, the Lombards, invaded Italy. They quickly overran most of northern Italy (which is now known as Lombardy for them) and also conquered Spoleto in Umbria and Benevento in the south. The Byzantines retained control of Ravenna, Rome, and a precarious strip of territory between the two, which divided the Lombard territories into two. The Byzantines also held on to the far south, along with the islands of Sicily and Sardinia. By playing a leading role in organizing defenses against the Lombards, the popes emerged as the effective rulers of Rome, under Byzantine sovereignty. The Lombard king Alboin (reigned 569–572 CE) established his capital at Pavia, but neither he nor his successors could impose their authority on Spoleto or Benevento, which became the centers of independent Lombard duchies.

During the reign of Liutprand (reigned 712–744 CE), the Lombards accepted Catholic Christianity (they had originally been Arians like the Ostrogoths or had followed local beliefs). The Lombards were also beginning to assimilate with the native Italian population and to speak Latin. Despite this, strong Germanic influences persisted in the Lombard kingdom, especially in its laws and its military and social institutions. Liutprand took advantage of the weakness of the Byzantine Empire to extend his territory, acquiring the region that is now Emilia Romagna. As a result, Byzantine influence in Italy was further reduced.

J. HAYWOOD

Early Medieval Italy

Through the early medieval period, Italy was dominated by conflicts between the Holy Roman emperors, the papacy, and the city-states of Lombardy. A pattern of geopolitical disunity on the peninsula emerged, which was to last for a millennium.

In 751 CE, the Lombard king Aistulf (reigned 749–756 CE) captured Ravenna, which had been the capital of the Western Roman Empire, and prepared to seize Rome. Ravenna and Rome, as well as a narrow strip of land between them, had remained part of the Eastern Roman (or Byzantine) Empire, which also retained Sicily and Sardinia. Deprived of Byzantine support, Pope Stephen II (reigned 752–757 CE) appealed to the Frankish king Pépin III (714–768 CE; reigned 751–768 CE), better known as Pépin the Short, for support. Pépin invaded Italy and forced Aistulf to return to papal control territories that the papacy claimed had been granted by Roman emperor Constantine I (c. 272–337 CE; reigned from 306 CE, undisputed in the west 312–324 CE, and in a reunited empire 324–337 CE).

In 773 CE, the Lombards again began to encroach on Rome. Following an appeal from Pope Hadrian I (reigned 772–795 CE), the Frankish king Charlemagne (from Carolus Magnus, meaning "Charles the Great"; 742 or 747 CE; reigned as Charles I, 768–814 CE) invaded and conquered the Lombard kingdom in 774–775 CE. Charlemagne further extended the papal territory but made it clear that the popes governed it as his subjects. The Lombard duchies of Spoleto and Benevento acknowledged Charlemagne as overlord but were never fully integrated into his kingdom. In 800 CE, Charlemagne was crowned emperor in Rome by Pope Leo III (reigned 795–815 CE). In time, Charlemagne's successors in this office became known as Holy Roman emperors.

THE ITALIAN KINGDOM

After the death of Charlemagne's son Louis the Pious (Louis I; 778–840 CE; reigned 814–840 CE), the Frankish empire was partitioned between his three sons. Further partitions followed until the empire was briefly reunited under Charles III (better known as Charles the Fat; 839–888 CE; reigned 876–888 CE). After Charles's death, the empire of the Franks broke up, and northern Italy became an independent kingdom under Berengar I (c. 845–924 CE; reigned 888–924 CE), a great-grandson of Charlemagne.

Throughout the ninth century CE, Italy experienced raids by Arab pirates from North Africa. In 846 CE, the pirates even sacked Rome. Between 827 and 878 CE, Arabs conquered and occupied the islands of Sicily (where they established the emirate of Sicily) and Sardinia, reducing the Byzantine hold on Italy to the regions of Calabria and Puglia in the south and a few ports, such as Naples and Venice. Venice was developing as an important maritime power by this time, and it had shaken free of Byzantine control by 1000 CE.

ITALY WITHIN THE HOLY ROMAN EMPIRE

In 950 CE, the principal claim to the kingdom of Italy was inherited by Adelaide (931 or 932–999 CE), daughter of Rudolf (reigned 922–926 CE; died 937 CE) and widow of Lothair II (c. 927–950 CE; reigned 947–950 CE). Her rival, Berengar II (c. 910–966 CE; reigned 950–951 CE), attempted to force Adelaide, who had many suitors because of her inheritance, to marry his son. When she refused and fled, she was eventually besieged by Berengar at Canossa. Adelaide asked German king Otto I (912–973 CE; reigned 936–973 CE) for assistance; he invaded Italy and married Adelaide himself, linking Italy and Germany for the remainder of the Middle Ages. In 962 CE, in conscious emulation of Charlemagne, Otto was crowned emperor in Rome, effectively founding the Holy Roman Empire.

The Holy Roman emperors spent most of their time in Germany. In their absence, the north Italian cities began to develop strong traditions of communal self-government under the leadership of the wealthy merchant class. Under more peaceful conditions in Europe in the eleventh century, there was a general economic recovery. Trade, banking, and textile manufacture flourished in the cities of Lombardy, making it the wealthiest region of western Europe. Cultural life also revived, and Europe's first university was founded at Bologna around 1088.

The later eleventh century was dominated by the Investiture Contest, a dispute with the papacy over rights to appoint bishops. A church reform movement had developed in the mid-eleventh century. Among its chief aims was to end lay influence over the church and to make the papacy independent of the Holy Roman Empire. The dispute broke out in 1075, when Pope Gregory VII (c. 1020–1085; reigned 1073–1085) abolished the right of secular rulers to appoint bishops. As bishops played an important role in the government of medieval states, this was not a right that the emperor, Henry IV (1050–1106; reigned 1056–1106), was willing to give up. The ensuing power struggle ended in compromise in 1122, but not before imperial authority in Italy had been severely damaged. The north Italian cities usurped many imperial rights and became autonomous city-states under only nominal imperial sovereignty. The popes, too, became effectively independent rulers of the Papal States in central Italy.

Miniature from a manuscript in the Vatican Library of Holy Roman emperor Frederick I Barbarossa (1122–1190; reigned 1152–1190) portrayed as a crusader with (right) Henry of Schäftlarn dedicating to him a copy of the History of the First Crusade by Robert of St. Remy.

NORMAN SICILY

While power in northern Italy became decentralized in the eleventh century, in the south a stronger centralized state emerged after the region was conquered by the Normans. In the early eleventh century, southern Italy was an area of conflict and competition between Lombard duchies, the Byzantine Empire, and the Arab emirate of Sicily. In 1017, Norman mercenaries were invited to settle in the area by the Lombard dukes. Following the arrival of Robert Guiscard (c. 1015–1085), an

adventurer and soldier and half-brother to the count of Apulia, the Normans began to conquer their own principalities in 1042. By 1072, the Normans had conquered the Lombard duchies and expelled the Byzantines and Arabs from Italy and Sicily. The Norman principalities were united by Robert's nephew Roger II (1095–1154; reigned 1105–1154), who was recognized by the papacy as king of Naples and Sicily in 1130.

GUELPHS AND GHIBELLINES

Holy Roman emperor Frederick I Barbarossa (1122–1190; reigned 1152–1190) attempted to recover the imperial rights lost during the Investiture Contest. Supported by the papacy, which feared a revival of imperial power, the northern Italian cities united to form the Lombard League and defeated Frederick at the battle of Legnano in 1176. Frederick was forced to recognize the cities' autonomy in return for their recognition of his sovereignty. The dispute divided Italians into rival parties of Guelphs (supporters of the papacy) and Ghibellines (supporters of Frederick's Hohenstaufen dynasty). Their rivalry would be a major factor in Italian politics into the Renaissance.

In 1186, Frederick found a new way to strengthen his dynasty's position in Italy when he arranged the marriage of his son, the future emperor Henry VI (1165–1197; reigned as Holy Roman emperor Henry VI, 1190–1197, and as Henry I, king of Sicily, 1194–1997), to Constance (1154–1198; reigned 1194–1198), the heiress to the Norman kingdom of Sicily and Naples. However, the Normans opposed Henry, as did the papacy, which feared it would lose its independence if it was surrounded by Hohenstaufen lands. Henry invaded and conquered Sicily in 1194, so bringing all of Italy except the Papal States under Hohenstaufen control. Three years later, Henry died of malaria at Messina, leaving as heir his infant son, Frederick II (1194–1250; reigned as Frederick II, Holy Roman emperor, 1212–1250, and Frederick I, king of Sicily and Naples, 1197–1250).

J. HAYWOOD

The Hohenstaufens in Sicily

In the late twelfth century, the German Hohenstaufen dynasty, whose members were Holy Roman emperors, acquired the throne of Sicily through marriage, transforming the balance of power in Italy.

Under the leadership of Robert Guiscard (c.1015–1085) and his successors, the Norman rulers of Sicily (which included Naples and southern Italy as well as the island of Sicily) transformed one of the most unstable areas of southern Europe into one of its most centralized and tightly organized kingdoms. The Normans proved to be effective allies of the popes in their struggles with the German emperors for power in Italy. However, the Hohenstaufen emperor, Henry VI (1165–1197; reigned as Holy Roman emperor Henry VI, 1190–1197, and as Henry I, king of Sicily, 1194–1997), succeeded to the Sicilian throne through his wife, Constance of Sicily (1154–1198; reigned 1194–1198). As a result, the kingdom of Sicily effectively became an arm of the Holy Roman Empire.

Remains of the castle at Melfi, located in the Southern Italian region of Basilicata. The walls were originally built by the Normans, but the doorway, known as Porta Venosina, was built by Emperor Frederick II. In 1231, Emperor Frederick II proclaimed the Constitutions of Melfi (or Constitutiones Augustales) in Melfi.

A FOREIGN DYNASTY

Many Norman barons in Sicily were enraged at the prospect of a foreign king, and the German troops he brought with him in 1194, when he claimed his throne, were widely detested. Henry imposed his will on his recalcitrant subjects with considerable brutality. His son, Frederick II (1194–1250; reigned as Frederick II, Holy Roman emperor, 1212–1250, and Frederick I, king of Sicily, 1197–1250), did attempt to rule well; in 1231, he issued the Constitutions of Melfi, a remarkably advanced written law code, which remained the basis of Sicilian laws until 1819.

However, Hohenstaufen power in Italy attracted the enmity of others. Successive popes were determined to oust them, and north Italian city-states, such as Milan and Venice, were only too willing to join coalitions hostile to the German dynasty. Frequent absences, in his German realm and on crusade in 1228, added to Frederick's problems in Italy. Sicily was too valuable a source of wealth to allow intentions of good government to interfere with collecting taxes. The Hohenstaufens imposed ruinous taxation on Sicily, which undermined economic development and threatened to provoke a peasant revolt.

Frederick inflicted a crushing defeat on his most formidable foe, the Lombard League, a coalition of several northern cities, at the battle of Cortenuova (1237). However, assuming that opposition was destroyed, he rejected peace offers from the city

of Milan, demanding abject surrender. Unable to accept such a humiliation and strongly supported by the pope, the Milanese fought on; in 1248, they delivered an equally crushing defeat on Frederick at the battle of Parma.

THE LAST HOHENSTAUFENS

In the long term, Hohenstaufen rule in Sicily was unlikely to survive. The implacable hostility of the popes and the determination of north Italian states never to permit a single ruler to dominate the Italian Peninsula were too formidable a combination. Through a lifetime of struggles, Frederick never really secured his position.

After Frederick's death, his most relentless enemy, Pope Innocent IV (c. 1195–1254; reigned 1243–1254) was determined to break Hohenstaufen power once and for all. The pope refused to recognize Frederick's heir, Conrad (1228–1254; reigned as Conrad IV, Holy Roman emperor, and as Conrad I, king of Sicily, 1250–1254), and offered the Sicilian crown to an English prince, Edmund "Crouchback" (1245–1296), the earl of Lancaster. Edmund never visited Sicily, and the offer was an empty gesture. A defiant Conrad was excommunicated shortly before his death, and neither his son, Conradin (1252–1268; reigned as Conrad II, king of Sicily, 1254–1258, and, contested, 1266–1268), nor his illegitimate half-brother, Manfred (1232–1266; reigned 1258–1266), were strong enough to hold on to Sicilian power.

Conrad II was the natural leader of the anti-papal Ghibellines party in Italy—the Ghibellines were opposed by the Guelphs (supporters of the papacy), and their rivalry was a major factor in Italian politics through the Middle Ages. Conrad was deposed by his uncle, Manfred, but, in 1265, the pope appointed Charles of Anjou (1226–1285; reigned as Charles I of Sicily, 1268–1282), son of King Louis VIII of France (1187–1226; reigned 1223–1226), as king. After Manfred's death, Conrad had to fight Charles for his throne. In 1266, at the battle of Benevento, Charles of Anjou, with strong papal backing, finally destroyed Hohenstaufen power in Sicily and established a new dynasty. Conrad was detained, handed to Charles, and executed in 1268.

J. SWIFT

Italy from the Twelfth through the Fifteenth Century

The medieval world saw the emergence in western Europe of several of today's unitary nation states, often with surprisingly durable frontiers. Yet in Italy, a patchwork of small states, the modern national border was not established until the nineteenth century.

Italy in the Middle Ages comprised hereditary duchies and principalities, the kingdoms of Sicily and Naples in the south, the Papal States in the center, and a number of city-state republics. There is considerable debate over the influence of various geographical, cultural, and political factors on medieval Italy's lack of political unity.

There were undoubtedly wide variations in climate and land use in Italy. A north-south divide still persists, if not as glaringly as in medieval Italy, when the north was the economic powerhouse of Europe and the birthplace of the Renaissance. The common view is that the south lagged, with its economy based mainly on agriculture and fishing. Even so, some contemporary accounts—such as the *Decameron* by Giovanni Boccaccio (1313–1375)—paint a vibrant picture of the south, especially Naples, during this period, leading some commentators to date the decline of the south only from the end of eighteenth century. Arabic and Byzantine cultural influences were seen in the south; northern European influences had more impact in the north. There was effectively no single language, but a collection of almost mutually unintelligible regional dialects of Italian. Although other nations, such as France, largely overcame similar divisions, Italy was prevented from emerging as a unitary state as political factors exacerbated regional divisions.

POPE AND EMPEROR

Early medieval Italy, in theory at least, was ruled by the German emperor, from the mid-tenth century known as the Holy Roman emperor. In 1046, Emperor Henry III (1017–1056; reigned 1046–1056) had exerted imperial authority when there were no less than three claimants to the papacy—he dismissed all three and selected his own candidate. However, such an assertion of power was unacceptable to the papacy, and, in 1075, Pope Gregory VII (c. 1020–1085; reigned 1073–1085) and Emperor Henry IV (1050–1106; reigned 1056–1106) entered into the Investiture Controversy. At issue was whether the pope or the emperor should appoint abbots and bishops in imperial lands. In essence, however, it was a battle for primacy between the two, which developed into a long, sporadic struggle by successive popes to exclude imperial power from Italy.

Rivalry between the papacy and the emperor characterized the political life of much of medieval Italy. Two parties emerged, the Guelphs, who supported the pope, and the Ghibellines, who favored the emperor. The defeat of Emperor Frederick II (1194–1250; reigned as Holy Roman emperor, 1212–1250, and as Frederick I, king of Sicily, 1197–1250) and his Italian Ghibelline allies in 1248 by a coalition of his enemies at the battle of Parma effectively marked a papal triumph. However, this struggle—which affected central and southern Italy more than the northern regions—allowed developments in northern Italy to proceed without interference.

NORTHERN ITALY

From the tenth century, various cities in Lombardy had begun expelling feudal overlords and establishing republican governments, where magistrates, for example, were elected. During the twelfth century, such communes (or city-states) developed across northern and central Italy. They began extending their authority into the *contando* (agricultural hinterland), seeking markets and investment opportunities, and offering a measure of security in return. Textiles, especially woolens, were the mainstay of their prosperity. The great ports of Venice, Genoa, and Pisa established a network of trading interests stretching from Africa to northern Europe, turning the Mediterranean into the economic center of the medieval world. These city-states often fought among themselves and formed coalitions to further their own immediate interests. However, they generally had a common interest in keeping imperial power weak in Italy because a strong emperor might crush their independence and tax them. As a result, many of the communes entered the Lombard League, which defeated imperial forces at Legnano, in 1176, and decisively at Parma in 1248.

Near constant conflict, however, did have often unfortunate consequences for the communes. From the thirteenth century, many were increasingly dominated by political struggles between nobles who controlled the government and the *popolo* (non-nobles), who included wealthy professionals, bankers, and merchants who wanted to enter the nobility, as well as artisans, who wanted fairer taxes and justice. In some cities, notably Florence, the *popolo* gained constitutional changes and dominated government through their guilds. Notwithstanding, in most city-states, the clamoring of the *popolo* allowed the emergence of a single great family, such as the Carrera in Padua and the Visconti and, later, the Sforzas in Milan.

By the fourteenth century, with the notable exceptions of Genoa, Siena, Lucca, Arezzo, Pisa, Florence and Venice, republican governments had given way to ducal and princely houses in most of the city-states. At the same time, the cities were being embellished with new churches and municipal buildings, and universities were established at Padua, Naples, and Rome. With comparatively high levels of literacy, the Italian Peninsula was ideal ground for the Renaissance, the period when interest in art, science, and discovery intensified, transforming European culture and science from the late fourteenth and fifteenth centuries.

THE PAPAL STATES

Central Italy—from Lazio (the region around Rome) through Umbria and Marche to Romagna (the southeastern part of the modern region of Emilia Romagna) in the north—lay outside

these geopolitical trends. The region, which had almost no city-states, was ruled as a sovereign territory by the popes. The papacy in Rome was determined to establish the Papal States as an effective power, within which the pope need never fear the domination of an emperor or a king again. In the process, individual popes became ever more worldly, more secular rulers than religious leaders. Pope Julius II (1443–1513; reigned 1503–1513), for example, led his troops into battle. Growing unease with an earthly politician claiming spiritual authority over the Christian world paved the way toward the Protestant Reformation from 1517.

THE SOUTH

In southern Italy, the demise of the Hohenstaufen dynasty allowed the installation of a French dynasty, the Angevins. However, the perceived misrule of the first king of the new dynasty, Charles of Anjou (1226–1285; reigned as Charles I of Sicily, 1268–1282), led to a massive uprising in Sicily, the Sicilian Vespers, in 1282. The result was partition, with Naples being ruled by Charles and his Angevins successors, while a (Spanish) Aragonese dynasty controlled the island of Sicily—Peter I of Sicily (Peter the Great; 1239–1285; reigned as Peter III of Aragon, 1276–1285, and as Peter I of Sicily, 1282–1285) was the son-in-law of Manfred (1232–1266; reigned 1258–1266), king of Sicily. As a result, Spanish monarchs ruled Sicily until the early eighteenth century. Subsequent hostility between the rulers of the kingdoms of Sicily and Naples resulted in ruinous overtaxation, destroying any chance of sharing in the prosperity of northern Italy. The impoverished peasantry of the south were left at the mercy of great landowners.

FOREIGN INTERVENTION

In northern Italy, rivalries between city-states and their constantly shifting alliances were to prove their undoing. In 1494, the duke of Milan, Ludovico Sforza (1452–1508; reigned 1494–1499), seeking advantage in his disputes with neighboring cities, took the fateful and ultimately disastrous step of inviting the French king, Charles VIII (1470–1498; reigned 1483–1498), to intervene in Italian affairs. The resulting invasion led to Spanish intervention and sparked off a series of wars that were to make Italy the battlefield of Europe. During these conflicts, the Italian city-states were reduced to political insignificance, and Italy's economic and cultural preeminence was destroyed.

Dante Alighieri (1265–1321), a poet from Florence, is considered to be the father of the Italian language.

J. SWIFT

The Papal States

Between the eighth and nineteenth centuries, the popes were not only the spiritual leaders of the Catholic Church but the temporal rulers of much of central Italy. Particularly in the Middle Ages, temporal concerns often seemed to outweigh spiritual ones.

From the fourth century CE, the popes had acquired considerable lands around Rome. Then, in 756 CE, Pope Stephen II (reigned 752–757 CE) received territory in the Donation of Pepin from the Frankish King, Pépin III (714–768 CE; reigned 751–768 CE). This grant gave the popes temporal (or political) authority over a strip of land that cut across the Italian Peninsula, from the coast west of Rome to the Adriatic Sea in the east. The degree to which that temporal authority was subordinated to the Frankish kings, and subsequently German emperors, remained unclear. The extent of this territory and the level of papal control over it varied greatly over the centuries. However, the Donation of Pepin did provide the basis on which succeeding popes could build an independent state.

THE PAPAL STATES AND THE GERMAN EMPERORS

In 1046, the church faced the embarrassment of no less than three people claiming to be the rightful pope. The German Holy Roman emperor, Henry III (1017–1056; reigned 1046–1056) acted as arbiter, dismissed all three, and appointed his own candidate. Such a display of imperial power fed a growing determination by succeeding popes to assert their independence. In 1073, Gregory VII (c. 1020–1085; reigned 1073–1085) was elected pope, largely through the acclaim of the Roman people and without consulting the emperor, Henry IV (1050–1106; reigned 1056–1106). Gregory, an astute politician and reformer, was soon locked in conflict with the emperor.

The Investiture Controversy (1075–1122) was ostensibly a quarrel over whether the pope or the emperor should appoint bishops and abbots in imperial territory. In essence, however, it was a struggle for supremacy between the two in Italy. Henry proclaimed Gregory deposed, while Gregory proclaimed Henry both excommunicated and deposed. Henry was humiliatingly forced to perform penance and beg forgiveness, standing barefoot in the snow at Canossa in 1077—but by 1084 he had occupied Rome and was crowned emperor by his own candidate to the papal throne, the so-called antipope, Clement III (c. 1029–1100; "reigned" 1080–1100). Gregory had to summon the Normans, who ruled Sicily, for rescue, but the Normans only marched when their leader, Robert Guiscard (c. 1015–1085), felt directly threatened by Henry, and Guiscard's troops took the opportunity to sack Rome.

This rivalry between the papacy and the emperor found expression in the emergence of two broad parties in medieval Italy: the Guelphs, who supported the popes, and their opponents, the Ghibellines, who favored the emperor.

Antagonism between Guelphs and Ghibellines underlay many of the conflicts and political arguments of the period in Italy.

Continuing conflict and cyclical swings in fortune emphasized to the popes the need for a solid territorial base and real temporal power. In no other way, it seemed, would the papacy ever be able to impose its authority over militarily powerful neighbors. This need was highlighted between 1194 and 1266, when members of the Hohenstaufen dynasty were not only emperors but also kings of Sicily. As a result, the papal territories were effectively surrounded by the lands of—or of those owing allegiance to—the Holy Roman emperor. In order to remove the perceived Hohenstaufen threat and to end this encirclement, successive popes entered into coalitions and military alliances and carried out covert diplomacy. As part of this campaign, in 1263, Pope Urban IV (c. 1195–1264; reigned 1261–1264) declared the Hohenstaufen king of Sicily dethroned and appointed in his place a French prince, Charles of Anjou (1226–1285; reigned as Charles I of Sicily, 1268–1282), to the Sicilian throne. Charles gained his throne through military action, removing the Hohenstaufens as the pope's southern neighbor.

PAPAL CAPTIVITY AND THE GREAT SCHISM

The end of Hohenstaufen power in Italy did not free the papacy; it simply left it at the mercy of French kings, who did not hesitate to pressure popes to serve their ends. Pope Boniface VIII (c. 1235–1303; reigned 1294–1303) had an uncertain temper, possibly because of a painful illness, and violently quarreled with King Philip IV of France (1268–1314; reigned 1285–1314). As a result, the French king detained the pope in France.

The fourteenth century saw seven French popes in succession. Meanwhile, the Papal States were becoming noted for their economic backwardness and internal strife. The Roman nobility could also threaten and intimidate popes, and some popes felt unsafe in Rome because of the power of the great Roman princely families.

In 1307, the French monarchy detained Pope Clement V (c. 1260–1314; reigned 1305–1314) in France after his election and required him to establish himself at Avignon in southern France. Consequently, Avignon and its surrounding district became part of the Papal States and remained a papal possession until the French Revolution. The popes were to remain in Avignon for the next 73 years, a period known as the Babylonian Captivity. The five popes following Clement were, like him, all French, but the last, Gregory XI (1329–1378; reigned 1370–1378), returned the seat of the papacy to Rome in 1377. In the absence of the pope, Rome had become chaotic. While the pope was in Avignon, a colorful Roman politician, Cola di Rienzo (c. 1313–1354), attempted to found a Roman republic in an effort to end the prevailing lawlessness.

Neglected, much of the city fell into decay. With the long absences of the popes, along with challenges to their legitimacy, the Papal States sank ever further into anarchy, with local nobles usurping the power of papal officials. Attempts to reimpose papal authority effectively amounted to wars of reconquest (1319–1334 and 1353–1363), which saw much loss of life and few achievements.

The papal return to Rome was followed by the Great Schism, a period when there were popes in Rome and rival antipopes in Avignon. Urban VI (c. 1318–1389; reigned 1378–1389) had been elected largely through the influence of the Roman mob. He subsequently ruled so severely that some cardinals withdrew their allegiance—an invalid action—and elected a rival. Antipopes "reigned" in Avignon until 1417.

RENEWED AUTHORITY AND DECLINE

Only in the fifteenth century did the popes fully reestablish their temporal authority and attempt to extend it across central Italy. To do so, they conducted themselves as the most secular of secular princes and exercised their power ruthlessly. This ruthless secularism reached its height with Julius II (1443–1513; reigned 1503–1513). Julius was a warrior prince, who glorified Rome with the best of Renaissance art, including the works of Raphael (Raffaello Sanzio; 1483–1520) and Michelangelo (Michelangelo di Lodovico Buonarroti Simoni; 1475–1564), and laid the foundation stone of the present Saint Peter's basilica. He also established the Swiss Guard, at the time a highly effective mercenary army, which he personally led into battle. Secular power, however, was won at the cost of spiritual authority. In 1527, owing to the unwise political maneuverings of Pope Clement VII (1478–1534; reigned 1523–1534), troops of the Holy Roman emperor Charles V (1500–1558; reigned 1519–1555) took it upon themselves to sack Rome, reducing much of the city to ruins.

Pope Sixtus V (1520–1590; reigned 1585–1590) rebuilt much of Rome, constructing broad new streets. He enforced the law and reordered the administration of the city and the Papal States as well as the church. Subsequently, prosperity returned to Rome and commerce developed. In a period of great cultural activity, the powerful princely families of Rome constructed large palaces. However, by this time, Rome was not even the leading city in Italy, and its influence decreased.

Thereafter, as the center of European political and economic power swung away from the Mediterranean to the Atlantic powers, the importance of the Papal States in international affairs declined. At the same time, the Reformation swept much of northern Europe, where Catholicism became a minority religion. As a result, the power of the pope further decreased. Increasingly within Europe, the Papal States were seen as a minor secular power, and the secular rights of the popes were often treated with indifference. Despite the often strenuous efforts of the popes, who built a more centralized and efficient administration, their domains remained economically backward.

Through the seventeenth and eighteenth centuries, the popes were primarily religious leaders. Their different character from the secular princes of the Renaissance is illustrated by the saintly reformer Innocent XI (1611–1689; reigned 1676–1689), who was known as the "Father of the Poor," and Benedict XIV (1675–1758; reigned 1740–1758), who is often cited as the greatest intellect ever to occupy the papal throne.

THE ROMAN REPUBLIC AND FRENCH RULE

From the sixteenth through eighteenth centuries, the borders of the Papal States remained stable, and the pope's sovereignty was exercised over Romagna, Marche, Umbria, and the area known as the Patrimony (present-day Lazio) plus two enclaves in southern Italy, Ponte Corvo and Benevento. In 1796, French revolutionary armies upset these territorial arrangements. Forces led by Napoléon Bonaparte (1769–1821) conquered the Papal States; in 1798, after riots in the city, the French occupied Rome and established the Roman Republic. Pope Pius VI (1717–1799; reigned 1775–1799) opposed the French and was deported by them to France, where he died.

The Roman Republic does appear to have enjoyed a degree of popular support, especially among a growing urban middle class, who embraced the ideals of representative government. However, the republic was short-lived and, in 1799, the pope's sovereignty was restored. Pope Pius VII (1742–1823; reigned 1800–1823) reached a concordat with France and, in 1804, he attended the coronation of Napoléon as French emperor. Pius later opposed the emperor's ambitions and was arrested and imprisoned. In 1809, the Papal States were annexed to France.

THE END OF THE PAPAL STATES

The Congress of Vienna, the international conference held after the Napoleonic Wars, restored the Papal States (1814–1815), and Pius VII became a secular ruler again. However, the liberal ideas of the French Revolution remained current. Papal secular rule appeared reactionary and ultraconservative to many of those who lived in the Papal States. Discontent led to political instability and, when revolts against absolute monarchies swept across Europe in 1830–1831, there was a renewed, short-lived attempt to recreate the republic in Rome. The election of Pope Pius IX (1792–1878; reigned 1846–1878) was briefly welcomed by Italian nationalists because he seemed sympathetic to Italian national unity. However, these hopes proved fruitless, and Pius was forced to flee Rome in 1849, when a revolt broke out following a second wave of revolutions across Europe in 1848–1849.

The ideas of the French Revolution spurred the concept of *risorgimento* ("resurrection"), the creation of a single state for all Italian speakers. The northern kingdom of Sardinia-Piedmont became one of the main centers of this movement. In 1859, its prime minister, Camillo Benso, count of Cavour (1810–1861; in office 1852–1859 and 1860–1861), used French support to bring about a war with Austria. Defeated at the Battle of Solferino and San Martino, Austria was

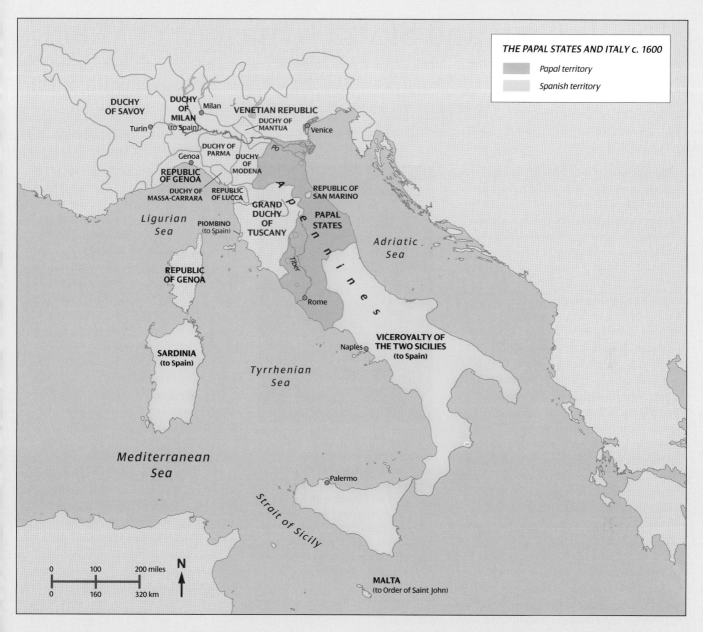

THE PAPAL STATES AND ITALY c. 1600

Papal territory

Spanish territory

DUCHY OF SAVOY

DUCHY OF MILAN (to Spain)

Milan

Turin

VENETIAN REPUBLIC

DUCHY OF MANTUA

Venice

Po

DUCHY OF PARMA

DUCHY OF MODENA

Genoa

REPUBLIC OF GENOA

DUCHY OF MASSA-CARRARA

REPUBLIC OF LUCCA

GRAND DUCHY OF TUSCANY

REPUBLIC OF SAN MARINO

PAPAL STATES

Ligurian Sea

PIOMBINO (to Spain)

Apennines

Adriatic Sea

REPUBLIC OF GENOA

Tiber

Rome

SARDINIA (to Spain)

Tyrrhenian Sea

VICEROYALTY OF THE TWO SICILIES (to Spain)

Naples

Mediterranean Sea

Palermo

Strait of Sicily

0   100   200 miles

0   160   320 km

N

MALTA (to Order of Saint John)

forced to relinquish Lombardy to Sardinia-Piedmont. At the same time, successful revolts against the rulers of the northern central duchies of Parma, Modena, and Tuscany had resulted in the flight of their rulers. Piedmontese troops occupied these states, which were annexed the following year. The people of the Legations—the part of the Papal States comprising Romagna, Marche, and Umbria—had also risen in rebellion and had expelled papal administrators. In 1860, the Legations were also annexed to Sardinia-Piedmont, and the Patrimony (Lazio) was all that was left of the Papal States.

Italian revolutionary Giuseppe Garibaldi (1807–1882) then launched a private invasion of Sicily. Against all odds, Garibaldi prevailed, establishing a base upon which to build a united Italian republic. This was a threat to the Piedmontese monarchy, and the government of Sardinia-Piedmont sent troops south to demand that Garibaldi surrender Sicily. The invasion of the Papal States that this troop movement involved was incidental. In 1861, the enlarged Sardinia-Piedmont joined with the Two

Sicilies (Naples and Sicily) to form the new kingdom of Italy, to which was added Venetia in 1866 (obtained after an alliance with Prussia in a war against Austria).

Under French protection and with a French garrison in the city, Rome itself was left in the hands of the pope. However, with the outbreak of the Franco-Prussian War (1870–1871), French forces withdrew from Rome, leaving what remained of the Papal States defenseless and allowing the Italians to seize Rome as their capital. Pope Pius IX could only excommunicate those responsible and forbid Catholics from taking part in the political life of Italy— leaving the church with no direct influence in the Italian Parliament until the 1920s. The pope had no secular power left. The Italian authorities offered him continuing sovereignty over the Leonine City (the Roman district of Borgo), the area surrounding the Vatican, but the pope refused and retreated into the Vatican, where he considered himself to be a prisoner.

J. SWIFT

The Visconti and Sforza Dynasties of Milan

From the fourteenth century, the city of Milan, under the energetic Visconti and Sforza dynasties, began to expand its territory in all directions.

The members of the Milanese Visconti and Sforza dynasties made their city the single most powerful city-state in Italy. Ultimately, however, Milan became so rich a prize that foreign powers would fight each other for the privilege of annexing it.

THE VISCONTIS

Ottone Visconti (1207–1295) was appointed archbishop of Milan by Pope Urban IV (c. 1195–1264; reigned 1261–1264) in 1262, in order to wrest control of the city from the ruling Della Torre family. After considerable fighting against the Della Torre faction, Ottone succeeded in the battle of Desio (1277) and became captain-general (ruler) of Milan. Afterward, he ignored the republican form of Milanese government and established a dynasty through his nephew, Matteo I (1250–1322; in office as captain-general 1287–1302 and 1310–1317; reigned as hereditary lord 1317–1322). From 1317, the head of the Visconti family ruled Milan as hereditary lord, and Giovanni Visconti (1290–1354; reigned 1339–1354), archbishop of Milan, extended his territory, acquiring much of Liguria and Emilia.

In 1395, Gian Galeazzo Visconti (1351–1402; reigned as lord 1385–1395 and as Gian Galeazzo I, duke of Milan 1395–1402), declared himself duke. He established the Viscontis as "royal" and married a French princess. Under Gian Galeazzo, Visconti Milan reached its greatest territorial extent, and he also founded the present Milan cathedral. The Viscontis were generally ruthless and competent rulers, and they had a reputation for cruelty. The dynasty greatly increased the wealth of Milan, where the economy was based on manufacturing armor and woolens and, increasingly, on banking. They used this wealth to finance wars of expansion, gaining control of much of Lombardy, and alarming neighboring Florence and Venice sufficiently to ally with the pope in order to contain Milan.

THE SFORZAS

The last Visconti, Filippo Maria (1392–1447; reigned 1412–1447), had no sons. With his death, a succession crisis opened the way

The altarpiece known as the Pala Sforzesca (completed in 1494) combines the religious theme of the Virgin and Child in conversation with Fathers of the Church, with detailed portraits of the artist's sponsor, Duke Ludovico Sforza (1452–1508; reigned 1494–1499), his wife Isabella d'Este, and their children. The artist is known as Master of the Pala Sforzesca.

for his son-in-law, Francesco Sforza (1401–1466; reigned 1450–1466), a successful *condottiere* (mercenary), to claim the ducal title. Initially, the Milanese attempted to reestablish a republic. However, anarchy and famine soon brought an end to republican rule, despite strong Venetian support. After this failure to reinstate republicanism, few cared to challenge Sforza, but because of his obscure origins, it was only in 1494 that the dynasty received recognition of the ducal title from the Holy Roman emperor—Milan nominally lay within the boundaries of the Holy Roman Empire.

Shrewd politicians and diplomats, the Sforzas increased the wealth of Milan and their own incomes through taxation. They continued the aggressive and acquisitive policies of the Viscontis. Duke Ludovico (1452–1508; reigned 1494–1499) was a sponsor of the arts and patron of Leonardo da Vinci (1452–1519), who famously painted *The Last Supper* in the church of Santa Maria delle Grazie, where Ludovico intended to establish the Sforza family burial site. Ludovico did much to bring the Italian Renaissance to Milan, but he did not share the political acumen of many of his predecessors. In 1494, seeking advantage over his local enemies, he encouraged the French king, Charles VIII (1470–1498; reigned 1483–1498), to intervene in Italian affairs. This was to prove a disastrous error. In 1499, Charles's successor and second cousin, Louis XII (1462–1515; reigned 1498–1515), whose grandmother had been a Visconti, seized Milan for himself, deposing and imprisoning Ludovico.

Several years of conflict between the Sforzas and the French saw Milan change hands a number of times. The French occupied Milan from 1499 through 1512, when, with Swiss military help, Ludovico's son, Massimiliano (1491–1530; reigned 1512–1515), was restored. He, in turn, was deposed by the French, who again occupied Milan from 1515 to 1525, when Milanese independence was restored, after the Battle of Pavia, under Ludovico's younger son, Francesco (1492–1535; reigned 1525–1535). Near constant warfare exhausted and impoverished the city, allowing the Spanish to seize control in 1535, ending Milanese independence forever.

J. SWIFT

Venice

The Most Serene Republic of Venice, sometimes called La Serenissima, grew from a small city-state to one of the great powers of the Middle Ages, establishing a territorial and trading empire in the eastern Mediterranean.

Venice probably began in the fifth century CE as a sanctuary for refugees from Hun and Lombard invaders of northeast Italy. A collection of islands and sandbanks protected by a lagoon, it was ideally sited for defense. The location also turned out to be suited for commerce. With easy access to the sea and to inland waterways, it became wealthy through the trade in commodities, such as grain, timber, wine, and salt.

EARLY VENICE

From the days of Byzantine Emperor Justinian I (c. 482–565; reigned 527–565 CE), Venice was a Byzantine city at the edge of the region of effective Byzantine rule. Its governor, or doge (duke), was initially a Byzantine official. Byzantine rule enhanced the city's prosperity. As a trading center, Venice imported goods, such as spices, from Asia and commodities, such as metals, from central Europe. Growing wealth was also accompanied by relative geographical and political isolation: Venice was effectively autonomous at the height of Byzantine power.

As Byzantine power began to decline, Venice was free to expand its territory and power into former Byzantine lands. The city first acquired the *dogado* (the strip of land surrounding the lagoon); by the late tenth century, Venice was actively imposing its authority along the Dalmatian coast (modern-day Croatia). The need to protect trade from piracy encouraged the city to develop formidable naval power. When the First Crusade captured Jerusalem (1099), new trade opportunities were opened for Venice. Political opportunities also were developing. During the twelfth century, the doge ceased to be an autocrat and became an elected official under a republican form of government.

AN INTERNATIONAL POWER

The growing power and international importance of Venice was evident when, in 1177, Doge Sebastiano Ziani (c. 1102–1178; in office 1172–1178) brokered a peace between Pope Alexander III (c. 1100–1181; reigned 1159–1181) and Holy Roman emperor Frederick I Barbarossa (1122–1190; reigned 1152–1190). By this time, Venice regarded Constantinople, the Byzantine capital, as a serious trading rival. In 1204, Doge Enrico Dandolo (also given as Dandalo; c. 1107–1205; in office 1192–1205) helped maneuver the knights of the Fourth Crusade into sacking the city. The

damage to Constantinople allowed Venice to be unchallenged in the eastern Mediterranean, and the city became an imperial power. With the (temporary) overthrow of Constantinople, Venice acquired a considerable area of former Byzantine territory. However, the extension of Venetian power made the city-state an object of fear and jealousy.

Between 1298 and 1381, Venice fought a series of four wars with Genoa, its main Italian city-state trading rival, for domination of Mediterranean trade. Venice suffered a number of heavy defeats and costly, indecisive victories. That Venice ultimately triumphed was widely credited to the strength, wealth, and, above all, the social harmony within the city.

THE VENETIAN GOVERNMENT

Venice was ruled by the doge in theory, but real power resided with the Great Council, which was elected by the most powerful aristocratic families. Within the Great Council was the Council of Ten, established in 1310 initially as a temporary body, in response to a revolt against the doge; the council, whose members were elected from the Great Council for one year, was

The fortified seaport of Nafplion in the Peloponnese in Greece was one of the strongholds built by the Venetians in the eastern Mediterranean.

An undated oil painting of the Venetian and allied fleet defeating the Turks at the Battle of Lepanto in 1571.

charged with maintaining the security of Venice. The office of doge was effectively restricted to members of a limited number of powerful families. The doge was indirectly elected in a complex manner through electoral colleges. Thirty members of the Great Council were chosen by lot, and then reduced by lot to 9, who elected 40 members, who were, in turn, reduced by lot to 12. The 12 members then elected 25 people, who were reduced by lot to 9; the group of 9 then elected 45 members, who were reduced by lot to 11. The 11 people, in turn, chose an electoral college of 41 members, who elected the doge.

The great majority of the Venetian population were excluded from political power, but they did benefit from a justice system far more equitable, and a network of charitable organizations far more comprehensive, than elsewhere in Europe. Popular acquiescence to this system of government survived and was reinforced by a secret police answerable to the Council of Ten, which could counter malcontents. Later, as the (Turkish) Ottoman Empire advanced through the Balkans, fear of Turkish conquest also deterred dissent.

THE HEIGHT OF IMPERIAL POWER

With the defeat of Genoa, Venice was free to undertake a new wave of expansion. A series of wars were fought to expand the city-state's territories in northern Italy, securing control of inland trade routes. As a result, Venice acquired most of northeastern Italy. The city-state also built an army formidable enough to encourage rivals into occasional alliances to contain its ambitions. In 1508, the League of Cambrai—including the Holy Roman emperor, the pope, the French, and the Spanish, alongside other Italian city-states—attacked Venice. Although suffering heavy defeats, the Venetians emerged from the conflict in 1509 largely unscathed, even though its landward expansion was brought to an end. At sea, Venice took full advantage of the final conquest of Constantinople by the Turks in 1453. Subsequently, Venice became the most powerful Christian state

in the eastern Mediterranean, annexing Cyprus in 1489. The Venetian Empire also included Istria (now part of Croatia), Dalmatia (the Croatian coast), what is now coastal Montenegro, several ports along the Ionian shore of Greece, the Ionian Islands (including Corfu), Crete, and a number of islands in the Aegean Sea. Consequently, the city-state stood in the forefront of the struggle against the Turks.

The great wealth and power of the city were reflected in its embrace of the Italian Renaissance, producing such artists as Giovanni Bellini (c. 1430–1516) and Titian (Tiziano Vecelli; 1488–1576). Its leading aristocrats also developed a taste for claiming a Roman heritage, and the city depicted itself as the heir of imperial Rome, which was ironic, given the city's Byzantine origins. For example, on the strength of similarity of name alone, the powerful Venetian

Genoa

The city of Genoa, along the Ligurian coast of northwestern Italy, was the greatest Italian rival to Venice. Emerging as a city-state before 1100, Genoa was one of the four states often known as the Maritime Republics: Venice, Genoa, Amalfi, and Pisa. Genoa was initially governed by consuls, who were elected by a popular assembly, although the city's bishop was nominally chief of state. Trade and shipbuilding brought prosperity to Genoa, which, like Venice, was effectively controlled by a small number of powerful aristocratic families including the Doria, Grimaldi, and Fieschi families.

Genoa acquired territory in Liguria and inland in Piedmont and also ruled the island of Corsica. By the twelfth century, the Genoese were dominant in trade in the Tyrrhenian Sea, and the collapse of the Crusader States in western Asia provided an opportunity for Genoa to acquire influence in that region. At the same time, Genoa built an empire that included islands in the Aegean Sea, trading bases in North Africa, and colonies in Sicily. This brought Genoa into conflict with Venice, which had similar ambitions.

The height of Genoese power came toward the end of the thirteenth century, when the Genoese fleet defeated Pisa in 1284. A subsequent military victory over Venice in 1296 seemed to mark Genoa's ascendancy. However, the tide turned, and the advent of the Black Death in the middle of the fourteenth century decimated the city's population. Subsequently, Venice gained military superiority over Genoa in the War of Chioggia (1378–1381), greatly reducing the power and status of Genoa, which lost its trading empire, except for the island of Corsica. Venetian dominance was acknowledged, and Genoa even adopted the Venetian system of government, rule by a doge. The Genoese republic remained independent, although much reduced, until the end of the eighteenth century.

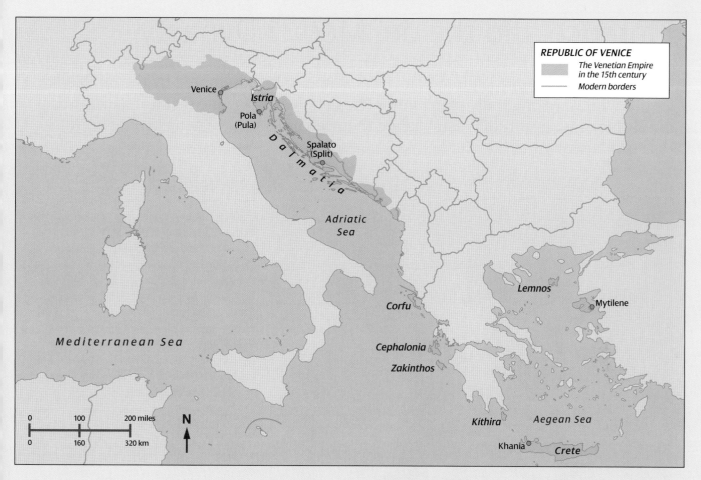

Cornaro family claimed descent from the Roman general and statesman Publius Cornelius Scipio (236–183 BCE).

Despite these cultural pretensions, Venice and its empire remained a commercial venture. Leading aristocrats ensured that the main commercial opportunities remained tightly in their grasp. Although the Venetians fought the Turks at times, these conflicts did not prevent them from trading with the Turks in peacetime. Venice had commercial interests stretching from Amsterdam (the Netherlands) to Alexandria (Egypt). Its coinage, the ducat, set the standards in Europe for stability and reliability. The city was also a major center of manufacture. In glassblowing and silk weaving, Venetian artisans were renowned across the continent. In the Arsenal, a vast dockyard and probably the greatest industrial complex in Europe, Venetians developed mass-production techniques, which in the sixteenth century employed 16,000 workers and could produce a warship within a day. Also at the Arsenal, Venetian artisans made great strides in producing handguns and field artillery.

THE DECLINE OF VENICE

Venice's greatness was not destined to last. The sixteenth century voyages of discovery and the opening of new trade routes, which moved the center of European economic power from the Mediterranean to the Atlantic powers, perhaps had less impact than once thought. Such trade routes remained expensive, and Venetian traders could still compete for a considerable period. What was perhaps more debilitating was the constant pressure from the Turks. In 1571, as part of the Holy League alongside Spain and the papacy, more than 100 Venetian warships contributed to a resounding naval victory over the Turks at the Battle of Lepanto. However, this victory could not compensate for the fact that the Turks had conquered Venice's colony of Cyprus.

Over succeeding generations, the Venetian maritime empire was whittled away by the Turks. In 1718, the Treaty of Passarowitz concluded another conflict between Venice and the Ottoman Empire, costing Venice its remaining territories in Greece, although it retained the Ionian Islands, including Corfu.

This steady loss of resources resulted in a decline in the economic and political importance of Venice. When, in 1796, the French army of Napoléon Bonaparte (1769–1821) entered northern Italy to challenge Austrian domination of the region, Venice tried to remain neutral. However, neither the retreating Austrians nor the pursuing French hesitated to violate Venetian territory. The Venetians were incapable of expelling large modern armies and stood by helplessly. Under the subsequent Treaty of Campo Formio (1797), Bonaparte awarded Venice to Austria. The little prosperity that was left to Venice subsequently went into precipitous decline, and the city would never know independence again.

J. SWIFT

Florence and the de' Medici Dynasty

The republic of Florence, founded in 1208, came to be dominated by the de' Medici family, who were originally merchants. The de' Medici became dictators, acquired a ducal title, and, eventually, established themselves as a royal dynasty, the grand dukes of Tuscany.

A bronze statue of Cosimo I de' Medici (1519–1574), the first grand duke of Tuscany, in the Piazza della Signoria, Florence. The statue was cast by Giambologna (1529–1608) and took seven years to complete (1587–1594).

Florence was a medieval manufacturing and banking center of continental importance, but in the aftermath of the Black Death, in the fourteenth century, a series of popular revolts shook the city's oligarchic government. In 1434, the oligarchs rallied behind a rich banker, Cosimo de' Medici (1389–1464; in office as leader of the Florentine Republic 1434–1464), to restore order. He had been proven correct in his doubts concerning the advisability of war against the rival republic of Lucca and, under his rule, the resulting stability coincided with an economic recovery.

THE FIRST DE' MEDICI RULERS

Cosimo de' Medici was briefly succeeded as ruler of the republic by his son, Piero I (1414–1469; in office 1464–1469). Piero's son, Lorenzo de' Medici (better known as Lorenzo the Magnificent; 1449–1492; in office 1469–1492) remained a commoner but took the initial steps toward establishing his family as princely, marrying a member of an ancient aristocratic Roman family and then marrying the daughter of the reigning duke of Savoy. Although he was the first citizen of a republic, Lorenzo the Magnificent, a great patron of the arts, was called the "ideal Renaissance prince."

Lorenzo's son, Piero II (1471–1503; in office 1492–1494), however, lost power in the wake of a French invasion in 1494. With the de' Medici family deposed, Girolamo Savonarola (1452–1498; in office 1494–1498) became the leader of the Florentine Republic. A great orator and the first vicar-general of the Dominicans, Savonarola tried to establish a Christian commonwealth in Florence. However, the extremity of his asceticism alienated the people of Florence—he destroyed great works of art in his "Bonfire of the Vanities" (1497). His unorthodox views and vehement criticism of the pope alienated the Roman Catholic Church. Consequently, Savonarola was deposed, tried for heresy, and executed.

After Savonarola, the Florentines attempted to restore the republic under the leadership of Piero Soderini (1471–1552; in office 1498–1512), but Spanish troops reestablished the de' Medici dynasty from 1512 to 1527—under four successive family members—until a new uprising sent the de' Medici into exile again. The republican restoration quickly led to factional infighting and political instability.

THE DUCHY OF FLORENCE

Unrest in Florence led to the intervention of Emperor Charles V (1500–1558; reigned as Charles I of Spain, 1516–1556, and Charles V, Holy Roman emperor, 1519–1555). With the support of Pope Clement VII (Giulio de' Medici; 1478–1534; leader of the Florentine Republic 1519–1523; reigned as pope 1523–1534), the emperor took Florence by siege in 1530. Charles V then established young Alessandro de' Medici (1510–1537; reigned 1530–1537), the illegitimate son of Lorenzo II de' Medici (1492–1519; in office as leader of the Florentine Republic 1514–1519) as hereditary duke of Florence, under the emperor's (nominal) control. Three years later, the new duke's legitimate half-sister, Catherine de' Medici (1519–1589), married the future Henry II of France (1519–1559; reigned 1547–1559). Although the bridegroom was not heir to the French throne at the time of the wedding, the marriage of the wealthy de' Medici commoner into the French royal house dramatically secured the status of the de' Medici.

Alessandro maintained republican institutions, which comprised patricians rotating through elected short-term offices. Florence governed the provinces by sending patricians to exercise justice there. Each town was largely self-governing, but there was considerable nostalgia for independence in the principal subject towns, like Pisa or Arezzo. Both Florence and its subject cities were kept in check by citadels garrisoned by the duke's soldiers.

Alessandro was assassinated in 1537, but leading patricians immediately established the adolescent Cosimo I de' Medici (1519–1574; reigned as duke of Florence 1537–1569 and as grand duke of Tuscany 1569–1574) in his place. Cosimo I retained the rotating magistracies but appointed key members of these committees himself from among eligible candidates. By the 1550s, the primacy of the de' Medici over their former peers was

A self-portrait (1516) of Leonardo da Vinci (1452–1519), in the Biblioteka Real, Turin.

striking. The dynasty derived crucial support from Emperor Charles V and his heir, Philip II of Spain (1527–1598; reigned 1556–1598), whose side they took in wars against France. Cosimo helped the emperor conquer the unstable republic of Siena and received it, as a fief, from Spain in 1557. Siena retained most of its institutions and was governed as an autonomous state (the Stato Nuovo, or new state) alongside the Florentine Stato Vecchio (old state). Good relations with the Austrian

Hapsburgs and the papacy were eventually rewarded by the conferral of the title of grand duke in 1569.

THE GRAND DUCHY OF TUSCANY

The acquisition of the grand ducal title firmly established the de' Medici family (former merchants) as royalty and placed the dynasty above most other Italian princes in status. Alongside the city government of patrician officeholders, Cosimo I created a court at the Palazzo Pitti, whose importance increased during the reign of his son, Francesco (1574–1587; reigned 1574–1587). De' Medici splendor reached its pinnacle during the reign of Ferdinand I (also known as Ferrante I; 1587–1609; reigned 1587–1609). Under Ferdinand, Tuscany was exceptionally prosperous and well-administered by the standards of the age, and Florence was a flourishing capital city of some 60,000 inhabitants. The Tuscan countryside was blessed by peace after a wave of banditry was quelled by the grand duke's peasant militia. This political and economic stability continued under Ferdinand's son Cosimo II (1590–1621; reigned 1609–1621).

A seventeenth-century copperplate engraving of Galileo Galilei (1564–1642).

The years after 1620 marked the onset of a long economic depression throughout southern Europe. Ferdinand II (1610–1670; reigned 1621–1670) could not reverse the collapse of urban industry or population decline, which led to the impoverishment of the region and its people. He kept Tuscan participation in the Thirty Years' War (1618–1648) to a minimum and vigorously defended state jurisdiction against encroachment from the papacy. Raising new taxes in a weak economy was done more smoothly than in other states, and, while the cities saw their manufacturing roles decline, the presence of the court and government institutions led to the expansion of service industries.

Florence remained a leading cultural capital until the 1660s. Ferdinand II promoted science, inventing a new thermometer and the condensation hygrometer. He protected and encouraged astronomer and physicist Galileo Galilei (1564–1642), even after his condemnation by the Inquisition (an organ of the Roman Catholic Church charged with suppressing heresy).

Cosimo III (1642–1723; reigned 1670–1723) was an extremely conscientious prince, whose austere Counter-Reformation piety led to a failed marriage with a French princess. Cosimo ruled his grand duchy with paternalistic absolutism, reining in more tightly the feudal institutions and strengthening the supervision of local government to control expenditures. He increased the role of professional bureaucrats, who continually marginalized the patrician committees, themselves weakened by a great decrease in the numbers of the traditional nobility as some ancient families became extinct. However, Cosimo's government became more aristocratic, and noble bureaucrats could accumulate offices and designate their own successors. The nobles sought government office and prized church appointments as ways to secure wealth and landed properties.

Neither of Cosimo's sons had children, and the family was about to become extinct, provoking a succession crisis. The last de' Medici grand duke was Gian Gastone (1671–1737; reigned 1723–1737), whose alcoholism, private life, and irreligion shocked the courts of Europe. On his death in 1737, Tuscany passed to the husband of the Austrian Hapsburg heiress Maria Theresa (1717–1780; reigned 1740–1780), Francis Stephen, duke of Lorraine (1708–1765; reigned 1737–1765). The last members of the de' Medici family were not consulted about the succession—Cosimo III had hoped to will Tuscany to his daughter, Anna Maria Luisa (1667–1743)—nor was the government of Tuscany. Francis Stephen, who was French, sent French-speaking functionaries to Florence to rule in his stead to break with the patrician habits of government the de' Medici tolerated. Tuscany became a Hapsburg possession, and Anna Maria Luisa, the last member of the de' Medici family, left all the personal possessions of the family to Florence.

G. HANLON

Wars in Italy and the Pax Hispanica

From 1494 through 1748, wars between the kings of France and the Hapsburg rulers of Austria (the Holy Roman emperor) and Spain dominated the political life of Italy.

Between the end of the fifteenth century and the mid-eighteenth century, the wars that were fought in Italy—between France and the Austrian Hapsburg emperors and the Spanish Hapsburg kings—were part of wider European hostilities. Although the Italian theater was often a sideshow, over time the dozen states of the Italian Peninsula were reduced to dependencies of France, Austria, and Spain.

FRENCH INTERVENTION

In 1494, Duke Ludovico of Milan (1452–1508; reigned 1494–1499) encouraged the young French king Charles VIII (1470–1498; reigned 1483–1498) to intervene in Italy. Charles duly took advantage of a dynastic dispute in Naples to invade southern Italy. In 1442, the king of Aragón (Spain) had won the kingdom of Naples (southern peninsular Italy) by force, displacing a French prince—both claimants had been left the throne in wills drafted by Queen Joan (Giovanna) II of Naples (1371–1435; reigned 1414–1435). Charles and his 30,000-strong army, complete with artillery, took the city unopposed in 1495. The adventure turned sour when a league of Italian states formed around Spanish king Ferdinand II of Aragón (1452–1516; reigned 1479–1516 and as Ferdinand V of Castile 1474–1504). Ferdinand, aided by the Hapsburg Holy Roman emperor, Maximilian I (1459–1519; reigned 1493–1519), closed in behind the French forces, which had to fight their way back to France.

Charles's successor and second cousin, Louis XII (1462–1515; reigned 1498–1515), claimed both the duchy of Milan and the kingdom of Naples, and occupied both. King Frederick of Naples (1452–1504) was deposed by the French and, from 1501 through 1504, France and Spain disputed Naples. Spanish forces finally swept the French from the kingdom in 1504, so bringing all of southern Italy under their control. The region remained under Spanish rule until the eighteenth century.

WARS IN LOMBARDY

Milan subsequently became the linchpin of hostilities in Italy. This prosperous duchy was seen by France as a bridgehead in Italy and by Austria as a buffer between itself and the Italian Peninsula. The different Italian states joined the French or the Hapsburgs, and often changed sides.

French forces occupied Milan from 1499 through 1512, when a coalition of the emperor, Venice, the papacy, and the Swiss ejected the French from Lombardy. However, the French returned under Francis I (1494–1547; reigned 1515–1547) in 1515 and

held Milan until 1522. In the meantime, both Ferdinand of Aragón and Castile and Maximilian of Austria had died, uniting their territories under their adolescent grandson, Charles V (1500–1558; reigned as Charles I of Spain, 1516–1556, and Charles V, Holy Roman emperor, 1519–1555). Charles V's army crushed the French at Pavia in 1525. In 1527, his forces sacked Rome. The following year, the republic of Genoa, still a significant naval power, switched sides and joined the Spanish. In 1530, unrest in Florence prompted Charles to intervene and restore the city to de' Medici rule. Finally, in 1535, he seized control of the duchy of Milan. With the Hapsburgs supreme in both northern and southern Italy, Italy ceased to be the principal battlefield between the French and the Hapsburgs. The financial strain on the French was such that they ceded control of Italy to Spain in the treaty of Cateau-Cambresis (1559).

THE PAX HISPANICA

Charles V divided his empire into two parts in 1555–1556: in the German territories, the imperial title passed to his brother Ferdinand (1503–1564; reigned 1555–1564), while his son, Philip II (1527–1598; reigned 1556–1598), became king of Spain, with the Italian territories (Sardinia, Sicily, Naples, and Milan), eastern Burgundy, and the Low Countries as Spanish dependencies. Under Hapsburg rule, the Spanish territories enjoyed a long period of relative peace and prosperity, often known as the Pax Hispanica (the Spanish peace). Spain's troops were thinly scattered around the Mediterranean, and only Milan had a substantial garrison. Spanish viceroys maintained good relations with the pope and other Italian princes. Only Venice was consistently hostile to Spanish Hapsburg power, but its focus was fixed on the eastern Mediterranean.

THE THIRTY YEARS' WAR

Spain was drawn into the Thirty Years' War (1618–1648) in 1620, and into renewed war with the Dutch soon after. King Louis XIII of France (1601–1643; reigned 1610–1643) and his first minister, Cardinal Armand Jean du Plessis de Richelieu (1585–1642), believed France to be encircled by Spain and her allies. Their strategy was to wage proxy wars on Spanish allies rather than by attacking Spain directly. In 1625, France, in alliance with Savoy-Piedmont, launched an unsuccessful attack on Genoa, a key Spanish ally. In 1627, the direct line of the Gonzagas, the rulers of Mantua, died out, and the duchy was inherited by a junior

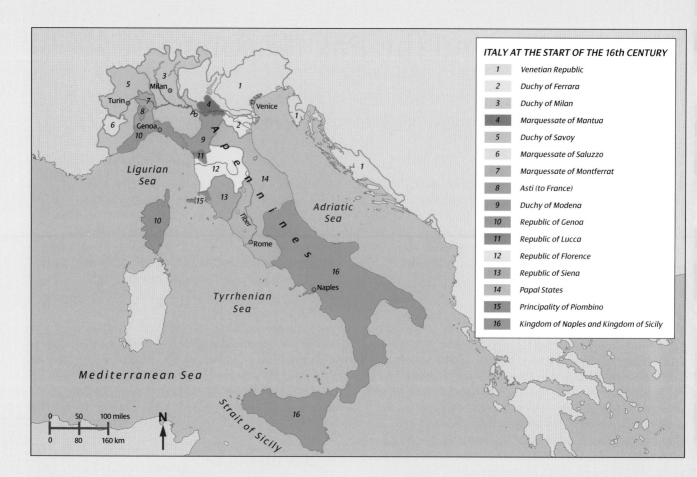

ITALY AT THE START OF THE 16th CENTURY

1	Venetian Republic
2	Duchy of Ferrara
3	Duchy of Milan
4	Marquessate of Mantua
5	Duchy of Savoy
6	Marquessate of Saluzzo
7	Marquessate of Montferrat
8	Asti (to France)
9	Duchy of Modena
10	Republic of Genoa
11	Republic of Lucca
12	Republic of Florence
13	Republic of Siena
14	Papal States
15	Principality of Piombino
16	Kingdom of Naples and Kingdom of Sicily

French branch of the family. Louis XIII dispatched forces to Mantua but hesitated to wage all-out war on the neighboring Spanish Hapsburg territory of Milan.

Savoy-Piedmont switched sides regularly during the Thirty Years' War, but, by 1631, French forces were entrenched in the Piedmontese fortress of Pinerolo, a key base for future invasions of northern Italy. The French were finally forced into war against Spain in Italy, forming an alliance with Savoy-Piedmont, Mantua, and Parma. Yet France did not have the resources to sustain far-flung campaigns. By 1636, Spain had regained the initiative in Italy. Piedmont descended into civil war and could no longer be relied upon as an ally. Spain was forced to withdraw resources from Italy to confront revolts in Catalonia and Portugal after 1640, but luckily for Spain, the Italian theater was of only secondary concern to France. Richelieu's Italian-born successor, Cardinal Jules Mazarin (Giulio Mazzzarino; 1602–1661), capitalized on a revolt in the Spanish-ruled kingdom of Naples in 1647. However, France itself was swept by civil unrest from 1648 through 1652, allowing Spain to recover most of its lost ground.

THE PAX GALLICA

After the end of the Thirty Years' War, France and Spain continued to wage war on a reduced scale until the end of 1658. Spain had mobilized hundreds of thousands of Spaniards, Flemings, Germans, Neapolitans, and Lombards to defend its Italian territories. These forces were supported by bands of peasant and town militias. Spain emerged from the war with its Italian territories intact, and France made no permanent gains from Spain, although it kept a foothold at Pinerolo.

The period 1659–1689 in Italy has been called the Pax Gallica (the French peace), for Spain was now gravely weakened and France had become the dominant power. Former Spanish allies, like Genoa, Parma, and Tuscany, let their allegiances lapse in the face of the power of French king Louis XIV (1638–1715; reigned 1643–1715). However, the peace in Italy was not to last; under Louis XIV, French aggression in Germany led to a series of major wars, beginning in 1689.

LATE SEVENTEENTH-CENTURY WARS

Duke Victor Amadeus II of Savoy-Piedmont (1661–1732; reigned as duke of Savoy-Piedmont, 1675–1713; king of Sicily, 1713–1718; king of Sardinia, 1718–1730) broke from the French alliance, and Spanish forces defended him against French attacks. More importantly, Holy Roman emperor Leopold I (1640–1705; reigned 1658–1705) sent a large German army to Italy and, claiming imperial rights, forced Italian princes to pay for its maintenance. Peace was established in 1697 but was short-lived. The War of the Spanish Succession (1701–1714) soon spread to the Italian Peninsula, with Austria becoming the main power there.

G. HANLON

Italy in the Eighteenth Century

In the eighteenth century, Austria replaced Spain as the dominant power in Italy. The Enlightenment stirred Italian thought, and there was a gradual revival of political, economic, and intellectual life.

After so many years of domination by Spain (which ruled the duchy of Milan and the kingdoms of Naples and Sicily), Austria became the dominant power in Italy after 1700. The eighteenth century also witnessed the development of the individual states of Italy and the rise of the kingdom of Piedmont-Sardinia.

THE END OF SPANISH POWER

In 1700, Spanish king Charles II (1661–1700; reigned 1665–1700) died, and the Spanish Hapsburgs became extinct. Spain's throne was contested by two principal claimants: a member of the Bourbon dynasty, a grandson of French king Louis XIV (1638–1715; reigned 1643–1715); and an Austrian Hapsburg archduke. The powers of Europe divided between the two factions, with many opposing the Bourbon inheritance, which was perceived as concentrating too much power in the hands of Louis XIV. France, Spain, and Bavaria, and initially Savoy Piedmont, supported the claims of the Bourbon Philip V (1683–1746; reigned 1700–1724 and 1724–1746) to the Spanish throne.

The dispute led to the War of Spanish Succession (1701–1714). Most Spaniards and Spain's Italian subjects rallied to the Bourbon king Philip V, but they showed only lukewarm support for French armies operating across northern Italy against Austrian forces. The imperial forces in Italy were unsuccessful against the French until Duke Victor Amadeus II of Savoy-Piedmont, (1661–1732; reigned as duke of Savoy-Piedmont, 1675–1713; king of Sicily, 1713–1718; king of Sardinia, 1718–1730) defected a second time from his alliance with France. Subsequently, the Austrian Hapsburg imperial army, led by general Prince Eugene of Savoy (1663–1736), won a decisive battle against the French under the walls of Turin (the Piedmontese capital) in 1706. French forces then withdrew in haste, and Austria occupied much of Italy, subjecting princes and even neutral states to heavy taxation. Austria's victory at Turin drove France's ally, Spain, from Italy and ensured Austrian ascendancy in the region for the next 150 years. Austrian Hapsburgs took over the thrones of Naples and Sicily, and Austrian forces occupied the duchy of Milan.

The Treaty of Utrecht (1713) reordered the territorial arrangements of Italy. Spain lost Milan to Austria, which also gained Mantua. While a Hapsburg ruled in Naples until 1735, Sicily was given to Victor Amadeus II of Savoy-Piedmont as a reward for his support against Louis XIV. The dukes of Savoy thus gained the royal title they had longed desired but, in 1718, Victor Amadeus was forced to exchange Sicily for Sardinia, which at least was much closer to his north Italian realm. Sicily then reverted to the Hapsburg emperor Charles VI (1685–1740; reigned as Holy Roman emperor, 1711–1740; as Charles III, king of Sicily, 1711–1713 and 1718–1735; and Charles VI, king of Naples, 1711–1735).

The Spanish Bourbons did not accept exclusion from Italy. In 1731, the ancient Farnese family, who were sovereign dukes of Parma, became extinct in the male line. Ambitious Elizabeth Farnese (1692–1766), wife of Philip V of Spain and sister of the last Farnese sovereign of Parma, was influential in gaining the throne of Parma for a younger son, Charles (1716–1788; reigned as Charles I of Parma, 1731–1735; as Charles IV of Sicily, 1735–1759; Charles VII of Naples, 1735–1759; and Charles III of Spain, 1759–1788). During the War of Polish Succession (1733–1738), Charles led a Spanish army to conquer the kingdoms of Sicily and Naples. The peace of 1738 established Charles as monarch of both kingdoms, although he lost Parma, which in 1748 (after Spain had been involved in another war against Austria) was secured for Charles's younger brother, Philip (1720–1765; reigned 1748–1765). On becoming king of Spain in 1759, Charles abdicated Naples and Sicily in favor of his third son. Thus, although descendants of the Spanish Bourbons ruled in Parma and in Naples and Sicily, Spain no longer held territory in Italy.

THE RISE OF PIEDMONT

The changing fortunes of the major European powers brought benefits to Piedmont. With its origins in Savoy, this northwest state became an important buffer between France and Austria. During the eighteenth century, Piedmont ably demonstrated its diplomatic skill to increase territory. Recognition as a kingdom—when its ruler gained Sicily in 1713—brought increased prestige. After 1718, when Victor Amadeus II exchanged Sicily for Sardinia, the Piedmontese state was generally known as Piedmont-Sardinia.

The Treaty of Aix la Chapelle in 1748 concluded the War of Austrian Succession (1740–1748), a major war that involved most of the powers of Europe. In the fifty years of peace that followed in Italy, the dozen Italian states could concentrate on internal reforms.

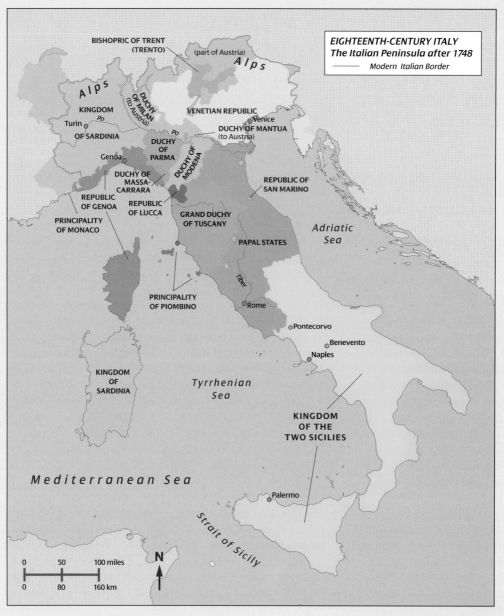

EIGHTEENTH-CENTURY ITALY
The Italian Peninsula after 1748
——— Modern Italian Border

If the Italian states were economically restricted, they were rich in other ways, and Italian influence in the arts was extensive. Visits to Italy's great treasures of art and architecture in Venice, Florence, and, above all, Rome, were the culmination of a classical education for many people of wealth. Known as the Grand Tour, these visits brought men and women from Great Britain, Germany, Scandinavia, and also later America. An emerging interest in archaeology and the excavations at Pompeii and Herculaneum caused much excitement. Italy was also exporting music, such as Neapolitan opera, particularly by Alessandro Scarlatti (1660–1725), inspiring a wave of Italian singers and opera companies in Europe. Great Italian composers of the period included Arcangelo Corelli (1653–1713), Antonio Vivaldi (1678–1741), and Giuseppe Tartini (1692–1770).

The second half of the eighteenth century saw increasing belief in rational inquiry—using reasoned thought rather than a blind view of tradition or superstition. The major centers of intellectual reform in Italy were Florence, Milan, and Naples. Writers, such as Cesare Beccaria (1738–1794), whose treatise *Dei delitti e delle pene* (On crimes and punishment) was a call for the reform of criminal law and the end of the death penalty, and philosophers, such as Antonio Genovesi (1712–1769), were influential. The reformers' targets were the taxation system, the rights of the aristocracy and the church over administration and legal jurisdiction, and the ownership of church land. The modernization of Italy was well under way but, while the population increased from 12 million across the century to 18 million, there was still considerable poverty and crime. Reforms were mainly to the internal workings of states, and the first time there was any suggestion of national unity was in the writing of Count Vittorio Alfieri (1749–1803), a dramatist, who was the first to mention the goal of national unity. Alfieri coined the concept *risorgimento* (resurgence) for unity.

THE ECONOMY AND CULTURE

Italy was not a rich region, and its only significant manufacture was silk weaving in the north. The main exports were raw materials: olive oil, wine, grain, wool, and raw silk. Agriculture dominated, and much of the land was still held under a form of feudalism, a system in which peasants worked the land for their local lords, who protected them but required their military service in time of war. The maritime republic of Venice, exhausted after wars with the Turks, had lost much of its foreign influence and empire in the eastern Mediterranean and was not the great trading center it once had been. In the eighteenth century, only the ports of Livorno and Genoa—which traded mainly in the western Mediterranean—were able to expand their mercantile activity.

H. DOE, G. HANLON

Italy in the French Revolutionary and Napoleonic Wars

The French invasion of Italy in 1796 by Napoléon Bonaparte (1769–1821; in office as French first consul 1799–1804; reigned as emperor 1804–1814 and 1815) had a powerful and lasting effect on the country. It broke up the old order of states, imposed new laws, and gave greater representation in government.

French rule in Italy from the 1790s through 1814 not only changed the map of Italy but also promoted a sense of being Italian rather than Sicilian, Tuscan, or Piedmontese. Under Napoléon, the name *Italian* was used to denote a political state in Italy for the first time.

INVASION AND THE REPUBLICS

The French Revolutionary Wars began in 1792 when France, threatened by Austria, Prussia, and other powers who were supporting the imprisoned French king, Louis XVI (1754–1793; reigned 1774–1792), went on the offensive. French forces were initially ineffectual along the German front but invaded Piedmont-Sardinia, occupying Nice and Savoy. Piedmont-Sardinia managed to withstand an attack by the French in 1794. However, in 1796, Napoléon Bonaparte was appointed commander of the French army, and his forces overran Piedmont, which was forced to allow free passage of French troops into peninsular Italy. Napoléon then took Milan and besieged Mantua. In 1798, King Charles Emmanuel IV of Piedmont-Sardinia (1751–1819; reigned 1796–1802) was forced to renounce Piedmont and take refuge in the other part of his kingdom, the island of Sardinia, where the Piedmontese kings remained until 1814. The French established a provisional government in Turin, which declared the annexation of Piedmont to France.

France established a number of puppet republics in northern Italy. In 1796, Bologna, Ferrara, Mantua, and Reggio were united as the Transpadane Republic, while Milan became the center of the Cispadane Republic. The following year, the two merged as the Cisalpine Republic; a constitution was drawn up, an assembly was elected, and Napoléon appointed Italians as ministers. Venice attempted to remain neutral, but in the peace terms negotiated with Austria in May 1797, the republic of Venice, which had survived for a millennium, was suppressed and was annexed to Austria. In that same year, Napoléon suppressed the ancient Republic of Genoa, creating the Ligurian Republic in its place, before leaving Italy for Egypt. In his absence, the domination of Italy by France continued. In the Papal States—the northern part of which had been annexed to

the Cisalpine Republic—the pope was deprived of his sovereignty, and the Roman Republic was established.

SOUTHERN ITALY

Southern Italy, comprising the kingdoms of Naples and Sicily, was ruled by a branch of the Bourbon family. Ferdinand IV of Naples and III of Sicily (1751–1825; reigned 1759–1816 in Sicily and 1759–1799, 1799–1806, and 1815–1816 in Naples) was encouraged by the defeat of Napoléon's fleet in the Battle of the Nile in 1798. Consequently, he attempted to oust the French from Rome. His campaign ended in a rout for the Neapolitans, and Ferdinand fled to Sicily. When order was restored, the kingdom of Naples was reorganized as the Parthenopean Republic, another French puppet state. In just two years, Italy had become a group of republics controlled by France.

FRENCH REVERSES AND ADVANCES

The tide turned in 1799, when Austrian, British, and Russian forces invaded northern Italy. There were uprisings in Tuscany, Piedmont, and Naples. The republicans were defeated in Naples; over 100 were killed, 220 sent to the gallows, and hundreds more exiled. The French had made themselves unpopular in Italy by looting art treasures, and the Italians were beginning to distrust any foreigner, whether French, British, Austrian, or Spanish. As a result, the beginnings of a nationalist movement were emerging. The allied forces pushed back the French in Italy, and Austria was able to restore the duchy of Milan to its rule. Also in 1799, the Hapsburg grand duke of Tuscany was briefly ousted and the Etruscan Republic was created, but, before the end of 1799, the Tuscan duke was restored.

In 1800, after the Battle of Marengo, the French reconquered the northern part of the Italian Peninsula. The pope's sovereignty was restored in the Patrimony (modern Lazio), Umbria, and Marche and the French also restored the Cisalpine Republic and suppressed the ancient republic of Genoa, creating the Ligurian Republic in its place. The following year, France again ousted the Hapsburg grand duke of Tuscany, creating the kingdom of Etruria

Joachim Murat, king of Naples (reigned 1808–1815).

for the heir to the duchy of Parma, which was annexed to France. Also in 1802, Napoléon presided over an assembly of the Cisalpine Republic, and he agreed to a suggestion that it should be renamed the Italian Republic with himself as president. This was the first time the word *Italian* was used to denote a modern political state, even if it was just a part of the peninsula.

THE NAPOLEONIC MONARCHIES

Republican Italy lasted only a couple of years. In 1804, Napoléon made himself emperor of the French and, soon, the republics of Italy were reborn as kingdoms, duchies, and principalities for himself, members of his family, and his allies. The republic of Italy became the kingdom of Italy with Napoléon as king; his son, Napoléon (1811–1832), would later be named king of Rome, although Rome itself was annexed to France in 1809, when the pope was again deprived of his sovereignty. Napoléon placed those he trusted in charge of the Italian states. His viceroy in the kingdom of Italy was his stepson, Eugène de Beauharnais (1781–1824); in 1806, Napoléon's elder brother, Joseph (1768–1844; reigned in Naples 1806–1808 and in Spain 1808–1813), became king of Naples. Joseph had studied at the University of Pisa and ruled in an enlightened way with a majority of Italians in his government. In 1808, he was made king of Spain and was replaced in Naples by Joachim Murat

(1767–1815; reigned 1808–1815), husband of Napoléon's sister, Caroline (1782–1839).

Other members of Napoléon's family and court were installed on minor thrones in Italy. The republic of Lucca was made a duchy for Napoléon's sister Elisa (1777–1820; reigned in Lucca 1805–1814 and in Tuscany 1809–1814), who was later given Etruria, renamed Tuscany as a revived grand duchy. Another sister, Pauline (1780–1825; reigned 1806), was given the tiny duchy of Guastalla but handed it back to her brother rather than leave Paris. Ponte Corvo and Benevento were made principalities, respectively for Marshal Jean-Baptiste Bernadotte (1763–1844; prince of Ponte Corvo, 1805–1810; reigned as Carl XIV of Sweden, 1818–1844) and for French foreign minister Charles Maurice de Talleyrand (1754–1838).

THE IMPACT OF FRENCH RULE

The impact of French control was significant. The elderly Pope Pius VII (1742–1823; reigned 1800–1823) was moved to France in 1808 and the influence of the church, already seriously weakened in the eighteenth century, was further reduced. By 1814, many monasteries had been suppressed, and the last remains of feudalism were abolished. Most reforms, such as the sale of church lands, benefited the emerging middle classes. New roads were built across the Alps and Apennines—these mountain ranges had been a hindrance to travel, trade, and armies. Napoléon introduced representative government in Italy for the first time, thus giving governmental opportunities to Italians. The law was standardized across Italy, and, in the kingdoms of Italy and Naples, the standardized Italian language was promoted. In administration, Napoléon relied upon the professional classes because many of the old aristocracy had left with their deposed rulers.

THE END OF NAPOLEONIC ITALY

French control of Italy came to an end with the downfall of Napoléon in 1814. Eugène de Beauharnais remained loyal to Napoléon and, when Austrian troops occupied Milan, he was allowed to go into exile to his father-in-law, the king of Bavaria. Elisa Bonaparte abandoned her brother but still lost her throne. Joachim Murat, king of Naples, went over to the allies against his brother-in-law and intrigued with whoever he felt might save his throne, but to no avail. He changed sides again, allying himself with the restored Napoléon in 1815; as a result, he lost his crown and his life, shot by the forces of the returning Bourbon king of Naples and Sicily. The Napoleonic states in Italy were swept away, but an important legacy in terms of reforms, laws, infrastructure, and concepts of governance remained.

H. DOE

Italy in the Early Nineteenth Century

After the end of Napoleonic rule in Italy, there was a return to the previous Austrian-dominated state system. Many Italians resented this move, and the period 1815–1848 saw the rise of secret societies determined to unite Italy and free the region from foreign domination.

In 1814, the Congress of Vienna, the conference that redrew the map of Europe after the Napoleonic Wars, restored Italy to much the same situation as it had been before the French invasion, except that the ancient republics of Genoa and Venice were not restored. Venice remained part of Austria, which also retained Lombardy. Genoa was annexed to the kingdom of Piedmont-Sardinia, and King Victor Emmanuel I (1759–1824; reigned 1802–1821) returned from exile in Sardinia to Piedmont, now enlarged and with access to the sea through the port of Genoa.

In southern Italy, King Ferdinand (1751–1825; reigned as Ferdinand III of Sicily, 1759–1816; as Ferdinand IV of Naples, 1759–1799, 1799–1806, and 1815–1816; and as Ferdinand I of the Two Sicilies, 1816–1825) was restored in Naples. In 1816, he combined the mainland state and Sicily under the title of the kingdom of Two Sicilies, a name it retained until 1860. The exiled grand duke of Tuscany was restored, as was the sovereign duke of Modena, and Marie Louise (1791–1847; reigned 1814–1847), the Austrian wife of French emperor Napoléon I (1769–1821; reigned 1804–1814 and 1815), became sovereign duchess of Parma for her lifetime.

The republic of Lucca, which Napoléon had made a duchy for one of his sisters, remained a duchy and was given to the exiled dowager queen of Spain; it would pass after her death to the Bourbon heir to Parma, until he regained his inheritance upon the death of Marie Louise of Parma. Several principalities, such as Piombino, were not revived, but the small republic of San Marino retained its independence. In central Italy, the papacy recovered all its former possessions.

AUSTRIAN DOMINATION

French rule in Italy may not have been popular, but those who had been officers in the army of the Napoleonic kingdom of Italy and other Italian states were now reduced in rank by the restoration of returning aristocrats. In government as well, the people drawn from the professional classes who had administered the various Napoleonic states in Italy were ousted in favor of the old nobility, but few of the returnees had had the benefit of the training afforded under Napoleonic rule. This return to an eighteenth-century mentality in government and the military stirred resentment. As a result, secret societies developed that plotted to overthrow aristocratic and foreign rule. Many of these societies had their roots in eighteenth-century Italian Freemasonry.

Overseeing this return to tradition was Austria. Austria directly controlled only parts of northern Italy (Lombardo-Venetia), but its influence was widespread, partly through the Austrian Hapsburg rulers of Tuscany, Modena, and Parma. Austrian foreign minister and later chancellor (first minister) Prince Klemens Wenzel von Metternich (1773–1859; in office as foreign minister 1809–1848 and as chancellor 1821–1848) saw Italian nationalism as a threat to the survival of the Hapsburg monarchy. Metternich sought an alliance with the restored rulers that they would uphold absolute rule, resist constitutional government, and suppress secret societies. A seemingly innocent request by Metternich for an agreement that all foreign postal correspondence would be channeled via Austria became an important political weapon—letters were opened, copied, and then resealed and forwarded, thus keeping Italy under the surveillance of the Austrian chancellor. Only the Papacy, Tuscany, and Piedmont-Sardinia refused to enter into the agreement, but a network of spies across the Italian Peninsula, reporting to the Austrian ministers in each state, ensured that all of Italy was effectively under Austrian supervision.

THE AGE OF CONSPIRACIES

The societies that Metternich was anxious to repress were a hotbed of Italian nationalism. Known as the Carbonari (literally, "charcoal burners"), they were most numerous in Naples and Piedmont. The activities of the Carbonari were condemned by the papacy because they were deemed anti-Catholic, but the ranks of these societies were swelled by disaffected former officers and others from Napoléon's Italian army and unemployed civil servants.

In 1820, discontent brought rebellions in Naples and in Piedmont. Ferdinand I of the Two Sicilies initially agreed to a new constitution, but he was not sincere and persuaded Austria to send in troops to repress the revolution and restore his absolute rule. The rebellion in Piedmont forced Victor Emmanuel to abdicate in favor of his brother, Charles Felix (1765–1831; reigned 1821–1831), who was at that time in Modena. However, the revolutionaries briefly succeeded in getting a new constitution granted with the aid of Prince Charles Albert (1798–1849; reigned 1831–1849), a distant cousin and heir to the throne. The Piedmontese rebels were also defeated by the intervention of an Austrian army, and Charles Albert fled.

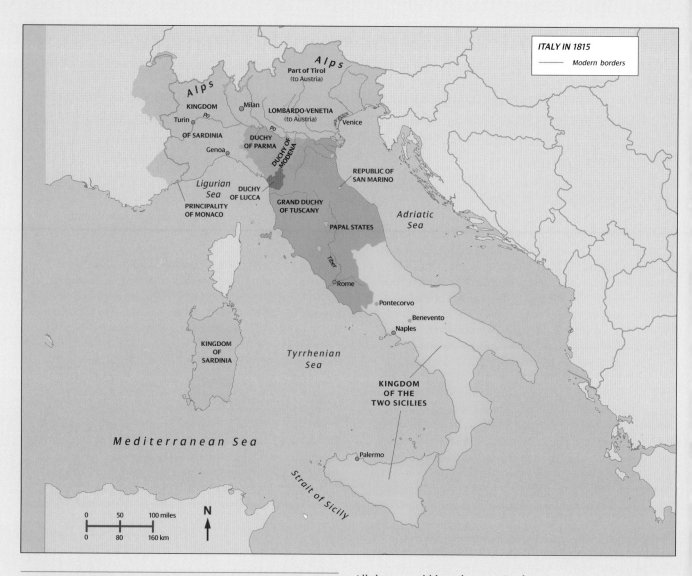

ITALY IN 1815
—— Modern borders

Alps
Part of Tirol
(to Austria)

Alps

KINGDOM
Milan
LOMBARDO-VENETIA
(to Austria)
Turin
Po
Venice

OF SARDINIA
Po
DUCHY
OF PARMA
DUCHY OF MODENA

Genoa

Ligurian
Sea
DUCHY
OF LUCCA

REPUBLIC OF
SAN MARINO

PRINCIPALITY
OF MONACO
GRAND DUCHY
OF TUSCANY

Adriatic
Sea

PAPAL STATES

Tiber

Rome

Pontecorvo

Benevento

Naples

KINGDOM
OF
SARDINIA

Tyrrhenian
Sea

KINGDOM
OF THE
TWO SICILIES

Mediterranean Sea

Palermo

0   50   100 miles
0   80   160 km

N

Strait of Sicily

YOUNG ITALY

The failure of these first uprisings against the restored regimes prompted the foundation, in July 1831, of a new secret society known as La Giovane Italia (Young Italy) by a Genoese lawyer, Giuseppe Mazzini (1805–1872). Mazzini had initially joined the Carbonari but found them too theatrical and ineffective. He sought the unification of the Italian nation as a democratic and class-free republic: he strove not just for independence from foreign rule, but for political unity and freedom for individual citizens.

Young Italy was a highly successful propaganda machine, but its attempts at revolution in 1833 and 1834 were failures. Consequently, Mazzini was forced to go into exile. In 1837, after a stay in Switzerland, he went to London, where he remained, apart from brief forays to Italy. In Great Britain, Mazzini attracted many to his cause, both Italian and British, and he continued to inspire rebellion in Italy. Other influential but more moderate theorists were the writers Vincenzo Gioberti (1801–1852), Count Cesare Balbo (1789–1853), and Marquis Massimo d'Azeglio (1798–1866), a romantic artist and novelist.

All three would later become Piedmontese prime ministers after 1848.

PIUS IX

In 1846, Pope Pius IX (1792–1878; reigned 1846–1878) was elected and set about dramatic reform in the Papal States. He released political prisoners, granted (limited) political freedom, permitted an independent press, allowed political clubs and demonstrations, and established an armed national guard. These unprecedented freedoms led to reverberations across Italy, and the cry of *Viva Pio Nono* ("Long live Pius IX") became a rallying cry. The nationalists assumed that Pius IX was sympathetic to Italian unity as well as being a reformer, but they would be disappointed. The pope would prove unwilling to contemplate the loss of his sovereignty in the cause of Italian unification. Metternich described Italy in 1847 as merely a "geographical expression," but this was also to prove wishful thinking; the political will to build an Italian state was now unstoppable.

H. DOE

Italian Unification

Italian unification was accomplished in a relatively short time, from 1859 through 1870, but its roots may be traced to the eighteenth century.

The unification of Italy was achieved through a combination of diplomacy, a strategic alliance between the kingdom of Piedmont-Sardinia and France, and strong leadership. In 1861, a united kingdom of Italy was proclaimed, under King Victor Emmanuel II of Piedmont-Sardinia (1820–1878; reigned as king of Piedmont-Sardinia 1849–1861 and as king of Italy 1861–1878). By 1870, for the first time since the sixth century CE, almost all of Italy was politically united. However, even after 1870, a few predominantly Italian-speaking territories, known as *Italia irredenta* (unredeemed Italy), still remained outside the new kingdom of Italy.

THE REFORMS OF 1848

Revolutionary pressures in the 1840s had brought constitutional reforms in the Papal States, Lucca, and Tuscany. In Piedmont-Sardinia, in 1848, King Charles Albert (1798–1849; reigned 1831–1849) signed a constitution that provided for a two-chamber parliament (legislature) with an elected lower house. Among the reforms was the granting of freedom of the press. One of the first newspapers subsequently to be published was called *Il Risorgimento*—the name by which the process of the reunification of Italy became known. The term *il risorgimento* was first used in this context by dramatist Count Vittorio Alfieri (1749–1803), who coined the concept *risorgimento* (resurgence or rebirth) for unity. One of the editors of the newspaper *Il Risorgimento* was Camillo Benso, count of Cavour (1810–1861; in office as prime minister of Piedmont-Sardinia, 1852–1859 and 1860–1861, and of Italy, 1861), who was to play a leading role in the unification of Italy.

The reforms were intended to slow the revolutionary movements to allow the rulers of the various Italian states to control the pace of change, but because the reforms did not go far enough to satisfy popular demands, the pressure only increased. In 1848–1849, revolution spread across Europe. The Hapsburg Austrian Empire was under threat from within as calls for political reform increased, and the reactionary Austrian head of government, the chancellor Prince Klemens Wenzel von Metternich (1773–1859; in office as foreign minister 1809–1848 and as chancellor 1821–1848), who perceived nationalism as a threat to the Austrian Empire, was forced to resign. A temporarily weakened Austria, which ruled northern and northeastern Italy and had much influence through Hapsburg rulers in two of the three central duchies (Tuscany and Modena), offered an opportunity for Italian nationalists to revolt.

THE REVOLTS OF 1848–1849

In March 1848, the people of Lombardy and Venice rose in revolt against Hapsburg rule and managed to drive the Austrians out of the city of Milan. They then asked the king of Piedmont-Sardinia for assistance. Encouraged by these events, Piedmont-Sardinia declared war on Austria and invaded neighboring Lombardy. The Piedmontese gained two initial military successes against the Austrians, but, after a crushing defeat at Custoza at the hands of an Austrian army commanded by Marshal Joseph Radetzky (1766–1858), Austria regained all of Lombardo-Venetia, except the city of Venice, which declared itself a republic under the leadership of Daniele Manin (1804–1857).

Meanwhile, revolts in Naples and Sicily forced a constitution from the archconservative Ferdinand II (1810–1859; reigned 1830–1859). Ferdinand was outspokenly contemptuous of the radicals and reformers and used bombs to suppress the revolt. As a result, he earned the nickname "Bomba."

Republican enthusiasm spread, and an insurrection in Rome in 1848 caused Pope Pius IX (1792–1878; reigned 1846–1878) to flee, following the assassination of his minister of justice, Pelligrino Rossi (1787–1848). Pius IX had been popular upon election and had granted a constitution, freedom of the press, the right to hold meetings of protest, and other reforms. However, he became alarmed by the revolts and, contrary to the expectations of the advocates of Italian unity, had no intention of surrendering papal sovereignty to a united Italy. After the flight of Pius IX, a republic was proclaimed in Rome (1849). Lawyer Giuseppe Mazzini (1805–1872), founder of the unification movement known as La Giovane Italia (Young Italy), was briefly a member of the triumvirate that ruled the Roman Republic from February 1849. Mazzini ruled in an enlightened, effective administration, but it was to last for only a few months because the French government became determined to restore the pope to his territory.

Mazzini was supported by the other great leader of the *risorgimento*, Giuseppe Garibaldi (1807–1882). Garibaldi had been a supporter of Mazzini in a failed uprising in 1834 and, like him, had also gone into exile upon its collapse. Garibaldi had been in South America, where he gained a reputation as a brilliant leader of guerrilla forces in Uruguay. In July 1849, Garibaldi and his small force in the Papal States held out against a larger French army for nearly a month. Garibaldi eventually left with just a few thousand men, and he went into exile again, this time to the United States and later to South America. The temporal authority of Pope Pius IX was restored in the Papal States, with French forces remaining to protect him.

RIGHT LEG IN THE BOOT AT LAST.

GARIBALDI. "IF IT WON'T GO ON, SIRE, TRY A LITTLE MORE POWDER."

A wood engraving cartoon from the British satirical magazine Punch *(November 17, 1860) of Giuseppe Garibaldi (1807–1882) and Victor Emmanuel II (1820–1878; reigned as king of Piedmont-Sardinia, 1849–1861, and as king of Italy, 1861–1878), depicting the reunification of Italy, as Garibaldi helps the king to put on the "boot" of Italy.*

While the Roman Republic was still in existence and the goals of unity and reform still appeared possible, Charles Albert of Piedmont-Sardinia again invaded Lombardy, only to be heavily defeated once more by Radetzky, this time at Novara. Consequently, Charles Albert abdicated. His son, Victor Emmanuel II, succeeded him in March 1849; he retained the relatively liberal constitution, which would eventually become the constitution of a united Italy.

Austrian forces besieged Venice, which capitulated in August 1849, ending the first attempt to oust Austrian domination and the Italian Peninsula's reactionary rulers. In 1848–1849, the unification of Italy had been a brief dream, but ten years later the project was rapidly carried through to a successful conclusion.

CAVOUR

In 1852, Cavour (Camillo Benso, one of the editors of *Il Risorgimento*) became prime minister of Piedmont-Sardinia, and his leadership and diplomatic skill succeeded where the

1848–1849 struggle for national unity had failed. Until his premature death in 1861, Cavour worked toward one aim: a united Italy under the leadership of the kingdom of Piedmont-Sardinia.

To achieve his ambitions, Cavour needed the support of the great European powers, and he sought friendship with both Great Britain and France. To win favor, Cavour brought about an alliance with the British and French in the Crimean War (1853–1856), against Russia in support of the (Turkish) Ottoman Empire. Cavour sent some 18,000 Piedmontese troops to Crimea in 1855, raising the profile of Piedmont-Sardinia and earning the support of Great Britain and France. This gave Cavour the opportunity to represent Piedmont-Sardinia at the subsequent Congress of Paris, in 1856, where he worked to gain support from his new allies for the overthrow of Austrian rule in Italy. At the same time, Cavour built up the Piedmontese army and navy.

In 1858, there was a secret meeting at Plombières (in eastern France) between Cavour and French emperor Napoléon III (1808–1873; reigned 1852–1870), who had belonged to the Carbonari (secret societies that sought Italian unity) in his youth. France agreed to support Piedmont in helping to drive the Austrians out of northern Italy, and, in return, France was to gain French-speaking Savoy and Nice from Piedmont-Sardinia. Savoy was the original home of the dynasty that ruled Piedmont-Sardinia, and Nice still had an Italian-speaking minority; the eventual cession of these territories to France would be unpopular in Italy, and both regions were subsequently regarded as part of *Italia irredenta*.

THE WAR OF 1859

By openly supporting revolutionary elements in Lombardy, Cavour successfully provoked the Austrians into a declaration of war in 1859. The French came to the assistance of Piedmont-Sardinia, and the Austrians were defeated in the two major battles of Magenta and Solferino (both in June 1859). Meanwhile, revolts in Tuscany, Parma, and Modena drove their rulers into exile in Austria, and an uprising took place in Romagna and Marche (the Legations, parts of the Papal States), where the papal authorities were ousted. Austria was forced to surrender Lombardy to Napoléon III, who transferred it to the sovereignty of Victor Emmanuel.

At this point, Napoléon III sought to end his involvement in the war, partly because he perceived that only a long war would oust Austria from Venetia. As a result, the Peace of Villafranca (July 1859), agreed between France and Austria without Piedmontese participation, did not give Cavour what he wanted. While Piedmont-Sardinia gained Lombardy, Venetia was still in Austrian hands, and, under the terms of the peace, the monarchs were to be permitted to return to Tuscany, Modena, and Parma. However, the central duchies were not restored because they immediately formed an armed league and requested the protection of Piedmontese troops. The local authorities organized plebiscites in these territories, and, in 1860, Tuscany, Parma,

Modena, and the Legations voted to unite with Piedmont-Sardinia. Austria now just held Venetia, and the only French presence on the Italian Peninsula was in Rome, where French troops remained at the request of the pope.

GARIBALDI AND SOUTHERN ITALY

Events in southern Italy were moving rapidly. In April 1860, two separate revolts broke out in different parts of Sicily. Garibaldi, the charismatic guerrilla leader who had returned from exile, had little patience with diplomats and legislatures, and he determined to intervene. In what became known as the Mille Expedition, Garibaldi set sail from Genoa in two hired merchant ships with 1,000 volunteers from across Italy to support the Sicilians. After defeating the numerically superior Neapolitan army and gaining control of Sicily within six weeks, Garibaldi then turned his eyes toward Naples.

Garibaldi's forces crossed the Strait of Messina into Calabria, quickly taking the city of Reggio di Calabria. Marching northward, the Mille Expedition met little resistance and much open support. By September 1860, Garibaldi's army was close to the city of Naples. Within the city, the fall of Sicily and a loss of confidence in the monarchy and the army (which had been weakened by the recall of Swiss mercenaries who had formed the most efficient element of the Neapolitan army) led to the effective collapse of the Neapolitan authorities. The army of the Two Sicilies retreated, initially toward Capua, enabling Garibaldi to enter the city of Naples to popular acclaim.

The Neapolitan army regrouped at Capua and, initially, could not be ousted by Garibaldi's volunteers. Garibaldi then announced his intention to march on Rome to end the territorial sovereignty of the papacy and to acquire Rome as the capital of a new Italian state. However, Cavour took action, and the Piedmontese army invaded the Papal States, ostensibly to protect the pope from revolution. The Piedmontese army and Garibaldi's forces met at Teano in October 1860, when the republican Garibaldi loyally surrendered his command to Victor Emmanuel. Garibaldi, refusing all honors or rewards, then retired to his island home, Caprera, near Sardinia.

Meanwhile, the king of the Two Sicilies, Francesco II (1836–1894; reigned 1859–1861), and his queen, Maria Sophie (1841–1925), had fallen back on the strong coastal fortress of Gaeta. There they held out until February 1861; the bravery of the queen during the siege earned admiration, even from opponents. With the fall of Gaeta, the former kingdom of the Two Sicilies was then effectively in Piedmontese hands.

THE KINGDOM OF ITALY

In February 1861, a national legislature was called in Turin, with delegates from the enlarged kingdom of Piedmont-Sardinia and from all the territory annexed by the kingdom. Victor Emmanuel was proclaimed king of Italy, and the Piedmontese constitution was extended to cover the new kingdom. Cavour was made prime minister of Italy.

The unity of Italy was now complete except for Venetia, which was still within the Hapsburg Empire; the Patrimony (the territory around Rome), which was all that was left of the Papal States; and *Italia irredenta*, Italian-speaking territories, such as the South Tirol (Alto Adige) and Istria. Cavour did not live long to enjoy his success. On June 6, 1861, some 16 weeks after assuming the office of Italy's first premier, the architect of the unification of Italy collapsed and died.

For subsequent history, see pages 787–799, 845, and 854.

H. DOE

Marble monument located in Turin, Italy, of Camillo Benso, count of Cavour (1810–1861), a native of Turin, and the statesman who played a leading role in the unification of Italy. The monument was produced by Italian sculptor Giovanni Dupre (1817–1882) and erected in 1873.

Peoples of Italy, Malta, and San Marino

Italy and its small neighbors are, at first glance, remarkably homogenous in population. However, there is some local diversity.

The population of Italy, which in 2007 stood at 59,131,000 (Italian government estimate), is 99 percent European, of which 94 percent are Italians. The remainder comprises migrants, mainly from Asia and Africa.

THE ITALIANS

The Italians are a Romance people who derived from several ethnic groups in ancient times: Romans, Etruscans, and, in the south, Greeks. The Germanic invasions of the Italian Peninsula, from the fourth century CE, introduced other elements, particularly the Lombards in the north. In southern and central Italy, the Byzantine Empire held large areas in the first millennium CE, fostering links with the eastern Mediterranean world. The intervention of Arabs, in the ninth century CE, and Normans (of Viking ancestry), in the eleventh century, in Sicily and the far south of the Italian Peninsula added to the diversity of that part of Italy.

Over time, different parts of Italy were subject to domination by other European powers. For most of the period from the thirteenth to the eighteenth century, southern Italy was ruled by the Spanish, and nobles, administrators, and traders from Spain settled in the region. From the sixteenth century, Austria was the dominant power in northern Italy and parts of central Italy; as a result, people from the Austrian Empire, mainly Austrians but also Hungarians and Slovenes, added to the ethnic mix in those parts of Italy.

Although the majority of Italians are dark-haired, have brown or black eyes, and are generally slightly shorter than the European average, taller, blond Italians, often with blue eyes, are relatively common in a number of regions. There is some diversity in ethnicity, but there is relative uniformity in language and in religion. However, although some 94 percent of the population speak Italian as a first language, this figure does include a number of Italian dialects, some of which are claimed by some linguists to be different enough to, perhaps, be considered as separate languages. In religion, Italians are overwhelmingly Roman Catholic, with 87 percent said to be Catholics; around 37–40 percent are practicing, if only irregularly in some cases.

ITALIAN LINGUISTIC AND ETHNOLINGUISTIC MINORITIES

Within Italy, significant linguistic and ethnic minorities are recognized. The largest is the Venetian linguistic minority, which may number up to 2 million. Spoken in Venetia and Friuli–Venezia Giulia, Venetian is usually considered to be a dialect of Italian even though it has differences in construction from standard Italian, and Venetians are not ethnically different from other Italians.

The second-largest linguistic minority is Sardinian, which is a dialect understood by nearly 1.3 million people, mainly in Sardinia. Sardinian is a Romance language that is archaic in its phonetics when compared with other Romance dialects and languages. Sardinian received official recognition in 1992. Virtually all Sardinians also speak Italian, the majority as a first language.

The Friulians, who number around half a million, live in the northeastern region of Friuli–Venezia Giulia. Friulian is a Rhaetian language, which has the same roots as Ladin (spoken in parts of northern Italy and also Switzerland), but is influenced by Italian, German, and Slovene. The Friulians are often said to be ethnically distinct from the Italians. Undisputedly different from the Italians in ethnicity as well as in language are the Albanians. Communities of Albanians, many of whom descend from mercenaries who came to Italy in the mid- and later Middle Ages, live in rural areas of Sicily and southern Italy, particularly in Puglia. Together, these dispersed Albanian groups number, perhaps, fewer than 300,000 people but, in modern times, the number of Albanians living in Italy has greatly increased as a result of economic migration.

The South Tirol, a region of the Austrian Empire added to Italy after World War I (1914–1918), is home to a substantial ethnic and linguistic minority, the German-speaking Tiroleans. Numbering nearly 300,000, German speakers in the northern Italian region of Trentino–Alto Adige (Südtirol) were resistant to inclusion in Italy but, since the establishment of the republic in 1946, have won a large degree of autonomy. The French speakers of the Val d'Aosta, in northwestern Italy, also have autonomy. They are the last remnant of the French speakers who formed the majority of the population of Savoy, the region west of the Alps (and now in France) that was home to the dynasty that united Italy in 1860–1861. Savoy was the region from which Piedmont, the kernel of modern Italy, evolved.

Other ethnic and linguistic minorities in Italy include Slovenes (numbering fewer than 100,000) in Friuli–Venezia Giulia; around 50,000–60,000 Ladins, in the mountain valleys of the same region; more than 100,000 Occitan speakers in a few remote districts of Piedmont (although most are primarily Italian speakers); a small Croat minority in Molise; tiny Greek-speaking pockets in the southern regions Puglia and Calabria (remnants of early medieval migration rather than ancient colonization); and an Aragonese dialect still spoken in a small area in northern Sardinia, the legacy of the island's long association with Spain. There are also around 120,000 Roma (gypsies) scattered across Italy.

Italy has for several centuries been a region of emigration. Since the 1970s, however, while some Italians still emigrate, the country has been receiving immigrants, mainly from other parts

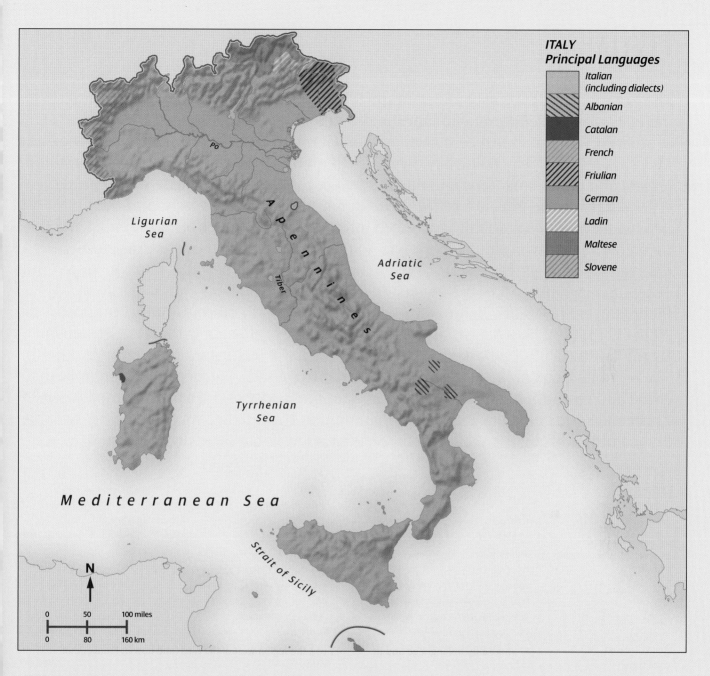

of Europe. The largest numbers of European immigrants come from less developed countries in southeastern Europe, particularly Romanians, Albanians, and Kosovars, who have settled in Italy in the twenty-first century. There has also been a much smaller movement of Poles into Italy.

At the same time, economic immigrants have arrived from Asia and Africa. From Asia, the largest group has been Filipinas, mainly temporary migrants working in hospitals and in service industries as well as in domestic employment. Smaller numbers of (mainly female) migrants have come from some other parts of Asia. By contrast, migration from North Africa, and in the twenty-first century also from sub-Saharan Africa, has been overwhelmingly male. Much of this migration is illegal, with economic migrants attempting to enter the country in small boats from northern Africa. Most African and

Asian migrants, whose total numbers are uncertain, live in the larger cities.

THE MALTESE

The people of Malta form a distinct ethnolinguistic group, which has diverse origins. The Maltese language, like the Maltese people, derives from Sicilian Italian and North African Arabic roots. Maltese is a Semitic language, the only one written in the Roman or Latin alphabet. The islands of Malta are also home to Italian and British minorities and, in modern times, have attracted illegal immigration from sub-Saharan Africa. Like the Italians, the Maltese are almost all Roman Catholics.

C. CARPENTER

Italy

The Roman Republic was founded in the fifth century BCE, and the Roman Empire included all the Mediterranean lands and much of western Europe from the first century BCE to the fourth century CE, when Germanic peoples invaded. From the early Middle Ages, Italy was politically divided into many different independent communes (cities) and larger kingdoms and duchies, while the Papal States rose to power in central Italy. In the fifteenth century, the Renaissance began in Italy, and the patchwork of states gradually coalesced into a smaller number of city-republics and hereditary duchies; but outside powers—Spain and France, and later Austria—intervened, occupying parts of the peninsula. Italy did not become a nation-state until 1859–1861, when most of the peninsula united under the kingdom of Sardinia-Piedmont. In the 1920s, Benito Mussolini (1883–1945; in office as prime minister 1922–1943) established a Fascist dictatorship, but his alliance with Nazi Germany in World War II (1939–1945) led to Italy's defeat and the ousting of the monarchy (1946). The republic faced political instability and many changes of government, organized crime and corruption, and great differences in prosperity and development between north and south. A major political realignment in the late twentieth and early twenty-first centuries brought greater stability and an embryonic two-party system.

GEOGRAPHY

Location	Southern Europe, a peninsula in the Mediterranean Sea plus Sicily, Sardinia, and many smaller islands
Climate	Mediterranean with mild, rainy winters and warm, dry summers; hot in the south in summer; temperate in the north; Alpine in the northern mountains
Area	116,324 sq. miles (301,277 sq. km)
Coastline	4,724 miles (7,603 km)
Highest point	Monte Bianco de Courmayeur 15,616 feet (4,760 m)
Lowest point	Mediterranean Sea 0 feet
Terrain	Mountainous and rugged in the north (the Alps) and through the center of the peninsula (the Apennines); river basins and coastal lowlands
Natural resources	Building materials and marble, natural gas, hydroelectric power potential, bauxite, iron ore, pumice, feldspar
Land use	
Arable land	26.4 percent
Permanent crops	9.1 percent
Other	64.5 percent
Major rivers	Po, Tiber, Arno
Major lakes	Garda, Maggiore, Trasimeno
Natural hazards	Earthquakes, landslides, floods, volcanism, drought

METROPOLITAN AREAS, 2006 POPULATION

Urban population	67 percent
Rome	3,402,000
Rome city	2,719,000
Milan	2,983,000
Milan city	1,300,000
Naples	2,229,000
Naples city	973,000
Turin	1,702,000
Turin city	908,000
Palermo	852,000
Palermo city	663,000
Genoa	611,000
Catania	477,000
Catania city	299,000
Florence	429,000
Florence city	365,000
Bologna	429,000
Bologna city	72,000
Bari	323,000

SWITZERLAND

Alps

AUSTRIA

Bolzano-Bozen

TRENTINO–
ALTO ADIGE/
SOUTH TIROL

★ Trento

FRIULI–
VENEZIA
GIULIA

Udine

SLOVENIA

★ Aosta
VALLE
D'AOSTA

Varese

LOMBARDY

Monza

Bergamo

VENETO

Vicenza

Treviso

Trieste ★

FRANCE

PIEDMONT

Novara

Milan

Brescia

Verona

Venice

Padua

CROATIA

Turin ★

Alessandria

Piacenza

Po

Parma

Modena

Ferrara

Gulf of
Venice

Genoa ★

Reggio nell'Emilia

Bologna

Ravenna

BOSNIA AND
HERZEGOVINA

LIGURIA

EMILIA-ROMAGNA

Forlì

Rimini

La Spezia

Massa

SAN MARINO

*Ligurian
Sea*

Lucca

Prato

Pesaro

Pisa

Florence ★

Apennines

Ancona

Livorno

Arezzo

MARCHE

*Adriatic
Sea*

TUSCANY

Elba

UMBRIA

Perugia ★

*Corsica
(FRANCE)*

Terni

Tiber

L'Aquila

Pescara

★

VATICAN CITY
Rome

ABRUZZI

LAZIO

Latina

Campobasso ★

MOLISE

Foggia

Caserta

Barletta

Giugliano in Campania

CAMPANIA

Andria

Bari

Sassari

Naples ★

Salerno

PUGLIA

SARDINIA

Potenza ★

Brindisi

BASILICATA

Taranto

Lecce

*Tyrrhenian
Sea*

*Gulf of
Taranto*

CALABRIA

*Ionian
Sea*

Cagliari ★

Catanzaro ★

*Mediterranean
Sea*

*Lipari
Islands*

Messina

Palermo ★

Reggio di Calabria

Marsala

Strait of Sicily

SICILY

Catania

Siracusa

Pantelleria

N

*Pelagie
Islands*

MALTA

| 0 | 50 | 100 miles |
| 0 | 80 | 160 km |

Legend:
★ National capital
★ Regional capital
● Other city
━━ National border
─── Regional border

Padua	322,000
Padua city	210,000
Bergamo	310,000
Bergamo city	116,000
Cagliari	298,000
Cagliari city	158,000
Brescia	290,000
Brescia city	190,000
Massa	281,000
Massa city	70,000
Verona	261,000
Venice	269,000
Messina	244,000
Caserta	239,000
Caserta city	79,000
Trieste	205,000
Taranto	195,000
Prato	186,000
Reggio di Calabria	186,000

Source: Italian government estimates, 2008

NEIGHBORS AND LENGTH OF BORDERS*

Austria	267 miles (430 km)
France	303 miles (488 km)
San Marino	24 miles (39 km)
Slovenia	144 miles (232 km)
Switzerland*	460 miles (740 km)
Vatican City	2 miles (3.2 km)

* includes enclave in Switzerland

POPULATION

Population	59,131,000 (2007 government estimate)
Population density	508 per sq. mile (196 per sq. km)
Population growth	-0.02 percent a year
Birthrate	8.4 births per 1,000 of the population
Death rate	10.6 deaths per 1,000 of the population
Population under age 15	13.6 percent
Population over age 65	20.0 percent
Sex ratio	107 males for 100 females
Fertility rate	1.3 children per woman
Infant mortality rate	5.6 deaths per 1,000 live births
Life expectancy at birth	
Total population	80.1 years
Female	83.2 years
Male	77.1 years

ECONOMY

Currency	Euro (EUR)
Exchange rate (2008)	$1 = EUR 0.68
Gross domestic product (2007)	$1.79 trillion
GDP per capita (2007)	$30,400
Unemployment rate (2007)	6 percent

Population under poverty line (2007)	N/A
Exports	$501.4 billion (2007 CIA estimate)
Imports	$498.6 billion (2007 CIA estimate)

GOVERNMENT

Official country name	Italian Republic
Conventional short form	Italy
Nationality	
noun	Italian
adjective	Italian
Official language	Italian
Capital city	Rome
Type of government	Quasi-federal republic; parliamentary democracy
Voting rights	18 years, universal; the voting age for senatorial elections is 25 years
National anthem	"Il Canto degli Italiani" (The song of the Italians), popularly known as "L'Inno di Mameli" (Mameli's hymn)
National day	Republic Day, June 2 (1946; foundation of the republic)

TRANSPORTATION

Railroads	12,095 miles (19,465 km)
Highways	301,171 miles (484,792 km)
Expressways	4,114 miles (6,621 km)
Other paved roads	297,057 miles (478,067 km)
Navigable waterways	1,492 miles (2,400 km); little used commercially
Airports	
International airports	24
Paved runways	101

POPULATION PROFILE, 2007 ESTIMATES

Ethnic groups	
Europeans	99 percent (of which Italians 94 percent; other Europeans 5 percent)
North Africans, Chinese, Filipinos, and others	1 percent
Religions	
Roman Catholic	87 percent; around 37–40 percent practicing
Sunni Islam and others	1 percent
Nonreligious	12 percent
Languages	
Italian	94 percent as a first language
German, French, Albanian, Romanian, Ladin, Friulian, and others	5 percent
North African languages	under 1 percent
Adult literacy	over 98 percent

CHRONOLOGY

c. 800–600 BCE	The Etruscan culture develops in central Italy. Greek colonies are established in Sicily.
5th century BCE	The Roman Republic is founded.
1st century BCE–4th century CE	Roman Empire includes all the lands surrounding the Mediterranean Sea and much of western Europe.
5th–8th centuries CE	An Ostrogoth kingdom is established in the north, while the Byzantine Empire gains part of southern and central Italy. A Lombard invasion ousts Byzantine influence from Italy in the eighth century.
756 CE	The papacy gains sovereignty over central Italy.
11th–15th centuries	Italy is divided into various city-republics, such as Venice, Pisa, Genoa, Florence, and Amalfi, and many small monarchical states. Venice and its commercial rival Genoa build empires in the eastern Mediterranean.
15th–16th centuries	The Renaissance spreads from Italy. French forces intervene in the north, while the Spanish intervene in the south, leading to the Italian Wars (1494–1559).
1559–1713	Spain is the major power in the Italian peninsula, particularly in the south.
1713–1796	Austria replaces Spain as the principal power in Italy.
1796–1814	French intervention in Italy brings the establishment of client republics and, in 1805, the puppet kingdom of Italy.
1815	The Congress of Vienna redraws the map of Italy: the kingdoms of the Two Sicilies in the south and Sardinia-Piedmont in Sardinia and the northwest; the papacy in central Italy; Austria in the north; and several central small states.
1830 and 1848–1849	Revolts against reactionary rulers and in favor of Italian unification are unsuccessful.
1859–1861	In a war against Austria, Sardinia-Piedmont (allied to France) gains Austrian Lombardy. After popular uprisings in northern and central Italy and against the Bourbon monarchy in the south, most of Italy is united.
1866	Italy, allied to Prussia, gains Venetia from Austria.
1870	Italian forces invade Rome. The Papal States are abolished.
1915–1918	Italy enters World War I (1914–1918), and gains Trentino, Istria, and other territories in 1918.
1922–1943	Benito Mussolini (1883–1945; in office as prime minister 1922–1943) establishes a Fascist dictatorship. Alliance with Germany leads to Italy's defeat and the ousting of the monarchy in 1946.
1946–mid-1990s	The Italian republic is unstable and suffers many changes of government. Organized crime and corruption decrease confidence in the state.
since mid-1990s	New political parties are formed, and a more stable governmental system emerges.
2008	A two-party system emerges in legislative elections, won by the (conservative) People of Freedom party over the (center-left) Democratic Party.

GOVERNMENT

The Italian parliamentary system was characterized by a large number of political parties, short-lived governments, and instability until the mid-1990s, when the parties that had flourished since the establishment of the republic in 1946 were replaced by newer parties.

Italy has a parliamentary system of government, one in which power rests with the legislature rather than the executive. The role of the chief of state, the president, is ceremonial. The president, who must be at least 50 years of age, is elected for a seven-year term by an electoral college, comprising both houses of the legislature and three members representing each of the 20 regional legislatures (except Valle d'Aosta, which has one regional elector). In the first round of voting, election requires a two-thirds majority, but the majority required is progressively lowered in each round of the election, until it reaches 50 percent plus one vote. Although there is no constitutional bar to reelection, no Italian president has served a second term.

The president, who stands above party politics, represents Italy abroad, appoints and receives ambassadors, is commander in chief of the armed forces, appoints principal public officers (upon the recommendation of the prime minister), and invites the leader of the largest party in the legislature to form a government. Advised by the premier, the president may dissolve the legislature and call an election and may also refuse to sign into law any measure that she or he considers to be unconstitutional.

THE GOVERNMENT AND THE LEGISLATURE

The government of Italy is responsible to the bicameral legislature, called the parliament (Parlamento Italiano). The legislature is elected by universal adult suffrage for five years. Legislation may be introduced in either house and must be approved by both to become law. Government ministers, who are chosen by the prime minister and appointed by the president, are normally members of the lower house.

The Senate (Senato della Repubblica; upper house) has 315 members directly elected under a system of proportional representation (with percentage thresholds for election) in each of the 20 regions. For senatorial elections, the voting age is 25 years and over. Former presidents and up to five other members chosen by the president are also senators.

The Chamber of Deputies (Camera dei Deputati) has 630 members elected by citizens aged 18 years and over under a system of proportional representation. Members are elected in 26 constituencies; each region is a single constituency, but heavily populated Lombardy is divided into three constituencies, and Piedmont, Lazio, Venetia, Sicily, and Campania are each divided into two constituencies. These constituencies elect 617 members. The region of Valle d'Aosta, which has a small population, elects one member, and 12 members are elected to represent Italian citizens living abroad. The winning coalition has the total of its domestic seats in parliament increased to 340, if necessary, in order to give it a working majority.

POLITICAL PARTIES

Public disillusionment with the traditional parties saw them gradually replaced by new political movements from the mid-1990s. In modern times, the two main political parties are the (conservative) People of Freedom (PdL) and the center-left Democratic Party (PD). The (northern regional autonomist) Northern League (Lega) and the small (southern regional autonomist) Movement for Autonomy (MpA) are allied to the PdL. The other parties represented in the legislature are the (populist anti-corruption) Italy of Values (IdV), the (Christian Democratic) Union of the Center, and the (South Tirol regionalist) South Tirolean People's Party (SVP).

LOCAL GOVERNMENT

Italy is divided into 20 regions, which each have an elected regional legislature, the Consiglio Regionale (regional council). The regional head of government is directly elected in each region, and she or he appoints the regional government (Giunta Regionale). There are two different types of regions: regions with ordinary statute (which have limited powers); and five regions with special statute, which retain between 60 and 100 percent of taxation raised locally and have extensive powers. These five regions are Valle d'Aosta (which has a French minority), Friuli–Venezia Giulia (with Slovene and Friulian minorities), Trentino–Alto Adige/Südtirol (with a German minority), Sardinia, and Sicily. In Trentino–Alto Adige/Südtirol, the powers normally exercised by regional authorities are assumed by the two provincial governments.

Below the regions, Italy is divided into 110 provinces. Lombardy has 12 provinces, while some regions have as few as two. In Valle d'Aosta, the provincial and regional authorities are merged. Since 1993, each province has a council (elected by proportional representation) and a directly elected president as well as a prefect (governor) appointed by the central government. Provinces are further subdivided into municipalities, 8,101 in all, each with an elected mayor and council.

C. CARPENTER

MODERN HISTORY

The Kingdom of Italy

In 1861, the kingdom of Italy was founded, uniting most of the Italian-speaking lands in one country for the first time, although Venetia was still under Austrian rule and the remainder of the Papal States had not yet been annexed. The next decades were spent promoting a sense of national unity, in particular addressing the problem of the underdeveloped south.

Italian unification was achieved by the northern kingdom of Piedmont-Sardinia, and the new state—created by Piedmont's annexation of Lombardy (1859) and central and southern Italy (1860)—was not renamed Italy until 1861. At the time, a considerable number of commentators saw unification as the outcome of a civil war rather than a struggle against foreign domination. Particularly in the south, many people perceived unification as a result of Piedmont's expansionist aims. As statesman and novelist Massimo D'Azeglio (1798–1866) stated, "while Italy was made, Italians still had to be made."

THE PROCLAMATION OF THE KINGDOM

When the first Italian parliament met in January 1861, it officially opened as "the eighth legislature of the parliament of Sardinia"—Sardinia was still the official name of the state—but it closed as the legislature of Italy. The assembly changed the name of the country to Italy, whose first chief of state was King Victor Emmanuel II of Piedmont-Sardinia (1820–1878; reigned as king of Piedmont-Sardinia 1849–1861 and as king of Italy 1861–1878). The alternatives to unification under Piedmont-Sardinia, such as the idea of a federal state or that of a state under the jurisdiction of the pope, were dismissed by the legislature without much debate. The body of laws and regulation known as Statuto Albertino, the constitution of Piedmont-Sardinia, was applied to the rest of the country; this measure arguably contributed to widening the gap between the north and the south of the country, a deep division that was destined to remain a characteristic of the new centralized state. The new nation was divided into provinces ruled by prefects appointed by the government and mostly coming from the north. For decades, the king showed his preference for a political elite and for civil servants from Piedmont with whom he could communicate in his own dialect.

Despite the proclamation of the kingdom of Italy, the nation was not complete. Venetia was still part of the Hapsburg Austrian Empire and that part of the Papal States surrounding Rome still remained the sovereign territory of the pope. These regions—and other areas that were home to Italian speakers, such as Istria, Trentino, and the Alto Adige/South Tirol—became known as *Italia irredenta* (unredeemed Italy).

VENETIA AND ROME

Italy gained Venetia, although not all of the region, from the Hapsburg Empire in 1866 after the new Italian kingdom formed an alliance with Prussia in the Austro-Prussian War. However, an Austrian army stopped the Italians at Custoza (June 1866), and an Austrian fleet was similarly successful at Lissa in the following month. A military force known as Cacciatori delle Alpi (the hunters of the alps), led by Giuseppe Garibaldi (1807–1882), whose 1860 campaign in southern Italy had toppled the kingdom of the Two Sicilies (Naples and Sicily), gained the only Italian victory of the war at Bezzecca. By this time, Prussia was already in peace negotiations with Austria, and Italy swiftly left the war. Rather than deal directly with Italy, Austria ceded Venetia to France, which then transferred it to Italy. The Cacciatori were close to taking the city of Trento, but the whole Trentino region remained Austrian for another half a century.

Prussia also played a role in Italy's acquisition of Rome. In 1870, because of the outbreak of the Franco-Prussian War, France had to reduce the number of its soldiers based in Rome to protect the pope's territories, leaving Rome vulnerable. In September 1870, at Porta Pia, Italian troops opened a hole in the Aurelian wall, as the city wall was called, and marched into Rome, which was regarded by most Italians as their future capital. The pope, Pius IX (1792–1878; reigned 1846–1878), protested the invasion, excommunicating those responsible.

Pius retreated to the Vatican, where he regarded himself as a prisoner, and refused the Italian offer of continued sovereignty over the Leonine City (the modern Roman district of Borgo), the area surrounding the Vatican and an area much larger than the present-day Vatican City State.

The pope's fierce refusal opened a period of tense relations between the papacy and the Italian state. After a long era of ideological debates and practical action to unify Italy, the conquest of Rome represented the end of an era. The annexation of the city, which was a symbol of the past glory of the Italian Peninsula dating back to the Roman Empire, represented the fulfillment of a project that had lasted for decades. At the same time, the acquisition of Rome was a high-water mark after which popular interest in political life in Italy steadily waned—the pope had also forbidden practicing Catholics from participating in the government of Italy, a measure that was, for the most part, ignored, but which prevented any direct influence of the church through a Catholic party until the 1920s.

THE SOUTHERN QUESTION

Italy was unified, but the country lacked unity. In 1874–1875, the "Southern Question," which refers to the gap in standards of living and education between the north and the south (which is frequently called the Mezzogiorno), became a national issue that had to be solved in order to build a common national identity. The profoundly different peoples of a recently united Italy would take decades to achieve a true national feeling. Politicians of the left, in particular, claimed the need not only for social reforms but also for promoting moral ideals, without which the already growing discontent in the south might spread through Italy, threatening the existence of the new state. For the left and liberals, the core of this set of values consisted mainly in loyalty and respect for the state and, at the same time, in a strong ideological and practical opposition to the Catholic Church.

While politicians and intellectuals engaged in a discussion concerning the values needed to found a nation and to provide its citizens with a strong feeling of belonging, Italy comprised people who were struggling to find better living conditions. Particularly in the south, the main problems were a lack of education and poor health care. Pellagra, cholera, and typhus, resulting from a poor diet and lack of hygiene, were the main causes of premature death in the Mezzogiorno. Some people in the south lived in caves or other inadequate housing, and, while around 78 percent of Italians were illiterate, the percentage rose to some 90 percent in the south.

The Casati law introduced in 1860, despite its many limits, was aimed at promoting the national language and making school attendance compulsory, although for only two years and in classes with as many as 70 students. This attempt to improve education provision faced several practical problems, among which was the lack of trained teachers and adequate facilities. Poor living standards contributed to a general state of social

unrest and to the spreading of a phenomenon known as brigandage—the action of groups of farmers in the countryside who started a series of riots. Subsequently, brigandage was repressed by the state with systematic violence.

THE CONSTITUTIONAL LEFT

In 1876, a government of the Historical Right (Destra Storica) was replaced by an administration of the Historical Left (Sinistra Storica) under Agostino Depretis (1813–1887; in office as prime minister 1876–1878 and 1881–1887). The Historical Left did not seem to a have a well-defined political program but rather stood in opposition to the Right and its harsh fiscal policies (implemented to confront the large public deficit); the Historical Left aimed to maintain the order and infrastructure of the Italian state as well as to protect agriculture and support industry. In 1877, disillusioned progressive liberals left the Historical Left to found the Radical Party.

A lack of discussion on reforms and the willingness of Depretis to seek agreements with his political opponents, such

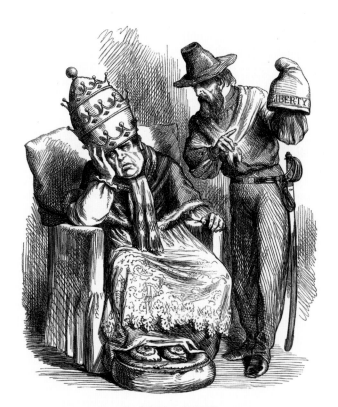

A GOOD OFFER.

GARIBALDI. "TAKE TO THIS CAP, PAPA PIUS. YOU WILL FIND IT MORE COMFORTABLE THAN YOUR OWN."

Cartoon of Pope Pius IX (reigned 1846–1878), the last temporal ruler of the Papal States. He became the "prisoner in the Vatican" after Italian forces took Rome in 1870.

as Marco Minghetti (1818–1886; in office as prime minister 1863–1864 and 1873–1876), in the 1882 legislative elections, inaugurated a phase of cross-party cooperation when the political Right and Left established an alliance to counter the rising appeal of socialism. The Left's foreign policy was influenced by a difficult relationship with France, which was seen as a potential enemy. Consequently, the Italian government tried to counterbalance the perceived French threat by signing a pact of mutual support with Germany and, later, Austria, known as the Triple Alliance. Many Italians were unhappy with the alliance with Austria, a former enemy that was still disliked, particularly as the Hapsburg Empire included areas inhabited by Italian speakers, districts regarded as part of *Italia irredenta*.

CRISPI

Francesco Crispi (1819–1901; in office as prime minister 1887–1891 and 1893–1896), who succeeded Depretis, tried to reestablish a clear difference between the Right and the Left. Deeply convinced that patriotism had to become the state theme and that loyalty toward the state had to be promoted, Crispi pursued an aggressive foreign policy, which put Italy at risk of a new war, at the same time that it was facing one of the bleakest economic phases in its history. Crispi's idea that a war would have represented a means to reinforce nationhood, along with his conviction that Italy could become a nation only at the expense of France, motivated his aggressiveness toward the French. France was seen as hostile to the new state for geographical and historical reasons, not least because of its recent interest in the former Papal States but also because Sardinia-Piedmont was forced to to cede Nice and Savoy. This French-speaking core around which Piedmont had developed was the price for French support in the war of 1859 that had liberated Lombardy from Austrian rule.

The idea that an authoritarian state was needed in order to pull the nation together became widespread. In his shift toward authoritarianism, Crispi identified a successful war in Africa as the best strategy to build a strong sense of national identity. As a result, Italy conquered Eritrea and what is now Somalia but was defeated by Ethiopia in the Battle of Adwa in 1896. The outcome of the colonial war in Africa, as well as the social unrest and the economic crisis of the 1890s, contributed to the downfall of Crispi's government in 1896 and created an atmosphere of disillusionment in a country that had forgotten the ideals of the *Risorgimento* (the struggle for national

The first king of Italy, Victor Emmanuel II (reigned 1861–1878).

unification in the first half of the nineteenth century) and was now struggling to assert itself as a nation.

GIOLITTI

Giovanni Giolitti (1842–1928; in office as prime minister 1892–1893, 1903–1905, 1906–1909, 1911–1914, and 1920–1921) dominated the political scene for more than two decades. Giolitti's first government (1892–1893) had a short life. Its end was brought about by economic problems, his refusal to repress riots with violence as Crispi had done, and the scandal of the Banca Romana (Roman Bank), when he tried to appoint the director-general of the bank—which had a reputation for corruption—to the Senate (upper house of the legislature) and abused his position as prime minister by obtaining documents referring to the case.

After a brief government led again by Crispi until 1896, Giolitti had three more discontinuous periods of government before World War I (1914–1918). Giolitti's administrations were characterized by a positive trend in the Italian economy. His governments aimed at developing industry rather than promoting agriculture, while retaining the protectionist policy introduced in 1887. The automobile corporation Fiat was founded in Turin in 1899, followed by Lancia and Alfa (in 1906), while tire company Pirelli emerged as a leading player in the national economy. The textile sector, particularly silk and cotton, grew as well, and Italy began to benefit from remittances (money sent home) from emigrants who had left the country and settled in the United States, Argentina, and other countries.

After the financial scandals of the 1890s, Giolitti's government introduced new rules on the printing of money and the reorganization of the banking system. The Banca Commerciale Italiana had been founded in 1884 in Milan with German capital and began a new trend of mixed banks, characterized by foreign participation. Despite growing urbanization and the employment of an increasing workforce in the cities, Italy was still a mainly rural country sustained by agriculture. Although school attendance figures improved in the country as a whole, the standard of living in the Mezzogiorno was still low, and the average wage covered only the cost of basic goods.

Giolitti's decision not to intervene in matters related to labor led to many strikes, which, in turn, led to the creation of labor unions in Italy. The government introduced a policy of social reforms that included banning children under age 12 from employment, the introduction of a compulsory day of rest in the workweek, and the creation of funds for ill and retired workers as well as a maternity fund. These measures, along with Giolitti's support of moderate socialist principles, provoked the resentment of employers and industrialists, while the more radical labor unions advocated the need for a new government led by the workers, under the guidance of the unions.

BAVA-BECCARIS AND UMBERTO I

In January 1878, Victor Emmanuel II died. The king had been genuinely popular for the role he had played in the unification of Italy. He had become a symbol of the *Risorgimento* and had won the admiration (although begrudging) of a republican such as Garibaldi, who surrendered the kingdom of the Two Sicilies to him in 1860. Victor Emmanuel made few public errors of judgment, except retaining the title Victor Emmanuel II, rather than calling himself Victor Emmanuel I of Italy in 1861, when the kingdom of Italy was founded—this suggested that the new state was a "greater Piedmont" rather than a new unified state for Italian speakers. Nevertheless, many Italians mourned his death. His son and successor, Umberto I (1844–1900; reigned 1878–1900), was unpopular. Perceived as reactionary, he came to be seen as an opponent of the workers and the left during a time of economic hardship.

In May 1898, serious riots took place in the northern industrial city of Milan, where the actions of the government of

Bust of Francesco Crispi (1819–1901). Crispi was instrumental in the formation of the united Italy and was its prime minister from 1887 until 1891 and again from 1893 until 1896.

Antonio Starrabba di Rudinì (1839–1908; in office as prime minister 1891–1892 and 1896–1898) were generally held responsible for a drastic rise in the prices of basic commodities, leading to hunger. Strikes and riots also broke out in Livorno, Naples, and Florence. In Milan, barricades were erected by the strikers, and artillery, infantry, and cavalry units were deployed in the city in an attempt to intimidate the demonstrators. Then, General Fiorenzo Bava-Beccaris (1831–1924) ordered his troops to fire against the unarmed demonstrators, whose number included women and seniors. The authorities stated that 118 people died; the protestors claimed 400. Hundreds were wounded. Filippo Turati (1857–1932), founder of the Italian Socialist Party, was arrested and charged with promoting the riots. Umberto I praised and decorated Bava-Beccaris, seriously compromising the monarchy. The king became a divisive figure and, in July 1900, Umberto was assassinated. As a result of Umberto's approval of the suppression of the demonstrations, the Italian monarchy forfeited support from the left and liberals.

THE EARLY TWENTIETH CENTURY

After Giolitti returned to office in 1903, the most active element of opposition was the Nationalists, who in 1910 founded their own party, the Italian Nationalist Association, promoting the need for a more authoritarian government. The Nationalists campaigned for a new colonial war as the means to achieve their ideals. In 1911, surrendering to this view of war and aiming to appease his opponents, Giolitti ordered the invasion and conquest of Tripolitania and Cyrenaica (modern Libya), which were then Turkish possessions. The successful colonial adventure did not prevent the collapse of support for Giolitti.

The portrayal of war as a valid means to unite the nation, the concept of violence almost as a necessary evil, and the creation of myths helped shape Italy's future. The acceptance of these ideas helped lead Italy into World War I.

E. GARAU

Italy in World War I

When World War I (1914–1918) broke out, Italy remained neutral. However, various political factions in the country advocated Italian participation both to promote national unity and to gain territory. Entering the conflict in 1915, Italy had little success and became disillusioned with the subsequent peace settlement.

In 1914, Italy was a young nation of great regional diversity, in peoples, dialects, development, and standards of living, with a deep economic and cultural gap between the north and the south. United only since 1861, Italy was still struggling to build a national identity. Many intellectuals and members of parties of the political left initially considered participation in the war—which many people in Europe believed to be inevitable—as the best means to provide Italians with a sense of nationhood. Later, support for war came from the right.

INTERVENTION OR NEUTRALITY

When World War I broke out, Italy was neutral. The country's alliance with Germany and Austria-Hungary, first signed in 1890, was still in force and had been renewed at regular intervals (the Austrian Empire had become the Austro-Hungarian Empire in 1867, when what became known as the Dual Monarchy was established). However, the pact guaranteed support to the allied countries only if one of them became the victim of an attack by another country. This was not the case for Austria-Hungary, which was the first to declare war, on Serbia, in 1914. Given the defensive nature of the Triple Alliance, and not having been consulted by Austria on the declaration of war, Italian political leaders did not feel they had any obligation to intervene, and they decided that Italy would not take part in the conflict.

The majority of deputies in the Italian legislature were against intervention. The Catholic Church and the recently resigned prime minister, Giovanni Giolitti (1842–1928; in office as prime minister 1892–1893, 1903–1905, 1906–1909, 1911–1914, and 1920–1921), who was the dominant political figure in Italy, also agreed that Italy should stay neutral and possibly use the opportunity to negotiate with the belligerents precisely because of its neutrality. Most people were against embarking on a struggle whose outcome was difficult to foresee.

Although the mainstream position on the war was one of non-intervention, some minority groups both in parliament and among Italian intellectuals started advocating active participation in the war, which they saw as an opportunity for Italy's affirmation as a nation. The supporters of the war were now mainly, but not exclusively, on the right. Some representatives of the Socialists, the most radical members, also joined the campaign to push the government toward an interventionist policy. Among them was future Fascist party leader Benito Mussolini (1883–1945; in office

as prime minister 1922–1943) who left the Socialist Party in protest and became, with intellectuals such as poet, dramatist, and adventurer Gabriele d'Annunzio (1863–1938), one of the strongest advocates of Italian participation in the war.

The Nationalists and the Futurists, an avant-garde group led by Filippo Tommaso Marinetti (1876–1944), also joined the interventionists. Futurist painter Umberto Boccioni (1882–1916), who was killed while serving as a cavalry officer, declared "We want to glorify war—the world's only hygiene." There was a general growing mood of excitement about the conflict, fueled by the romance of speed, the new phenomenon of aviation, and technology in weaponry. At the same time, participation in the war was promoted as a unifying moment for the nation. Other supporters of the war included groups of industrialists who saw in it a chance to increase their profits, a prediction that was soon proved correct.

GOING TO WAR

Italian prime minister Antonio Salandra (1853–1931; in office 1914–1916) and minister of foreign affairs Sydney Sonnino (1847–1922; in office as prime minister 1905–1906 and 1909–1910 and as foreign minister 1914–1919), started a process of covert consultations with the two opposing factions to see what advantages would derive from taking part in the war with one or other alliance. Sonnino initially favored the Triple Alliance powers, but, eventually, in April 1915, Italy signed a pact with France and Great Britain, known as the Treaty of London, and left the Triple Alliance; in the treaty, Italy was promised territory along the Adriatic should the allies emerge victorious. The pact was signed despite being an open violation of the constitution, whose fifth article stated that an involvement in a conflict needed to be supported by a majority in the national legislature. Italy officially entered the conflict on May 23, 1915, declaring war on the Austro-Hungarian Empire and, later, in 1916, on Germany. This decision contributed to a weakening of the constitution.

ITALY AT WAR

The advocates of war had predicted that the conflict would be short and that Italians, inspired by national fervor, would prevail. Neither prediction proved correct. Italian troops faced a

November, Austrian forces pushed the Italians back to the Piave River, taking much of Venetia, and the city of Venice seemed about to fall. After Caporetto, General Armando Diaz (1861–1928) succeeded General Luigi Cadorna (1850–1928) as the head of the Italian troops. Limited Allied forces (British, French, and U.S.) strengthened the line along the Piave river, where the Italians had stopped the Austrian advance.

The Austrians launched what was supposed to be a definitive attack for final victory in June 1918 in the Battle of the Solstice, which lasted eight days. However, the Italians resisted the assault. Italian forces then began a counteroffensive against the Austrians, who were now demoralized and economically weak. At the Battle of Vittorio Veneto (October 24–November 3,

At the Battle of Caporetto in 1917, Austro-German forces broke through the Italian lines, routing the Italian army.

1918) Italy gained a victory against an Austro-Hungarian army that was collapsing. The Italians advanced toward Friuli, and an armistice with Austria-Hungary was signed, near Padua, on November 3.

long series of bloody, inconclusive battles on the Isonzo River, along the main front against Austria-Hungary, in the northeast of the country. The Italian soldiers, involved in what became a long trench war, came mainly from the south of Italy. This shaped a general feeling of confusion and disillusion among these southern Italian forces, who were fighting for a territory that they did not perceive as their homeland. Although Italy had been united for two generations, regionalism was strong, and the sense of national unity was not deep.

Low wages in the army, poor conditions, and a lack of commitment contributed to a high level of desertion, even though defection was harshly punished by court martial. However, during the conflict, Italian industry grew exponentially as a result of a careful organization which, among other things, saw the state involving all the firms needed for the war as auxiliaries. In some facilities, where production was seen as part of the war effort, workers were placed under the discipline of the army, which controlled the distribution of raw materials and imposed fixed prices on armaments.

The most dramatic defeat for Italian forces was at Caporetto (October–November 1917; now Kobarid in Slovenia), and the Austrians subsequently reached the city of Udine. In mid-

THE PEACE SETTLEMENT

In November 1918, Italy occupied Trento and the South Tirol, and Italian forces went on to occupy all of the Tirol north of the Brenner Pass, including the city of Innsbruck. Italian forces also entered Trieste, Rovigno, Zara, and Lissia, all territory promised to Italy by the Treaty of London. The terms of the treaty were not, however, fully respected; although Italy finally gained Istria (now part of Croatia), neither the Dalmatian coast (now coastal Croatia) nor the Italian-speaking city of Fiume (now the Croatian city of Rijeka, which was claimed by Italy even though it was not mentioned in the treaty) were annexed to Italy. The shock of crushing defeat at Caporetto, where Italy suffered one-fifth of its casualties in the war, including 275,000 troops taken as prisoners, and the inequitable peace, which fell far short of what Italy had been promised by France and Great Britain in 1915, helped shaped Italy's future course. Subsequently, Italy built up its armed forces and eventually looked toward a German alliance rather than one with World War I allies.

E. GARAU

Italy between the Wars

After World War I (1914–1918), Italy became economically and politically destabilized.

In 1915, Italy signed the Treaty of London with France and Great Britain, under which Italy would receive Italian-speaking regions of the Austro-Hungarian Empire, including areas with an Italian minority, such as South Tirol and Dalmatia (now coastal Croatia). Although Italy received Friuli, Istria, and all of South Tyrol (including areas with a German-speaking majority) in the peace treaty, Dalmatia was not ceded, nor was Fiume (now Rijeka, Croatia), which had an Italian-speaking majority. Italian-speaking Zara (now Zadar, Croatia), along the coast of Dalmatia, was finally ceded to Italy in 1920, but the failure to acquire other Italian-speaking areas was poorly received in Italy.

At the same time, left-wing movements grew, alarming the authorities, business, and the middle class. The Communist Party (PCI) was founded in 1921, and more workers organized themselves in labor unions. The seizure of power by the Communists in Russia in 1917 persuaded many Europeans that similar revolutions would occur through the continent.

THE FIUME CRISIS

The postwar settlement gave Italy most of the Austrian territory that had been promised in 1915 but little of the expected land from Hungary. Consequently, Italian nationalists took action, promoting an audacious march on Fiume. Fiume had been awarded to the new nation of Yugoslavia (officially called the Kingdom of Serbs, Croats, and Slovenes until 1929). The march on Fiume was secretly organized and led by poet, dramatist, and adventurer Gabriele d'Annunzio (1863–1938), who left Venice on September 11, 1919. Despite the disapproval of the Italian government and a prohibition against members of the armed forces taking part, many followed the poet, including soldiers. The expedition received widespread public support as well as encouragement from industrialists.

Italy's prime minister, Francesco Saverio Nitti (1868–1953; in office 1919–1920), decided not to send the army to stop d'Annunzio because he feared a mutiny if he did so. As a result, d'Annunzio's volunteers entered Fiume in September 1919. D'Annunzio declared Fiume a separate state and he became a symbol of Italian nationalism. His rousing public speeches from balconies provided an example for Fascist leader Benito Mussolini (1883–1945; in office as prime minister 1922–1943). In November 1920, Italy and Yugoslavia agreed that Fiume and contiguous Croat-speaking Susak should form an independent country, the Free State of Rijeka/Fiume. D'Annunzio resisted by force and was ousted by Italian troops. In March 1924, the free state was partitioned by Italy and Yugoslavia, with Fiume becoming Italian and Susak Yugoslav. The whole episode had demonstrated growing Italian nationalism.

POLITICAL AND SOCIAL DEVELOPMENTS

Italy's political life was transformed by the introduction of universal male suffrage in 1918 (the voting age had previously been 30) and the growth of a new party, the Italian People's Party (PPI). Led by a priest, Don Luigi Sturzo (1871–1959), the PPI was close to the Catholic Church although not strictly confessional. In legislative elections in 1919, the PPI and the Socialist Party became the two largest parties, at the expense of the liberals.

Mussolini's Fasci di combattimento (the Fascist party), founded in March 1919, fared poorly in these elections and, as a result, he dropped the left-wing elements in the Fascist program to mark more clearly the difference between his party and the Socialists. Mussolini soon started attracting the most conservative fringes of society.

The spread of popular resentment that followed the war was due not only to disillusionment with the peace settlement but also to social discontent. The war lasted much longer than the political elite had expected, leaving the country economically weakened. Industrialists saw their profits grow consistently during the war, but other social classes were seriously damaged. The majority of Italians suffered deprivations, and the standard of living declined. The daily calories in the diet of the average Italian amounted to just one-fifth of those in the British diet, and British salaries were three times those of Italian ones. Italy was consuming far more than it was producing, and imports and public debt grew. At the same time, the demobilization of the wartime army greatly increased unemployment.

The power of labor unions increased, and employers perceived as weak the reaction of the government of Giovanni Giolitti (1842–1928; in office as prime minister 1892–1893, 1903–1905, 1906–1909, 1911–1914, and 1920–1921). Consequently, workers in Turin, under the leadership of the Communist Antonio Gramsci (1891–1937), launched the experiment of the factory councils, which hinted at revolution along the Soviet model. Fascism, with its strong militaristic character, increasingly attracted support as a reaction to the perceived threat of revolution, despite its violent militia, the MVSN (Milizia Volontaria per la Sicurezza Nazionale), usually known in English as the Black Shirts.

MUSSOLINI IN POWER

The National Fascist Party, formed in 1921, combined elements of anticommunism, populism, nationalism, and support for territorial expansion with promotion of workers' welfare and social progress. The movement managed to appear revolutionary

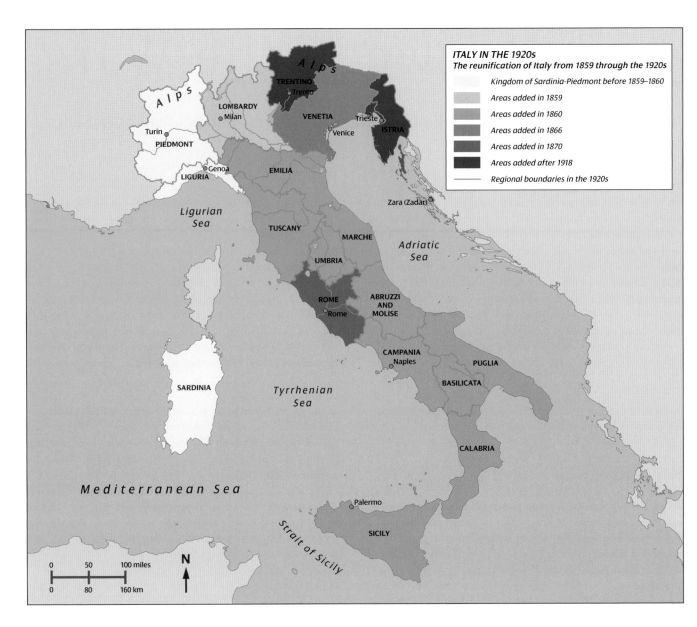

ITALY IN THE 1920s
The reunification of Italy from 1859 through the 1920s

- Kingdom of Sardinia-Piedmont before 1859–1860
- Areas added in 1859
- Areas added in 1860
- Areas added in 1866
- Areas added in 1870
- Areas added after 1918
- Regional boundaries in the 1920s

to workers and conservative to the middle class, and it gained support for its promise to restore order. In October 1922, the Fascist militia marched on Rome, undermining the government and effectively staging a coup. King Victor Emmanuel III (1869–1947; reigned 1900–1946) withdrew support from the weak government of Luigi Facta (1861–1930; in office 1922), refused to deploy the Italian Army, and offered the premiership to Mussolini.

The 1923 Acerbo Law entrenched the Fascists by making Italy a single electoral constituency and allocating two-thirds of the seats in the legislature to the largest party gaining more than 25 percent of the national vote. A coalition led by Mussolini won nearly two-thirds of the vote. Following the political assassination of an opponent, Socialist deputy Giacomo Matteotti, by a group of Fascists, opposition parties boycotted the legislature, giving Mussolini a free hand. The regime became increasingly dictatorial from 1925, although the centralization of the state and curtailment of individual rights were carried out over a relatively long period.

Mussolini's strong government embarked on a program of public works. Abroad, colonial expansionism was seen as evidence of a strong nation. Italy invaded and annexed Ethiopia (1935–1936) and, in Europe, neighboring Albania (1939). Fascism exalted the myths of military strength, but despite this exaltation of war, the main battles Fascism had to fight were internal and were directed against Communism and the PPI—both of which were banned, along with all other political parties and trade unions.

In the Spanish Civil War (1936–1939), Mussolini sent Italian troops to support the Nationalists against the (largely) Socialist and Communist Republicans. Italy's relations with Nazi Germany became closer, and Mussolini started talking about a Rome-Berlin Axis. In 1937, during a visit to Berlin, he declared support for German dictator Adolf Hitler (1889–1945). Fascism became influenced by Nazism, and, in 1938, Mussolini introduced the Manifesto of Race, which deprived Jews of Italian citizenship.

E. GARAU

Italy in World War II

When World War II (1939–1945) began, Italy at first was not ready for combat and remained neutral. In June 1940, Italy entered the war as an ally of Germany, but its participation led to defeat, division, and national humiliation before the final ousting of the Fascist dictatorship.

Fascist leader Benito Mussolini (1883–1945; in office as prime minister 1922–1943) believed that, despite the loss of human lives, the common struggle of participation in the war would forge the nation and provide Italians with a sense of loyalty toward the state. Instead, the conflict would prove a disastrous experience for Italy and leave a humiliating legacy of military inadequacy for decades.

ENTERING THE WAR

At the beginning of the war, the Italian army, navy, and air force were ill-equipped and weakened by rivalry and lack of cooperation. Not only did Italy have insufficient aircraft of all types, its forces also suffered from poor logistics. In 1936, Mussolini had formed an alliance with Nazi Germany, the Rome-Berlin Axis. In 1939, Italy overran and annexed neighboring Albania in five days, and Mussolini and German dictator Adolf Hitler (1889–1945) signed the Pact of Steel, under which Italy would have to support Germany in case of war and vice versa.

Mussolini was aware that the country was not ready to fight a war but, at the same time, he seemed impressed by the strength and the successes of the German army, which soon appeared invincible. By early June 1940, Germany had conquered not only Poland and Czechoslovakia, but also Denmark, Norway, Belgium, the Netherlands, and Luxembourg and had invaded France. Mussolini became concerned that Italy might lose its international role and might be excluded from the distribution of territories at the end of the war. Reassured by the dominant position of Germany in Europe, on June 10, 1940, Mussolini declared war on France and Great Britain. Mussolini subsequently declared war against the Soviet Union in June 1941 and the United States in December 1941.

Mussolini's ambition was Italian domination of the Mediterranean region, an aim that he had negotiated with Hitler, whose expansionist aims were concentrated on eastern Europe. Mussolini wanted to reclaim the territories known as *Italia irredenta* (unredeemed Italy), comprising Savoy, Nice, and Corsica from France; Malta from Great Britain; and the Dalmatian coast from Yugoslavia. With the addition of other territories, such as Albania, Tunisia, and some Greek islands, he wished to establish a new Roman Empire in the region.

ITALY AT WAR

The Fascist rhetoric on war as a means to fortify the nation was not enough either to motivate the Italian troops, who lacked strong leadership and preparation, nor to compensate for the inadequacy of equipment. This was confirmed during the invasion of Greece in the late fall of 1940, when the Italian troops proved unable to complete their objective and Germany had to intervene, conquering Yugoslavia and invading Greece in a few days. In 1941, Italian troops accompanied German forces in the invasion of the Soviet Union, where (mainly) German armies marched on Moscow and Stalingrad (modern Volgograd) but were defeated and forced to withdraw in February 1943.

By this time, Italian forces had already suffered major reverses elsewhere. In 1935–1936, Italy had overrun Ethiopia, adding it to the existing Italian colonies of Eritrea and what is now Somalia to form Italian East Africa. However, in 1941, British forces liberated the entire region. In North Africa, the situation was critical. Italian and German troops suffered a severe defeat in El Alamein (October–November 1942) and, after more than 30 years, Italy lost its North African colony, Libya, in 1943. In May 1943, Italian and German forces were also ejected from Tunisia.

A DIVIDED COUNTRY

By the summer of 1943, Italy was in crisis, facing invasion. Discontent had grown, food was in short supply, and, in March 1943, strikes had been held in northern Italy. Fearing the collapse of Italy, Germany greatly increased its military presence there. The German forces, which increasingly came to be seen as an army of occupation, were resented, and support for Mussolini evaporated. Italians turned to Vatican Radio and Allied radio stations for trustworthy news.

On July 9, 1943, U.S., British, Canadian, Australian, and South African forces landed in Sicily and were (largely) greeted as liberators. On July 24, Mussolini's government split, with the majority advocating his removal. On July 25, Mussolini was dismissed by the king, Victor Emmanuel III (1869–1947; reigned 1900–1946), on whose orders he was arrested. The king appointed a new prime minister, Marshal Pietro Badoglio (1871–1956; in office 1943–1944). In early September, U.S. forces

The final battle for Monte Cassino (1944); a British soldier brings in two German prisoners.

Italy was now divided in two: the Fascist Republic of Salò (1943–1945), a German puppet state, in the north; and the Allied-controlled zone in the south. A resistance movement began, and partisans fought alongside the Allies against the Fascists and Germans. From January through May 1944, Allied forces were in action against the Gustav Line at Cassino, and it was thought that German forces were in the historic Monte Cassino monastery, where Saint Benedict (c. 480–c. 547 CE) had first established Western monasticism. U.S. planes bombed and destroyed the monastery, one of the most controversial Allied actions of the war in Europe. In 1969, the U.S. Army official record was made public, revealing that the monastery had been unoccupied by Germans at the time of the bombing.

After Cassino, the Germans were pushed back, and Rome had already fallen on June 4. The Germans to the north at first responded to resistance with violent reprisals, often against civilians, but on April 25, 1945, German forces in northern Italy surrendered, and the cities of Milan, Genoa, and Turin were taken by Allied forces. Mussolini, whose government was centered in Salò, near Lake Garda in Lombardy, attempted to escape north to Switzerland. At Dongo, near the Swiss border, he was arrested and executed by partisans. Italy was finally liberated on April 25, 1945.

The Resistance, eventually coordinated by the Committee of National Liberation, played a crucial role in the defeat of the Fascist regime, despite the sometimes poor relations between its various strands. Its activities were carried out by individuals and groups of different political views including Communists, Catholics, Socialists, anarchists, monarchists, and liberals, united in the struggle against Fascism. In modern times, some historians have attempted to minimize the role of the Resistance by attributing the defeat of the regime exclusively to the intervention of Allied troops. However, most observers acknowledge that the Resistance contributed to the development of a strong sense of nationhood that Italy had lacked until then. The course taken by republican Italy in the aftermath of the war was largely determined by those who took part in the Resistance movement.

E. GARAU

came ashore on the Italian mainland at Salerno, near Naples, while British troops landed at Taranto, in Puglia. By the end of the month, some 190,000 troops had landed, and U.S. forces took Naples in October. The Germans prepared a strong line of defense, the Gustav Line, across the peninsula, centered on Cassino.

An armistice and Italy's unconditional surrender were announced by U.S. commander Dwight D. Eisenhower (1890–1969; in office as U.S. president 1953–1961) on September 8, 1943. The same day, the cessation of hostilities against the Allies in Italy was proclaimed, while Badoglio and the king traveled to the city of Brindisi in the south, which was controlled by Italian forces. On September 12, Mussolini was set free by the Germans and conducted to Munich, where Hitler invited him to reconstruct the Fascist government. After six days, Mussolini announced from Munich the constitution of a new Fascist republican state, the Italian Social Republic, usually known as the Republic of Salò.

Italy since 1945

After World War II (1939–1945), Italy faced the need for reconstruction following the Fascist dictatorship. A republic was founded in 1946, and the political framework and parties established between 1946 and 1948 lasted until the collapse of existing political movements in the early 1990s.

At the end of World War II, the Italian political elite was concerned with regaining international credibility after the fall of the Fascist regime. On the domestic front, the partisans and other groups and individuals who had taken part in the Resistance were involved in the reconstruction of the nation and set about building a new state structure. Italy was also destabilized by what became known as the "Southern question," the cultural and economic divide between the south (commonly known as the Mezzogiorno) and the north of the country.

In 1945, King Victor Emmanuel III (1869–1947; reigned 1900–1946) was discredited, having appointed Benito Mussolini (1883–1945; in office as prime minister 1922–1943) to the premiership in 1922. The king was tainted by his support for the Fascist regime, and he lost more support by subsequently fleeing to Brindisi, in Puglia, rather than remaining in Rome, when German forces effectively occupied northern and central Italy. Victor Emmanuel made his son, Umberto (1904–1983; reigned May–June 1946), regent in all but name and promised a referendum on the form of government after the war.

A referendum was held in 1946, but Victor Emmanuel abdicated before the vote. The result was tight, with a small majority in favor of a republic, but the vote is now regarded by many commentators as flawed. Millions were not on the electoral roll; Italy's postwar borders had not been fixed and some regions were excluded from the vote; and, in some areas, Communist officials rigged the vote. However, the royal family went into permanent exile and, so insecure was the subsequent republic that they were banned from entering the country.

The first postwar elections, which preceded the legislative elections and referendum of 1946, showed an electoral divide in which the left-wing parties—the Communist Party (PCI) and Socialist Party (PSI)—gained more votes in parts of the north and in central Italy, while the (conservative) Christian Democrats (DC) were dominant in other parts of the north. With the exception of left-wing votes in larger cities, the south supported the DC. The referendum on the monarchy, which had taken place at the same time as the legislative elections, had shown a deep regional divide. The areas that voted for the DC also broadly voted for the monarchy; those districts that supported the PCI and PSI were more republican. The Mezzogiorno was largely monarchist.

THE SOUTHERN QUESTION

In 1946, the secretary of the Italian Communist Party and newly appointed minister of justice, Palmiro Togliatti (1893–1964), declared an amnesty for Fascist collaborators, even though many ex-partisans and political leaders, such as former partisan Resistance leader and founder of the Action Party, Ferruccio Parri (1890–1981; in office as prime minister 1945), advocated a radical purge of the bureaucracy and action to be taken against those who did not voice opposition to the former regime. However, the moderate wing prevailed, many state officials kept their jobs, and the bureaucracy maintained its organization.

The center for change and reform in Italy was the north. The northern regions (where the partisans had fought the occupying Germans) were ready for a new start based on the values of the Resistance, but the Mezzogiorno had gone through a different experience from 1943 through 1945 under the control of the Allies and had not taken part in the partisan struggle. In 1945, Italy was a deeply divided country, socially, economically, and politically. Those who drafted the new republican constitution recognized these deep divisions and advocated local democracy and promoted regionalism to avoid fragmentation and possible secession.

Sicily reacted to the presence of the CLN (Comitato di Liberazione Nazionale, the multiparty committee formed by the partisans) and the CLN's involvement in the administration of the island. Riots broke out, backed by landowners and the Mafia. Opposition to the new order in Sicily was led, among others, by bandit Salvatore Giuliano (1922–1950), who was part of a movement seeking independence for Sicily. Sicily had always resisted outside or foreign domination, but the violence of Giuliano's campaign lost support for him and the goal of independence. The new Italian constitution addressed the strong regionalism in Sicily by granting the island autonomy. A similar status was accorded to Sardinia, Valle d'Aosta (which had a French-speaking majority), Trentino–Alto Adige/Südtirol (South Tirol) with its large German-speaking community and, later, Friuli–Venezia Giulia, which was home to Slovene, Friulian, and Ladin minorities. The new 1948 constitution recognized the importance of historic regions and loyalties and instituted a new level of regional administration, although it was only in 1970 that these provisions of regional government were extended to the other regions.

THE NEW POLITICAL ORDER

In 1945, there were three dominant powers in Italy: the CLN with its coalition of left-wing movements and parties and Catholic elements; the Allied Military Force (largely U.S. and British), which still controlled public life and whose main interest was prevention of a Communist takeover; and, finally, the state apparatus. The latter, less visible than the other two elements, played a crucial role in the provision of welfare, public transportation, the application of the law, and other facets of daily life.

Under the new constitution, Italy was to be a parliamentary republic (one in which power resided in the legislature and not with the executive). The parliament (Parlamento Italiano) was to have two houses, and the chief of state was to be a largely ceremonial figure with limited powers. The system of government instituted in 1945–1948 remained largely unchanged until the 1990s, when various constitutional reforms were introduced as a result of a political crisis. In June 1946, Italy became a republic, with Enrico de Nicola (1877–1959; in office 1946–1948) as the first president, but the new constitution, which took time to gain approval, did not come into force until 1948.

In postwar Italy, where the political divide between left and right was deep, the only possible way to give the country a stable government seemed to be a coalition between the main political parties: the DC, PSI, and PCI. However, the electoral campaign in 1948 centered on a choice between Communism and the anticommunist DC. The DC won and—sustained by farmers, small landowners, the middle class, and also by big industry—the party was to stay in power for decades.

THE FIRST REPUBLIC

From 1948 through 1992, Italy was governed by the DC, nearly always in coalition with other parties. The party gradually lost electoral support, and public confidence in the system suffered. No matter what the result of legislative elections, the DC remained in power, bolstered by other parties in coalitions to keep the parties of the left out of power. The political division of the nation remained, with the PSI and PCI strong in the north and northwest and also in the "Red Belt" of Tuscany, Emilia Romagna, and Umbria, where the traditional sharecropping method of landholding (where tenants paid a proportion of the crop as rent) kept small farmers poor. By contrast, the DC had support in the northeast and the south. The Catholic Church intervened in politics, declaring that anyone supporting the PCI would be excommunicated, although this was often ignored.

Internationally, Italy's borders were settled. Some border areas in the northeast, including Istria and the port cities of Zara and Fiume, were lost to Yugoslavia; the Dodecanese Islands (occupied by the Italians since 1912) were restored to Greece; and Italy lost its colonies, although Somalia remained Italian as a United Nations trust territory. The city of Trieste, first declared part of a Free Territory, was assigned to Italy in 1954. Italy joined NATO (the North Atlantic Treaty Organization) on its foundation

in 1949, and funds made available through the Marshall Plan (a program of U.S. economic aid for the reconstruction of Europe from 1948 through 1952) helped rebuild the nation's economy.

Italy experienced the beginning of what came to be known as the Economic Miracle, a period when industrialization and internal migration changed the face of the nation. Industrial development in the north attracted waves of people from the south, in search of employment. At the same time, Italy experienced large-scale emigration, much of it from the north. Land and legal reforms transformed the status of sharecroppers and redistributed land, but the Mezzogiorno remained much poorer and less developed than the rest of Italy.

The poverty of much of the south, particularly Calabria, Naples, and Sicily, encouraged crime in these regions. There, the Mafia grew more powerful, influencing local government decisions and the awarding of contracts; different Mafia factions competed to control illegal activities, such as the drug trade from North Africa. In the early 1960s, violence between rival Mafia clans in Palermo, the capital of Sicily, culminated in the Ciaculli Massacre (June 1963), when seven police and military officers were killed by a bomb intended for a Mafia boss. The Antimafia Commission attempted to regain power from criminal elements in the south, but the civil authorities had difficulty prevailing. Some figures, such as Palermo mayor Salvatore Lima (1928–1992), were perceived as having Mafia links. In 1992, the Mafia assassinated Lima, an event widely regarded as a turning point in southern politics and the beginning of a decline in Mafia influence.

Nationally the DC continued to lose support from an increasingly disillusioned electorate. Coalitions were short-lived and ever broader across the political spectrum. In 1960, a proposal by some DC members to include the neo-Fascist National Social Movement (MSI) in the coalition led to riots. The PSI was largely seen as subordinate to the PCI and was excluded from power. However, by 1963, the PSI had moved toward the center and entered the anticommunist coalition. This extension of the coalition was known as the *apertura a sinistra* (opening to the left).

A program of long-needed reforms in education, taxation, and the provision of infrastructure through the 1960s helped bring a more equitable distribution of income and economic opportunities. However, discontent grew, finding expression in student and worker unrest and later the creation of small terror cells from 1968 onward.

THE YEARS OF LEAD

The discredited system of unstable, short-lived coalitions and no real prospect of change led to the growth of illegal political activity. Political violence increased through the 1970s and 1980s, which were called the *anni di piombo* (literally, "years of lead"), when political assassinations and outrages, bombings and shootings, were carried out by left- and right-wing terror groups, resulting in several hundred deaths.

The violence began in December 1969, with bombings in Rome and Milan, which claimed 16 lives. The Italian secret service (Servizio per le Informazioni e la Sicurezza Militare; SISMI) became involved in protecting right-wing terrorists; in 1970, there was a planned right-wing coup, which became known months after it was called off. One right-wing terror movement, Ordino Nuovo (New Order), collaborated with SID (Servizio Informazioni Difesa, the Italian military secret service). Although there were more left-wing terror bombings than those by groups on the right, right-wing groups—aided by the SID and later SISMI—also committed violent acts and attempted to blame them on the left.

By the late 1970s, the PCI (the largest Communist party in western Europe), under the leadership of Enrico Berlinguer (1922–1984), was largely independent of Moscow, pursuing its own reform agenda, and providing efficient local government in Emilia Romagna, Tuscany, and Umbria. Consequently, DC leader Aldo Moro (1916–1978; in office as prime minister 1963–1968 and 1974–1976) attempted to open up the ruling coalition even further by including the PCI. Through the 1970s and 1980s, the coalition, with its stance against terror, was supported across the political spectrum in the legislature, including the PCI, which strongly opposed the left-wing terror groups. However, the PCI was never included in the government. In 1978, the Red Brigades (a left-wing terror group) kidnapped and assassinated Moro.

The history of the 1970s and 1980s is complex and still disputed. The motives for many actions and responsibility for them are still not clear. Violence continued in the early 1980s. In 1980, a bomb planted by a neo-Fascist group destroyed the Bologna railroad station, killing 85 people and wounding hundreds. In 1984, a bomb on a train between Florence and Rome killed 16 and wounded around 200; the attack was held to be the responsibility of the Mafia and a right-wing group. In 1981, a secret anticommunist group, centered in the Propaganda Due (P2) Masonic lodge, supported by elements within the Italian secret services and covert U.S. operations, was discovered. The whole structure was dedicated to preventing, by any means, the PCI from coming to power. The discovery of this covert network shook Italy and coincided with a major banking scandal involving the Banco Ambrosiano.

The instability of the political system and its growing corruption are illustrated by the career of DC politician Giulio Andreotti (born 1919). As prime minister, Andreotti led seven coalition governments in 1972, 1972–1973, 1976–1978, 1978–1979, 1979, 1989–1991, and 1991–1992. Eventually, Andreotti was charged with having links to the Mafia and was indicted in 1995. He was also tried for complicity in the murder of an investigative journalist. Initially acquitted, Andreotti was retried and sentenced, and then, in 2003, acquitted again.

The weakening of the DC allowed politicians from other parties to lead coalition governments: Republican Party leader Giovanni Spadolini (1925–1994; in office 1981–1982), the first non-DC premier since World War II, and the socialist Bettino Craxi (1934–2000; in office 1983–1987), who later fled Italy for Tunisia rather than face corruption charges. Under Craxi, Italy's economic grew and Italy joined the G7 nations, the world's leading economies.

The fall of the Soviet Union in 1991 changed the politics of Italy. Since World War II, coalitions had been formed to keep the PCI, which by 1984 was the largest party in Italy, out of government. The end of Soviet Communism removed the threat from such an eventuality. In early 1992, police caught a Socialist politician accepting a large bribe. Public prosecutors in Milan began investigating corruption and, before the end of the year, ministers, heads of parties, and politicians in all parties (except the PCI) were implicated in corruption. The trials of public figures began, and electoral support for the major parties rapidly diminished. The *Mani pulite* (literally, "clean hands") investigation uncovered a web of irregularities and corruption, a system that came to be dubbed *Tangentopoli* ("bribesville").

THE SECOND REPUBLIC

In the wake of corruption scandals, a public backlash against existing political parties led to the disbanding of some parties, such as the PSI, and the fracturing of others, such as the DC, into various factions, with the largest faction becoming the Partito Popolare Italiano (Popular Party; PPI). The PCI reformed, renamed, and became a Socialist party before it, too, vanished. New parties and new political leaders emerged. The neo-Fascist MSI reformed as the National Alliance, discarding much of its right-wing political baggage at the same time that a reformed, more moderate Democratic Party of the Left was formed by ex-Communists. A new populist right-wing movement, Forza Italia, founded and led by business and television station and newspaper owner Silvio Berlusconi (born 1936; in office as prime minister 1994–1995, 2001–2006, and after 2008), became one of the largest parties, while in Lombardy and other northern regions, a regionalist movement, the Northern League, emerged as a dominant force.

The period since 1992 is commonly called the Second Republic, even though the previous constitution is still in force. However, significant constitutional changes reduced the degree of proportionality to ensure fewer and larger parties in the legislature. By the twenty-first century, many of the parties had coalesced into two electoral alliances, the (center-left) Ulivo coalition and the (center-right) Casa della Libertà coalition, with the heirs of the DC splitting between the two sides.

Berlusconi was a controversial leader; his position as head of a media empire led to accusations of conflicts of interest, and investigating magistrates have questioned him regarding business practices in the past. He alternated in power with a center-left coalition, led by Romano Prodi (born 1939; in office as prime minister 1996–1998 and 2006–2008). By 2008, the political landscape had changed again with the merging of parties to form five principal parties: Berlusconi's People of Freedom (which includes the former Forza Italia and National Alliance); the Northern League; the (center-left) Democratic Party (including the former liberals, republicans, Socialists, and ex-Communists, among others); the (populist anticorruption) Italy of Values (IdV) party; and the centrist Union of the Christian and Center Democrats (UDC).

E. GARAU

CULTURAL EXPRESSION

Literature

Italian literature has its roots in the literature of ancient Rome and of the Renaissance, when Italy was an important cultural center, spreading its literary influence throughout Europe.

The Italian language derives from Latin, the language of ancient Rome: some 89 percent of the vocabulary of modern Italian derives from Latin. Although the Roman Empire fell in the fifth century CE, Latin was used long afterward in society and literature, and Latin literature has remained central to Western civilization even in modern times.

EARLY MEDIEVAL LITERATURE

Medieval literature in Italy was also written in Latin, as in the rest of western Europe. Boethius (480–524/525 CE) was a Christian philosopher famous for *Consolatio philosophiae* (Consolation of Philosophy), one of the most important works of early Christianity. Gradually, a new vernacular, Italian, grew from Latin, and the twelfth and thirteenth centuries saw the adoption of vernacular Italian as a common literary and commercial language. However, the classical tradition was kept alive by monastic orders and royal courts, where many scholars and writers continued to write in Latin. Collections of songs and poems and French literature, based mostly on medieval epics, inspired poets and writers to use vernacular Italian along with Latin. After the Norman conquest of Sicily, King Frederick I (reigned 1197–1250) surrounded himself with artists and poets, the so-called Sicilian School. Sicilian writers codified a new language, based on Latin and southern dialects, but borrowing terms, themes, and grammar from French. Thirteenth-century authors like Giacomo da Lentini (dates unknown) composed love songs that were strongly influenced by chivalric values. Sicilians are also credited with codifying the *sonetto* (sonnet), a 14-verse poem that continues to represent the most important standard in short poetry.

The center of literary production then shifted to the city-states of central Italy. Authors treating religious subjects started to use vernacular Italian: Saint Francis of Assisi (1181–1226), for example, composed *Laudes creaturarum* (Praise of the creatures; translated as *Canticle of the Sun*). Street performers contributed to popular literature, and Cecco Angiolieri (1260–1312) was the most well-known satirist of his times. In this favorable environment for artists and writers, the *dolce stil novo* (sweet new style), codified by Guido Guinizzelli (1230–1276), was an important literary movement. Refined poetry presented an introspective combination of pure spiritual love and strong earthly passions.

Giovanni Boccaccio (1313–1375) was a storyteller and author of the Decameron, a collection of one hundred short stories.

THE TUSCAN REVOLUTION

Guinizzelli strongly influenced a group of authors who lived in Tuscany. The work of Dante Alighieri (1263–1321), considered the greatest Italian poet, made the Tuscan vernacular Italy's standard literary language. Dante wrote the epic *Commedia* (*Divine Comedy*), an imaginary voyage between hell and paradise, in which many historical and fictional characters (kings, sinners, saints, and mythological creatures) illustrate an impressive human array of passions, vices, virtues, and regrets.

The classical epic, influenced by Christian theology and medieval values, found new voices. Petrarch (1304–1374) and Giovanni Boccaccio (1313–1375) were, along with Dante, the most important writers of the thirteenth and fourteenth centuries. Petrarch was passionate about the study of linguistics and literature, and he revived ancient Greek and Latin works and developed an introspective, elegant poetry in his *Il Canzoniere* (Song book). Boccaccio wrote the *Decameron*, a collection of short novels that had enormous influence in Europe. This prose masterpiece, criticized for profanity, brought human beings and their passions to the center of literature.

Roman Literature

In the Roman era, poets, writers, and philosophers, like Horace (65 BCE–8 CE) and Virgil (70–19 BCE), created an impressive canon of poetry and prose, which borrowed heavily from Greek themes and epics but had an original character and style. The principal works of the early period of Roman literature are the six surviving comedies of Terence (195/185–159 BCE) and 21 works, also comedies, by Plautus (c. 254–184 BCE). The prose of Cato (234–149 BCE), including histories and *De agri cultura* (On farming), is also from the early period.

The Golden, or Classical, Age of Roman literature ran from the first century BCE through the late first century CE. The Latin in which the works of this period was written is a stylized literary language, different from the earlier version used by Plautus and Cato. From the second century CE onward, what came to be known as Vulgar Latin, the spoken language of the ordinary people, evolved as separate from heightened literary language. The principal poets of the Classical Age were Lucretius (c. 99–c. 55 BCE), who is remembered for his long poem *De rerum natura (On the Nature of Things)*. Catullus (c. 84–c. 54 BCE) wrote short and long poems, as well as epigrams (short poems with a witty twist). The zenith of poetry in this period was attained by Virgil, Horace, and Ovid (43 BCE–17 CE). Virgil wrote the epic the *Aeneid* (the legend of the travels of Aeneas). Horace, the greatest of the Roman lyric poets, wrote poems in Greek meter, odes, and satires. Ovid composed long poems that had mythological subjects. Important prose writers included Cicero (106–43 BCE), whose judicial and political writings survive, and Julius Caesar (100–44 BCE), whose accounts of his military campaigns in Gaul (modern-day France) give precise detail. The works of historians, such as Livy (59–17 BCE), who wrote *Ab urbe condita*, a history of the city of Rome, and Sallust (86–34 BCE), have also been preserved.

After this Golden Age, some writers attempted to copy the styles of previous authors, while others were more given to experimentation. Notable writers of the period include Pliny the Elder (23–79 CE), Pliny the Younger (63–c. 113 CE), Juvenal (dates unknown), Lucan (39–65 CE), and Tacitus (c. 56–c. 117 CE). Also in this period, the first Latin novels were written: *Asinus aureas* (*The Golden Ass*) by Apuleius (c. 125–c. 180 CE) and *Satyricon* by Petronius (c. 27–66 CE).

THE RENAISSANCE AND COUNTER-REFORMATION

The fifteenth and sixteenth centuries saw the rebirth of science, arts, economics, and literature in Europe. This new vision of the world, based on the revaluation of the dignity, freedom, and creativity of the human being, was promoted by the ducal and other courts like the de' Medici in Florence and the Sforza in Milan. The classical heritage was rediscovered and widely researched by scholars, serving as a model for poets, writers, and essayists.

In *De hominis dignitate oratio* (Oration on the Dignity of Man), Giovanni Pico della Mirandola (1463–1494) wrote a philosophical foundation of humanism and the Renaissance. Niccolò Machiavelli (1469–1527) wrote *Il principe* (The prince) and *Discorsi sopra la prima deca di Tito Livio* (Discourses on Livy), two innovative, controversial works of history and political philosophy. In literature, the most important works were those of Ludovico Ariosto (1474–1533), who perfectly embodied the new classical style in his epic *Orlando furioso*.

This innovative period lasted until the second half of the sixteenth century. Spanish domination in large areas of Italy and the Counter Reformation (a reform movement within the Catholic Church) constrained scientific and literary research. Galileo Galilei (1564–1642), a writer of history and pioneer of the scientific method, was arrested and jailed for astronomical theories perceived as heretical. Torquato Tasso (1544–1595) was the last great poet of the era: his *Gerusalemme liberata* (Jerusalem delivered) is a poem inspired by the Crusades, with some sensual elements that perfectly fit into a strongly twofold epic of love and war.

DECLINE AND REBIRTH

Partly as a result of the political crises affecting Italy through the sixteenth and seventeenth centuries, Italian literature went into a decline. Authors became obsessed with elaborate linguistic forms and figures of speech. Giambattista Marino (1569–1625) wrote *Adonis*, a masterpiece of Italian baroque literature, and, perhaps, one of the few works from the period to have survived with its reputation intact. The Arcadia Academy, established at the end of the sixteenth century, advocated a return to pastoral poetry.

In the eighteenth century, Italian literature recovered its vigor. Poet Giuseppe Parini (1729–1799) promoted an innovative style and political engagement, opening the road for pre-Romantic poetry, such as the works of Ugo Foscolo (1778–1827). Vittorio Alfieri (1749–1843) and Venetian playwright Carlo Goldoni (1707–1793) restored the status of Italian drama. The prose works of philosopher Giambattista Vico (1688–1744) particularly his *Scienza nuova* (1725; New science) and those of Cesare Beccaria (1738–1794), author of *Dei delitti e delle pene* (1764; On crimes and punishments), a treatise that criticized torture and the death penalty, were milestones in modern thought.

NINETEENTH-CENTURY LITERATURE

Following the spread of Romantic ideals through Europe, Italian writers in the nineteenth century created outstanding works. The *Risorgimento*, the struggle for national independence and the unification of Italy, served as a powerful inspiration in literature and the arts. In 1822, Alessandro Manzoni (1785–1873) wrote *I promessi sposi* (The betrothed), in which the historical novel is perfectly blended with popular realism and political messages. The poetry of Giacomo Leopardi (1798–1837), in his *Cantos* (1818 and 1823–1832), blends a strongly pessimistic view of life with a gentle and elegant style.

In the second half of the nineteenth century, Giovanni Verga (1840–1922) was the leader of a literary current called *verismo* (*vero* means "true"); *I vicerè* (1894; The viceroys) by Federico De Roberto (1861–1927) was a controversial, powerful work associated with the movement. Giosuè Carducci (1835–1907) was an influential poet and, in 1906, the first Italian to win the Nobel Prize for Literature. Many types of literature flourished in this period. One author of the time, C. Collodi (Carlo Lorenzini; 1826–1890), won international fame for a single book, the children's story *Pinocchio* (1880).

C. Collodi (Carlo Lorenzini; 1826–1890) is the most famous Italian children's author and the creator of Pinocchio.

THE MODERN ERA

In the early years of the twentieth century, the main literary current in Europe was Decadentism (a genre that promoted irrationalism), of which the standard bearer was Gabriele D'Annunzio (1863–1938), renowned for his linguistic virtuosity. It was also the era of avant-garde, and Italian literature embraced experimentalism. The Futurist movement, originating in the writing of Filippo Tommaso Marinetti (1876–1944), was a violent celebration of modernity and militarism. Giuseppe Ungaretti (1888–1970) tried to create a new style focusing on the evocative power of the single word, while Eugenio Montale (1896–1981), best known for *Le occasioni* (1939; Occasions), wrote what was deemed the finest Italian poetry of the century. The influence of psychoanalytic theories was notable in *La coscienza di Zeno* (1923; Zeno's conscience) by Italo Svevo (1861–1928); in this influential novel, the character Zeno Cosini describes his life to a psychoanalyst. Other psychoanalytical works were the drama and prose of Luigi Pirandello (1867–1936), such as the play *Sei personaggi in cerca d'autore* (1921; Six Characters in Search of an Author; 1922).

In the postwar era from 1945, Neorealist novelists flourished, marking the country's recovery from Fascist censorship and military defeat. The writer, movie director, and poet Pier Paolo Pasolini (1922–1975) was influential; Italo Calvino (1923–1985) introduced postmodernism into literature by means of fables that use metaphors. Umberto Eco (born 1928), essayist and writer, wrote novels that won international acclaim, such as *Il nome della rosa* (1980; *The Name of the Rose*, 1983), a medieval mystery, and *Il pendolo di Foucault* (1988; *Foucault's Pendulum*, 1989). Andrea Zanzotto (born 1921) became the main exponent of postwar avant-garde poetry.

Six Nobel Prizes for Literature have been awarded to Italians: Giosuè Carducci in 1906; novelist Grazia Deledda (1871–1936), whose works describe the lives of Sardinian peasants, in 1926; Luigi Pirandello in 1934; poet Salvatore Quasimodo (1901–1968) in 1959; Eugenio Montale in 1975; and playwright Dario Fo (born 1926) in 1997. Fo is best-known for his 1974 play *Non si paga! Non si paga!* (*We Won't Pay! We Won't Pay!*). Other leading modern Italian writers include Carlo Levi (1902–1975), who described the poverty of rural life in southern Italy in *Cristo si è fermato a Eboli* (1946; Christ Stopped at Eboli, 1947); Giuseppe Tomasi di Lampedusa (1896–1957), whose *Il gattopardo* (1958; *The Leopard*, 1960) is an account of Sicilian life; the short-story writer Alberto Moravia (1907–1990); poet and novelist Natalia Ginzburg (1916–1991); and Primo Levi (1919–1987), who wrote of his imprisonment in a concentration camp in World War II. Among contemporary authors, Antonio Tabucchi (born 1943) writes detective novels; novelist Francesca Duranti (born 1935) won fame for her dreamlike *La casa sul lago della luna* (1984; *The House on Moon Lake*, 1986); and Paola Capriolo (born 1962) is best-known for her novel about an actor who becomes obsessed with a member of the audience, *La spettatrice* (1995; *The Woman Watching*, 1998).

S. BRUNO

Art

As the center of the Roman Empire, Italy shaped a sophisticated visual culture that held sway across much of western Europe in ancient times. Italian art again attained broad cultural influence from the mid-fourteenth century, when Italy became home to the cultural flowering known as the Renaissance.

Italian artists, particularly those of the sixteenth century, were products of the Renaissance, a period of renewed intellectual and artistic vigor that was inspired by the physical remains of ancient Rome and the arrival of refugee scholars and artists of the Byzantine Empire from Constantinople when that city fell to the Ottoman Turks in 1453. In this revival of artistic traditions, Italy became a center of artistic excellence, a role that it has retained to varying degrees over the centuries.

ROMAN SCULPTURE AND PAINTING

By the third century BCE, the Romans had secured control of all of Italy, and, in the following centuries, conquered the Mediterranean Basin and much of North Africa and western Europe. Their military triumphs, trade, and taxation afforded the Roman elite great wealth, and they spent lavishly on the arts. The Romans drew on the expertise of decorative artists throughout their vast empire but, above all, were influenced by the culture of the ancient Greeks. Collectors prized Greek works of art, many of which were brought back from conquered lands, and workshops turned out copies of Greek sculptures to furnish Roman villas.

Of all the Roman art forms, sculpture survives in the largest quantity. Statues and carvings dominated Roman cities, both public spaces and private villas. Public sculptures celebrated the military conquests and supremacy of the Roman Empire, the virtues of its emperors and leading citizens, and their achievements. They ranged from freestanding statues, such as a monumental bronze erected in Rome in 176 CE showing Emperor Marcus Aurelius (121–180 CE; reigned 169–180 CE) on his prancing steed, to relief carvings (designs cut into flat panels) on huge triumphal arches and columns, such as those covering Trajan's Column (113 CE) in Rome. Rome is particularly known for its highly realistic portrait busts (sculptures showing the head and shoulders) of prominent citizens, as well as carvings and sculptures of classical gods and mythological themes, based on Greek examples.

While far fewer paintings survive, color was an important part of the Roman world, and sculpture and architecture were often painted. Excavations at the Roman towns of Pompeii and Herculaneum have also revealed richly colored murals on villa walls. They show landscapes, gardens, and scenes of everyday life and classical mythology, all set within frames and columns painted onto the wall to look like marble. The decorative arts also flourished across the Roman Empire: stunning examples of glasswork, jewelry, cameos, ceramics, silver vessels, textiles, and mosaic survive in large quantities.

EARLY CHRISTIAN ART AND THE MIDDLE AGES

Although the Romans perfected the art of mosaic, some of the most stunning examples were created after the disintegration of the Western Roman Empire. Dating from the sixth century CE, glittering mosaics were made to adorn the walls and ceilings of early Christian churches in Ravenna, then a flourishing port and part of the Byzantine (Eastern Roman) Empire. They feature clear, almost diagrammatic, designs showing the holy figures of Christianity rendered in small pieces of brilliantly colored or gilded glass.

With the exception of these mosaics, the period between the end of the Roman Empire and the emergence of strong city-states in the thirteenth century is traditionally regarded as a low point in Italian art. These centuries of political fragmentation and warfare were less conducive to large-scale investment in the arts. Nonetheless, painters and sculptors continued to create a wealth of work on religious themes. Their activity was centered

The remains of a household interior in Herculaneum, featuring mosaics.

The Holy Family with a Shepherd *(c. 1510), an oil painting by Titian (Tiziano Vecelli; 1488–1576).*

on the adornment of churches, on frescoes (murals), altarpieces (paintings on wooden panels to stand on or behind altars), and carvings, notably above the main entrance, on column capitals, fonts, and pulpits.

ART OF THE RENAISSANCE

By the mid-fourteenth century, the relative stability and increasing wealth of city-states in northern and central Italy contributed to a period of cultural brilliance and confidence that was unrivaled elsewhere in Europe. Scholars, artists, and their princely patrons looked back to the glories of ancient Greece and Rome and sought to emulate them, not least through the creation of new paintings and sculptures.

In an age when the church remained central to people's lives, the majority of new frescoes, panel paintings, and sculptures continued to be made for religious settings. However, secular (nonreligious) monuments for public squares and buildings were also created as a means of proclaiming the power and wealth of the cities. Decorative elements for palaces and villas were also important, and the decorative arts flourished, from fabulous velvet and silk textiles, gold and silver jewelry, sumptuous hand-illustrated manuscripts, to marquetry and furniture, majolica pottery, bronze statuettes, and medals. Portraits, landscape paintings, and works of art with themes from classical mythology also became popular with wealthy patrons.

A key theme of Renaissance art was the study of antique works, many of which could be seen in Rome, and the incorporation of ideas and motifs derived from them. Another was the accurate portrayal of subject matter based on direct observation and sketches, rather than on the stylized, symbolic types favored by the medieval church and its decorative artists. At this time, Filippo Brunelleschi (1377–1446), one of the major architects of the Renaissance, developed linear perspective, a mathematical system that enabled artists to recreate accurately

the appearance of three-dimensional space on the flat picture surface.

The study of nature and classical (ancient Greek and Roman) ideals came together in the portrayal of the nude human body. The nude became the ultimate subject for the expression of ideas about beauty and ideal form, as well as an expression of the mastery of the artist in the depiction of anatomy and complex poses.

EARLY RENAISSANCE ARTISTS

Painter and architect Giorgio Vasari (1511–1574) was the first commentator to write about the Renaissance, its values and its artists, and his research and views have shaped much subsequent thought. The art of the period is generally charted from Giotto (Giotto di Bondone; c. 1270–1337), through the work of other Florentine artists such as Filippo Brunelleschi, Donatello (Donato di Niccolò di Betto Bardi; c. 1386–1466), Masaccio (Tommaso Cascai; 1401–1428), Fra Angelico (Guido di Pietro; c. 1395–1455), and Sandro Botticelli (c. 1445–1510).

Giotto was responsible for one of the greatest masterpieces of the early Renaissance, the decoration of the Scrovegni Chapel in Padua with a series of frescoes illustrating the lives of Christ and the Virgin Mary. Painter and sculptor Donatello is known for his work in a shallow relief form of sculpture, known as *basso relievo* (bas-relief), but his most famous work is the bronze statue of David made for his Florentine patron Cosimo de' Medici (1387–1464). Massaccio was one of the most influential early Renaissance painters, known for the *Trinity* fresco (1428) in Santa Maria Novella, in Florence, and for frescoes in the Brancacci Chapel, Florence. Fra Angelico, a member of the Dominican order, painted the altarpiece and a cycle of frescoes in San Marco, Florence, and brightly colored frescoes in the Niccoline Chapel, in the Vatican. The work of Botticelli, which is sometimes overshadowed by the giants of the later Renaissance, is characterized by linear grace, of which his paintings *Primavera* (Spring; 1477–1478) and *Birth of Venus* are outstanding examples.

THE MASTERS OF THE HIGH RENAISSANCE

The great Italian artists of the High Renaissance are among the most influential of any period and any nation. The zenith of the Renaissance was reached in in the masterpieces of Leonardo da Vinci (1452–1519), Raphael (Raphael Sanzio; 1483–1520), Titian (Tiziano Vecelli; 1488–1576), and, above all, Michelangelo (Michelangelo di Lodovico Buonarroti Simoni; 1475–1574).

Leonardo was supremely gifted in many different fields: science, invention, math, music, and engineering. As a painter, he is best-known for the unfinished *Adoration of the Magi*; the two versions of the *Madonna of the Rocks* (1483–c. 1486 and 1483–1508); and, above all, for *The Last Supper* (c. 1495–1498), in the church of Santa Maria delle Grazie in Milan, and the enigmatic *Mona Lisa* (c. 1503), a portrait that is part of the collection of the Louvre museum, Paris.

The paintings and drawings of Raphael are known for the grace of their lines and the perfection of their composition. The harmony of his work served as a model for later artists. Raphael was celebrated for his wall paintings in the Vatican, including *The Parnassus*, *The School of Athens*, *Triumph of Religion*, *The Deliverance of Saint Peter*, and *The Miracle of Bolsena* (all 1508–1511). These large, complex works decorate the rooms sometimes known as the Raphael Rooms but more generally as the Stanza della Segnatura.

Venetian artist Titian created dreamlike pastoral scenes and was renowned for his use of color and the free handling of paint. His painting methods and skill profoundly influenced not only other artists of the Renaissance but painters of later generations. Titian's most famous works include *Venus and Adonis* (1554) and the altarpiece, *The Assumption of the Virgin* (1516–1518) in the church of Santa Maria Gloriosa dei Frari, in Venice.

Michelangelo, the great rival of Raphael, was the foremost painter and sculptor of his age. He created what are often claimed to be the most influential frescoes in Western art, scenes from Genesis on the ceiling of the Sistine Chapel in the Vatican, painted 1508–1512, and *The Last Judgment* (1536–1541), on the altar wall of the same chapel. Michelangelo's *Pietà* (1499), a marble statue of the Virgin Mary holding the body of Christ crucified, is in Saint Peter's basilica in the Vatican. The statue achieves a fine balance between naturalism and classical beauty. Strength and youthful beauty are captured in his statue *David* (1501–1504) in Florence.

Between 1842 and 1856, 28 marble statues of notable Tuscans were placed in niches outside the Uffizi Galleria in Florence, including this one of Donatello (c. 1386–1466).

ROME AND THE BAROQUE STYLE

While the Renaissance was a high point in the arts, it by no means marked the end of artistic innovation and creativity. In the seventeenth and eighteenth centuries, Rome, as the home of a rejuvenated Roman Catholic Church committed to promoting faith through art, continued to be the focus of European art.

Startlingly realistic paintings of sacred subjects by Caravaggio (Michelangelo Merisi da Caravaggio; 1571–1610) comprise one example of this originality. His striking compositions and dramatic effects of light and dark (*chiaroscuro*) became important features of the style that came to dominate seventeenth-century art: the baroque. Characterized by its confidence, accomplishment, and large-scale compositions, the baroque was favored by the Catholic Church as a means of engaging worshippers. Working in Naples and Rome, Gianlorenzo Bernini (1598–1680) created some of the most flamboyant works, uniting sculpture and architecture in dynamic arrangements, while painters such as Pietro da Cortona (1596–1669) combined fresco and stucco work (molded plaster) to create ceilings that looked as if they were open to the heavens.

At the same time, Italy became a place of pilgrimage for artists and connoisseurs from across Europe. Inspired by Rome's classical traditions, French painters Claude Lorraine (1600–1682) and Nicholas Poussin (1594–1665) trained and spent much of their careers in the city. A whole new trade also grew up in the provision of paintings, prints, and sculptures as mementos for tourists, and artists such as Antonio Canaletto (1697–1768)—who was noted for the topographical quality of his paintings (such as Venetian canal landscapes)—made their name as landscape painters. By the late eighteenth century, however, Italy's greatest artistic achievements were in the past, receiving one last revival in the virtuoso sculpture of Antonio Canova (1757–1822).

MODERN TIMES

By the nineteenth century, Paris was firmly established as the center of the European art world. Nevertheless, Italy continued to produce a number of innovative artists. In the second half of the nineteenth century, they included the group known as the Macchiaioli painters, who created fresh, vivid canvases using patches of color, rather than the highly finished style then popular.

In the early twentieth century, the Futurist group (founded 1909) embraced the fractured forms of Cubism to convey their belief in modern technology. Other artists, such as members of the Novecento ("twentieth century"; formed 1922) movement looked back to Italy's artistic traditions for their inspiration. In the years after World War II (1939–1945), sculptors such as Marino Marini (1901–1980) and Giacomo Manzù (1908–1991) most successfully realized this aim. Since 1895, Italy has hosted one of the world's most prestigious art events, the Venice Biennale, which has focused on contemporary art since 1948.

R. BEAN

Architecture

Italy's architectural heritage embraces a tradition of classical architecture that spans some two millennia, from the buildings of ancient Rome, through the Renaissance, to the present day.

At varying times, the work of the Roman and Italian architects, builders, and theoreticians have had a wide-ranging influence on built environments not only in the Mediterranean region and Europe but in the entire world. From the late fourteenth century, Renaissance Italy became the cradle of a renewal in art and architecture that replaced Gothic styles with classicism, a genre that has lasted for both public and private buildings to modern times.

ROMAN ARCHITECTURE

The Romans secured the Italian Peninsula and its islands by the third century BCE. By the second century CE, Rome controlled an empire that stretched from Syria in the east to Spain in the west, and from Egypt in the south to Britain in the north. In a physical sense, the Romans united these diverse regions with ambitious civil engineering projects, roads, and bridges, and stamped their authority through grand

The Pantheon in Rome was built as a temple around 125 CE, dedicated to all of the Roman gods. It is now used as a church.

architecture, which emanated from Rome and was remarkably consistent through the empire. This architecture owed much to ancient Greece, whose artistic achievements the Romans revered, although it also encompassed the Roman flare for organization and practicality, not least in the development of new building techniques and materials.

For their public buildings and temples, such as those of the Imperial Forum (c. 27 BCE–14 CE) in Rome, the Romans relied heavily on Greek examples, as they did for the external trappings of much of their architecture. They borrowed the classical orders—for columns and related building parts such as entablatures (that part of a classical structure above the columns) and pediments (low-pitched gables, usually triangular)—of Greece (the Doric, Ionic, and Corinthian), to which they added two more styles of their own: the Tuscan and composite. However, while the orders were integral to the structure of Greek buildings (which, at their heart, relied on

vertical posts supporting horizontal beams), more often than not these features were just surface decoration on their Roman equivalents.

Roman builders developed a different structural system based on rounded arches, and with them vaults and domes, and perfected the use of concrete. Both these advances facilitated the construction of the large-scale engineering projects and enormous public buildings with which Imperial Rome is particularly associated, from aqueducts to theaters, amphitheaters, *thermae* (bath complexes), temples, and triumphal arches and other enormous monuments to celebrate Roman leaders and military achievements. Famous examples include Rome's huge elliptical amphitheater, the Colosseum (72–82 CE); the massive circular, domed temple, the Pantheon (literally "temple of all the gods"), which was rebuilt around 125 CE and has survived intact because it has been used as a church since the seventh century CE; and the Baths of Caracalla (212–216 CE), also in Rome.

CHURCH BUILDING IN THE MIDDLE AGES

After the collapse of the Western Roman Empire in the fifth century CE, Christianity became the chief impetus for architecture, and in Italy, as across Europe, the Middle Ages are distinguished above all by their religious buildings, their churches, monasteries, and cathedrals. The design of early Christian churches was based on Roman buildings with similar requirements, and the need to accommodate large assemblies of people gave rise to churches called basilicas. Basilicas were typically rectangular, divided into a tall main space (the nave) separated from narrower side aisles by rows of columns, with a raised apse at the east end, where the altar was sited.

Reflecting Italy's political fragmentation, the appearance of medieval churches varied across the country. In Ravenna and Venice, which at various times had close links with the Byzantine Empire, the conventions of the Eastern church had a considerable impact. They included technical innovations, such as the pendentive (triangular sections of vaulting), which enabled builders to place a dome on top of a square base (Roman builders had supported the huge dome of the Roman Pantheon on a circular, drum-shaped wall). The Byzantine churches of Ravenna were also characterized by decorative features such as glittering mosaics of gold and glass.

By the time Byzantine artisans were building Saint Mark's Cathedral in Venice in the eleventh century, masons in Pisa were constructing one of Italy's best-known groups of buildings: the cathedral, baptistry, and bell tower, the famous "leaning tower" (1063–1272). With their marble cladding and rows of columns supporting round-headed arches, one above the other, Pisan buildings are famous examples of the Romanesque style, a wide-ranging term used to describe architecture that began to revive Roman features. Separate baptistries and bell towers (*campanile*) are typical of Italian church design.

THE RISE OF THE CITY-STATES AND URBAN ARCHITECTURE

With the gradual rise of towns and cities in northern and central Italy from the thirteenth century, increasing resources were also spent on secular architecture. The distinctive hill towns of Tuscany began to evolve, often perched high on rocky outcrops and surrounded by fortified walls for defensive purposes. In some, such as San Gimignano, rival families built fortified tower houses. The small town of San Gimignano has preserved 14 medieval towers, whereas many of the towers erected in other Italian cities were destroyed in wars. The tallest tower in the town is the Torre del Podestà, which was constructed in 1311 and rises to 177 feet (54 m).

In the larger, more powerful, and wealthy cities, civic pride inspired city governments to construct grand public squares and city halls, such as the Palazzo Pubblico in Siena (1298). With the pointed arches of its window and door frames and the crenellations of its roof line and tall bell tower, Siena's city hall is typical of the Gothic style that predominated in medieval Europe (originating in France). Italy's greatest Gothic building, constructed by German masons and not completed until 1485, is Milan Cathedral. Other important medieval buildings include the splendid merchants' houses that line the Grand Canal in Venice and the Doge's Palace (1309–1424) in the same city.

ARCHITECTURE OF THE RENAISSANCE

The continued growth of towns and cities in the fifteenth and sixteenth centuries gave impetus to the Renaissance, a cultural flowering based on a revival of ancient Greek and Roman art and contemporary creativity that received some of its finest expressions in architecture. The early center of the movement was the burgeoning republic of Florence; it was followed by the papal city of Rome, where the rebuilding of Saint Peter's Basilica took place throughout the sixteenth century, employing Italy's leading architects. After Rome, Venice became the next major center of grand Renaissance architecture.

Villa La Rotonda, near Vicenza, is a Renaissance villa designed by Andrea Palladio (1508–1580).

The Renaissance was inspired and nurtured by many factors: by the emergence of a new class of rulers and patrons, many of whom had grown rich as merchants and bankers; by the revival of learning about classical texts and civilization (in part spurred by an influx of scholars and decorative artists fleeing Constantinople, when that city fell to the Ottoman Turks in 1453); and by a new conception of people's potential, which was fostered by humanism. Against this backdrop, art and architecture—and the individuals who created them—were accorded greater status, and both were used to express the commercial, cultural, and intellectual prowess of their patrons.

Architects such as Filippo Brunelleschi (1377–1446), Donato Bramante (1444–1514), and Leon Battista Alberti (1404–1472) studied Roman buildings, ruins of which they could see throughout the country, particularly in Rome, as well as a treatise on architecture written by the Roman architect and theorist Vitruvius (active 46–30 BCE). They adapted many Roman features to their own buildings, adorning their churches, palaces, city halls, and villas with classical orders and façades based on temple fronts and triumphal arches. They also developed classical (ancient Greek and Roman) ideas about geometry and harmony, favoring certain mathematical ratios and shapes, notably the square and circle, which they considered to be ideal, or perfect.

Brunelleschi is best known for the great dome (1419–1436) of Florence Cathedral, an innovative double shell of brickwork supported on ribs. The city authorities had forbidden the use of buttresses to support the tower and dome, and Brunelleschi, who had journeyed to Rome to study Roman buildings, used mathematical methods to devise ways of constructing the largest dome since classical times. He was also responsible for two of the major landmarks of Renaissance architecture: the basilica of San Lorenzo in Florence (1419–c. 1480) and the church of Santo Spirito (1441–1481), in the same city.

Bramante was largely responsible for introducing Renaissance architecture to Milan and, later, the magnificent architecture of the High Renaissance to Rome. Bramante, originally a painter, used perspective and illusion in his designs, the most famous of which is Saint Peter's Basilica in Rome.

However, a much smaller building by Bramante, the Tempietto di San Pietro in Montorio, in Rome, is often said to be one of the finest High Renaissance buildings, even though it is only 15 feet (4.5 m) in diameter.

Alberti was a writer and humanist and, arguably, the principal founder of Renaissance architectural theory in Italy. His works include the façade of the Palazzo Rucellai (1446–1451), in Florence; San Sebastiano (begun 1458), in Mantua; and Sant'Andrea (begun 1471), in the same city.

HIGH RENAISSANCE AND PALLADIANISM

As time went on, architects such as Michelangelo (Michelangelo di Lodovico Buonarroti Simoni; 1475–1564), Sebastiano Serlio (1475–1554), and Andrea Palladio (1508–1580) added new features such as the giant order (devised by Michelangelo), in which huge columns or pilasters were used to span several stories. They also evolved the style known as mannerism, in which classical elements are used in new ways, for example by exaggerating particular features. Although mannerism spread through much of western Europe, it remained a particularly Italian architectural language.

Michelangelo designed the dome of Saint Peter's Basilica, in Rome, taking up a project that had been begun by Bramante. Also in Rome, he created an innovative public space, the Piazza del Campidoglio, in the shape of a rhomboid, which united the major buildings on the Capitoline Hill. Its shape cleverly counters the effects of perspective. In Florence, Michelangelo designed the Medici Chapel and the Laurentian Library, characterized by a long line of windows in bays above a cloister.

Serlio's publications described the classical orders and were highly influential; it was his writing, rather than any finished building, that attracted the attention of King Francis I of France (1494–1547; reigned 1515–1547), who commissioned Serlio to advise him on the construction and building of the palace of Fontainebleau. Serlio's manuscripts, drawings, and published books were instrumental in bringing the architecture of the Renaissance to France, the Low Countries, and England.

Palladio revolutionized classical architecture, using its elements in ways in which the Romans would have never done. However, this was achieved through a strict system of rules of proportion. Palladian architecture is refined and always harmonious and is best represented by the elegant villas built for Venetian nobility on the mainland. They include the beautiful Palazzo Chiericati and the domed Villa Capra (called La Rotonda), both outside Vicenza. Villa Capra has been the inspiration for many buildings since, but Palladio drew his inspiration for the structure, now a UNESCO World Heritage site, from the Pantheon in Rome.

The Palazzo della Civiltà Italiana is an example of the monumental Fascist architecture of the EUR (Esposizione Universale Roma) in Rome.

BAROQUE ARCHITECTURE

The free interpretation of classical architecture was taken further in the seventeenth and eighteenth centuries by architects working in the baroque style. The baroque departed from the Renaissance concern with symmetry and harmony, taking a grand, theatrical approach to building and urban design, and it is distinguished by its curvaceous and sculptural forms and abundant sculpted, painted decoration. It was favored by the Roman Catholic Church for much building work in Rome as well as by wealthy individuals for their palaces. Leading baroque architects were Gianlorenzo Bernini (1598–1680), whose projects include the sweeping colonnades (begun 1656) built around the square in front of Saint Peter's Basilica, and Francesco Borromini (1599–1667), whose reputation rests on such churches as San Carlo alle Quattro Fontane (begun 1638), also in Rome.

ENDURING TRADITIONS

The classical tradition in its various forms has remained strong in Italy. It has also shaped architecture farther afield. From the seventeenth century, Italy, and Rome in particular, became a place of pilgrimage for architects wishing to study its classical, Renaissance, and baroque heritage. As a result, Italian architecture gave rise to classical revival architecture across the world, from government buildings (such as the state capitols of many U.S. states) to stately homes in the British countryside, and museums, galleries, and other public buildings in major cities across Europe and North America.

Classicism also became the language for later political regimes in Italy: from the vast Vittorio Emanuele monument (1895–1935) erected in Rome to commemorate the country's unification in the mid-nineteenth century, to the more pared down interpretation favored by Benito Mussolini (1883–1945; in office as prime minister 1922–1943), who remodeled parts of Rome, creating boulevards and new quarters such as the EUR (Esposizione Universale Roma, but always referred to by its initials), which contains simplified, monumental, pseudoclassical designs. Classical architecture's emphasis on geometry and ideal forms also informed the work of those architects known as rationalists in the second half of the twentieth century. Foremost among them are Aldo Rossi (1931–1997), Giorgio Grassi (born 1935), and Mario Botta (born 1943). Rossi created the Carlo Felice opera house in Genoa, behind the remains of its war-damaged classical façade.

R. BEAN

Music and Performing Arts

Music and the performing arts in Italy reflect strong regional variations but they have also, over time, served as a means of binding Italians together in a rich national heritage and as participants in a vibrant culture.

Italian music and the performing arts have been said to have a dual nature: much of Italian music is sacred, but both opera and drama frequently highlight the foibles of human nature. These two threads were epitomized in the past by a musical tradition that evolved from medieval Gregorian chant and a taste for comedy that was rooted in the buffoonery of commedia dell'arte, a form of popular entertainment from the sixteenth through eighteenth centuries, featuring stock characters such as Harlequin, Columbine, and Punchinello.

OPERA

Artistic dualism is evident in the distinction between *opera buffa* (comic opera) and *opera seria* (serious opera). Opera had its origins in Italy, developing from musical drama presented at the court of the de' Medici dynasty in Florence, which evolved into a theatrical art in seventeenth-century Venice. Opera remains a much-loved art form, whose devotees transcend class boundaries. The nation boasts several of the great opera houses of the world, including Teatro della Scala (La Scala), Milan; Teatro San Carlo, Naples; Teatro dell'Opera, Rome; and Teatro La Fenice, Venice. There are also annual summer opera productions in the Roman arena in Verona.

The international profile of Italian opera has been enhanced by acclaimed performers such as tenors Enrico Caruso (1873–1921) and Beniamino Gigli (1890–1957), and, in modern times, sopranos Mirella Freni (born 1935) and Renata Scotto (born

The Verona Arena is a Roman amphitheater, where opera performances are staged in the summer.

1934), mezzo-soprano Cecilia Bartoli (born 1966), and tenors Luciano Pavarotti (1935–2007) and Andrea Bocelli (born 1958). These tenors, in particular, have done much to popularize classical music to a wider audience; Pavarotti most notably through his singing of *Nessun Dorma* at the 1990 (soccer) World Cup in Italy, and through his performance as one of the Three Tenors, alongside the Spaniards Plácido Domingo (born 1941) and José Carreras (born 1946). Italian song is characterized by bel canto, a style of singing that originated in multipart music and courtly solo singing in the sixteenth century and that was developed in opera between the seventeenth and early nineteenth centuries.

THE CLASSICAL COMPOSERS

Italians have been at the forefront of operatic composition. Giuseppe Verdi (1813–1901) was the most successful nineteenth-century composer of Italian opera. From the staging of *Nabucco* (1841) through the first performances of *Il trovatore* (1852), *La traviata* (1853), *Aida* (1871), and *Falstaff* (1893), Verdi's operas became a national music.

The other great opera composers of the century included: Gioacchino Rossini (1792–1868), who wrote *Il barbieri di Siviglia* (1816; *The Barber of Seville*), *La gazza ladra* (1817; *The Thieving Magpie*), and *Guillaume Tell* (1829; *William Tell*); Gaetano Donizetti (1797–1848), who is best known for *Lucia di Lammermoor* (1835); Vincenzo Bellini (1801–1835), who wrote *Norma* (1831); Giacomo Puccini (1858–1924), the composer of *La Bohème* (1896) and *Tosca* (1900); Pietro Mascagni (1863–1945), who wrote *Cavalleria rusticana* (1890); and Ruggero Leoncavallo (1857–1919), who wrote *Pagliacci* (1892). Italian composers had been making a major contribution to European music since the Middle Ages, when, in the fourteenth century, plainsong diversified through the introduction of the style known as *ars nova*, which incorporated innovations in rhythm and harmony. Composers of the period and through the fifteenth to seventeenth centuries wrote much sacred music; their number included Giovanni Palestrina (c. 1525–1594), Claudio Monteverdi (1567–1643), and Gregorio Allegri (1582–1652).

Alessandro Scarlatti (1660–1725) developed the Italian opera overture, which was the forerunner of the symphony, while his son, Domenico (1685–1757), wrote 550 harpsichord sonatas. Giovanni Gabrieli (c. 1557–1612) was known for his motets, which featured rich orchestral accompaniment, while Arcangelo Corelli (1653–1713) established the form of the concerto. Antonio Vivaldi (1678–1741) was a prolific composer of sacred music, 94 operas (of which 45 survive), and more than 460 concertos. Later composers, such as Luigi Cherubini (1760–1842), also wrote much sacred music as well as operas. In more modern times, Ottorino Respighi (1879–1936) wrote ballets and orchestral suites; the music of Luigi Nono (1924–1990) has a severe modernity, and Luciano Berio (1925–2003) experimented with electronic music. Italy has also produced famous musicians, such as violinists Niccolò Paganini (1782–1840) and Salvatore Accardo (born 1941) and pianist Maurizio Pollini (born 1942), as well as conductors, such as Claudio Abbado (born 1933) and Riccardo Muti (born 1941), and is home to great orchestras.

POPULAR SONGS

Italian popular songs have their roots in what is known as Neapolitan music (*canzone Napoletana*), originally serenades for the solo male voice. Neapolitan music is often said to be exemplified by the famous song *O sole mio*. The genre was made popular through radio, song festivals, and emigrant communities of Italians in other parts of Europe and the Western Hemisphere. Serenades and ballads remained an important part of Italian popular music, and many were part of the repertoire of actor and singer Totò (Antonio De Curtis; 1898–1967), a favorite entertainer of the early twentieth century.

Italian popular singers have enjoyed enduring favor, although few are widely known in English-speaking countries. The most successful include Domenico Modugno (1928–1994); Gianni Morandi (born 1944); Mina (Anna Maria Mazzini; born 1940), the only Italian artist to top the album charts in every decade from the 1960s; and celebrated singer, actor, comedian, and director Adriano Celentano (born 1938). Rock singer Zucchero (Adelmo Fornaciari; born 1955) mixes different genres in his music, including blues. Other popular artists include Vasco Rossi (born 1952), whose lyrics court controversy; Eros Ramazzotti (born 1963); rock artist Ligabue (Luciano Ligabue; born 1960); and rapper Jovanotti (Lorenzo Cherubini; born 1966). Although these singers may not be famous outside mainland Europe, many of their songs have become internationally popular, including Modugno's *Nel blu dipinto di blu* (known internationally as *Volare*) and *Piove* (called *Ciao, ciao bambina* outside Italy) and Mina's *Parole, parole*, which was a major chart hit across Europe for other artists.

Popular music writers and singers in Italy are promoted by the country's well-known song festivals, which have an avid following. The most famous festival is the Festival of San Remo (Festival della canzone italiana; founded 1951), which, like most events of its type, does not feature the latest music trends. Italian pop bands, such as Madreblu, are famous only in Italy, but Italian pop has been receptive to global influences and reflects all the major forms of recent pop music, including gangster rap (exemplified by the Sardinian group La Fossa), techno, trance, and electronica.

FESTIVALS, JAZZ, AND FOLK MUSIC

The Festival of the Two Worlds (Festival dei due mondi), held at Spoleto, features an eclectic mixture of concerts, opera, dance, drama, and sculpture. The Umbria Jazz Festival, held in summer in Perugia, attracts performers and spectators from around the world. The Italian jazz scene also flourishes through many other festivals and through clubs in virtually every city. A key figure in this field is the Sicilian Enzo Rao (born 1957), the leader of the Shamal project, which promotes a jazz-based fusion of the Arabic, African, Spanish, French, and Balkan musical influences of the region. Other luminaries of the Italian jazz scene include pianist Danilo Rea (born 1957), trumpeter Paolo Fresu (born 1957), and saxophonist Stefanodi Battista (born 1969).

Jazz is not alone in seeking to synthesize a range of styles including traditional music. In the pop world, this synthesis is particularly associated with patchanka-style music, which is characterized by an energetic, sometimes chaotic, mixture of folk-rock styles. Exponents of this musical mix include the Modena City Ramblers and Banda Bassotti.

Traditional folk music in Italy displays great diversity, in part a reflection of the country's fragmentation until the mid-nineteenth century. Northern Italy favored choral music, while the south was generally characterized by solo performance. Northern music usually featured a strict tempo, while music in the south is in *tempo rubato* (literally, "stolen time") in which the music speeds or slows. Folk music is nearly always sung in local dialect and almost never in standardized Italian. Local specialties include the tarantella dance, which originated in Puglia, and the distinctive polyphonic chanting (composed of independent melody lines or parts) and the bagpipes of Sardinia.

DANCE AND THEATER

Dance has long been an important part of the nation's culture, both through folk dance and ballet. Ballet in Italy dates from the fifteenth century; some of ballet's pioneers were Italian, such as choreographer Filippo Taglioni (1777–1871). The most famous Italian dancers include Maria Taglioni (1804–1884), Virginia Zucchi (1849–1930), and Carlotta Grisi (1819–1899). Today, the Aterballetto modern ballet company is a pioneer, now under the direction of choreographer Mauro Bigonzetti (born 1960).

Renaissance drama developed in Italy from the fourteenth through sixteenth centuries, and a neoclassical style evolved in Italian drama, which spread through the rest of Europe. Popular tastes in drama in Italy have long favored comedy; the improvisational style known as the Commedia dell' Arte, which features stock characters such as the clown Arlecchino (Harlequin) and the old miser Pantalone began in Italy in the sixteenth century and is still performed today. Leading dramatists, such as Luigi Pirandello (1867–1936) and Dario Fo (born 1926), have contributed innovative plays to the national canon. The nation has many theaters, 15 of which, in major cities, are state-funded.

J. PLOWRIGHT/C. CARPENTER

Film

Italian cinema is one of the most innovative and respected in Europe. Italian film won an international reputation in the 1950s through movies that boldly depicted social conditions.

By 1910, the Italian film industry was a major player in world cinema, after having initially lagged behind competitors. In the production of full-length feature films, Italy led the field, with *La Gerusalemme liberata* (internationally released as *The Crusaders*) and *L'inferno* (*Dante's Inferno*), both of 1911. The 1913 version of *Quo vadis?* by Enrico Guazzoni (1876–1949) was, in its day, the second-longest film ever made.

In the early days, comedies, documentaries, and historical films were particularly popular. Among the latter, *Quo vadis?* attained cult status and enjoyed critical and commercial success at home and abroad. However, World War I (1914–1918), which Italy joined in 1915, virtually halted moviemaking, followed by 15 years of decline (despite the development of sound in 1930). This period was characterized by increasing fragmentation of the Italian movie industry.

FILM AND DICTATORSHIP

The Fascist Party of Benito Mussolini (1883–1945; in office as prime minister 1922–1943) came to power in 1922, but the impact of the regime on film was gradual, with censorship imposed in 1923 and state control of newsreels in 1924. In 1931, a law assigned 10 percent of box office takings to reinvestment in the industry, and a series of protectionist measures culminated in 1938 with restrictions on U.S. movies, which provoked a Hollywood boycott. Mussolini constructed a complex of studios outside Rome, known as Cinecittà, in the hope that cinema would mold the national character politically, but the overwhelming majority of films in Fascist Italy were escapist confections.

POSTWAR REALISM

After World War II (1939–1945), escapism in Italian movies was replaced by social awareness. *Roma città aperta* (1945; *Rome Open City*), directed by Roberto Rossellini (1906–1977) marked the advent of neorealism, a loosely defined movement that addressed current issues. This movement, which focused international attention on Italian movies, also featured films by actor-director Vittorio De Sica (1901–1974) and director Luchino Visconti (1906–1976), who is best known for

Obsessione (1942) and *Morte a Venezia* (1970; internationally released as *Death in Venice*).

In 1955, box-office receipts in Italy reached their all-time peak, and the Cinecittà studios were making epics for the international market. Art house cinema was invigorated in the 1960s by the emergence of figures such as director Federico Fellini (1920–1993), who made the 1959 movie *La Dolce Vita*; Michelangelo Antonioni (1912–2007), whose influential movies featured a detached style and, seemingly, aimless characters; Pier Paolo Pasolini (1922–1975); Franco Zeffirelli (born 1923), who directed *Romeo and Juliet* (1963); and Bernardo Bertolucci (born 1940), who won international acclaim for English-language films such as *The Last Emperor* (1988). At the same time, Italian actors became famous outside Italy, appearing in English-language movies; they included Marcello Mastroianni (1924–1996), Vittorio Gassmann (1922–2000), Gina Lollabrigida (born 1927), and Sophia Loren (born 1934).

MODERN MOVIES

Popular cinema was also innovative, most notably in the genre that came to be called spaghetti Westerns, which achieved both critical and commercial success in the hands of Sergio Leone (1929–1989). However, the Italian film industry, in common with that of most European countries, suffered a severe setback from the 1970s, with

Sophia Loren (born 1934) found fame both at home and internationally.

ticket sales falling more than 500 percent from 1976 through 1992. Despite this, Italian cinema continues to produce internationally renowned directors, such as Giuseppe Tornatore (born 1956), who won the Academy Award for best foreign language film with the 1989 movie *Nuovo cinema paradise* (*Cinema Paradiso*) and Gabriele Salvatores (born 1950), who won the same award in 1991 with *Mediterraneo*.

One of the most acclaimed Italian movies of recent years, *Il Postino* (1994; *The Postman*), had a British director, Michael Radford (born 1946). Other acclaimed modern Italian films include *I cento passi* (2000; *The Hundred Steps*) directed by Marco Tullio Giordana (born 1950); *La vita è bella* (1997; *Life Is Beautiful*), directed by actor Roberto Benigni (born 1952), who also appeared in the movie; and *Pane e tulipani* (2000; *Bread and Tulips*) directed by Silvio Soldini (born 1958).

J. PLOWRIGHT

Festivals and Ceremonies

Because of its rich history, its former division into many different small states, and the long-time dominance of Catholicism, Italy celebrates many different festivals and ceremonies, with much local variety.

Three historically distinct, but now often overlapping, forms of festival are celebrated in Italy: *sagre*, which have their roots in pre-Christian times; religious festivals; and *feste*, which are expressions of civic pride, having their origin in the city-states of the late medieval and early Renaissance era. *Sagre* developed to mark the changes of the seasons, and most such festivals now celebrate seasonal produce, such as wine or fruits.

RELIGIOUS FESTIVALS

Although Easter and Christmas are the principal religious feasts, there is a profusion of saints' days throughout the year in Italy. Saints, often local, are celebrated with Masses, parades, and other events in different towns and cities. Carnevale (carnival), in preparation for the self-denial of Lent, has become the most exuberant of festivals. The main celebrations are Settimana grassa (literally, "fat week") and the final day of Carnevale, Martedì grasso (Mardi Gras). The famous masked balls of Venice, traditionally featuring the characters of commedia dell'arte (a popular art form in Italy from the sixteenth through eighteenth centuries), are the best-known expression of carnival, when, over 12 days, partygoers wear costumes, take part in parades, and attend dances.

Saints' days and feast days are most commonly commemorated by a religious parade, although there are many local variations, such as the feast of San Gennaro at Naples Cathedral, where crowds gather to witness the liquefaction of the saint's dried blood. At the Corsa dei Ceri (candle race) in Gubbio

The world-famous Palio horse race is held twice a year in Siena.

in Umbria, three wooden "candles," up to 23 feet (7 m) high, are paraded and, finally, raced through the streets of the city.

Saint Joseph's festival, on March 19, provides a welcome and widely celebrated break in Lenten fasting. The feast usually includes a dramatic performance, with children representing the Holy Family, and a meatless meal (Joseph being patron saint of pastry chefs). Easter is marked with solemnity, parades, dramatic performances, and a wide variety of local traditions, such as the *Scoppio del carro* (literally, "explosion of the cart"), the climax of which is a fireworks display in the piazza between the baptistry and the cathedral (the Duomo) in Florence.

CITY AND PUBLIC HOLIDAYS

Feste celebrate the history of different cities and the rivalries of the ancient quarters (city wards), into which cities were divided. One of the most famous competitions between city quarters is the Palio horse race in Siena. Held twice each summer in Piazza del Campo, ten costumed riders compete against each other, racing around the tight corners of the downtown square. A number of cities have flag-throwing festivals in which young men, in Renaissance costumes, parade and throw large traditional flags on long poles.

Rome celebrates its foundation on April 21; four days later, Venice celebrates the festival of Saint Mark, the patron saint of the city. In Pisa's Game of the Bridge, rival teams from different quarters of the city compete for possession of a bridge over the Arno River. Ivrea carnival includes the battle of the oranges, in which rival teams throw oranges. In addition to traditional events, there are modern food and wine festivals, music and film festivals, such as the Umbria Jazz Festival and the Venice Film Festival, and sports festivals.

Italy celebrates 12 public holidays, fewer than in the past. Religious holidays include Epiphany (January 6), Easter Monday, Assumption Day (August 15), All Saints' Day (November 1), All Souls' Day (*Il giorno dei morti*; November 2), the Immaculate Conception (December 8), and two days at Christmas. Secular public holidays include New Year's Day; Liberation Day (April 25), commemorating the anniversary of the overthrow of the Nazi-backed Republic of Salò (1943–1945) by anti-Fascist Italian forces; and May Day (Labor Day; May 1). The National Day is June 2, which is Republic Day, the anniversary of the establishment of the republic in 1946.

J. PLOWRIGHT

Sports

Passion for sports is part of the Italian character, and few sports arouse as much excitement in Italy as soccer.

Italians enjoy soccer and other team sports, such as rugby, as well as sports in which competition is on an individual basis, such as motor racing, cycling, skiing, and tennis. The country has a medal-winning record in the Olympics that is out of proportion to the size of its population.

SOCCER

Italy claims to have invented soccer in the form of *pallone*, one of many medieval games involving a ball. By 1600, a loose set of rules had evolved for what came to be known as *calcio* (still the Italian name for soccer). Modern soccer clubs emerged in northern Italy by the 1890s. Corporate interest began early, with tire corporation Pirelli subsidizing F.C. Internazionale Milano (commonly known as Inter Milan) and the Fiat automobile corporation's Agnelli family purchasing Juventus (of Turin). Major players are public figures, including Roberto Baggio (born 1967), acknowledged as technically one of the best players in the world in the 1990s, and former goalkeeper Dino Zoff (born 1942). Many Italians consider Valentino Mazzola (1919–1949), captain of Torino, which won the national championship for five consecutive years in the 1940s, to be the greatest Italian soccer player.

Italy is the most successful soccer nation in Europe, having won the (soccer) World Cup (held every four years) four times, in 1934, 1938, 1982, and 2006. In modern times, Italian teams are wealthy, attracting top players from other countries across the world. The top professional competition, the National League (Liga nazionale) comprises Serie A (upper division, with 20 teams), and Serie B (lower division, with 22 teams). Serie A has produced more finalists in the European Cup (the main European club competition) than any other league in Europe. Below Serie B is the Lega Pro, with five divisions of professional teams. There is promotion and relegation throughout the system.

Serie A is characterized by rivalry between clubs in the same city—Roma and Lazio in Rome; Inter Milan and AC Milan; Torino and Juventus in Turin. In 1986, the commercialization of soccer entered a new phase with the acquisition of AC Milan by Silvio Berlusconi (born 1936; in office as prime minister of Italy 1994–1995, 2001–2006, and from 2008). Capitalizing upon Italy's third World Cup victory (1982) and his media empire, Berlusconi made AC Milan a model Italian team commercially and in competition (with four Serie A and three European championships in six years). Soccer became big business. However, several leading teams experienced financial difficulties, and allegations of match-fixing were made.

OTHER SPORTS

Italians enjoy the partnership of high-performance machinery and daring individuals, focused upon aviation in the 1930s and, since then, upon Formula One motor racing, dominated by the Ferrari team. By the time Enzo Ferrari (1898–1988) died, his team had won more Grand Prix victories and more world championship points than any other. A similar combination of competitor and machine is the attraction of cycling. The first Giro d'Italia (Tour of Italy) was in 1909, and the race's most successful champion was Alfredo Binda (1902–1986), who won the Giro five times and was three times world champion (1927, 1930, and 1932). Angelo Fausto Coppi (1919–1960) equalled Binda's Giro record and, in 1949, became the first Italian to win the Tour de France.

Yachting has a growing following, in part because of international success, including Italian yachtsmen twice winning the Louis Vuitton Cup (1992 and 2000), which, apart from the America's Cup, is yachting's most prestigious competition. Skiing is popular in the Alps, and Italy has twice staged the Winter Olympics, most recently at Turin in 2006. Italian Alberto Tomba (born 1966) became the first Alpine skier to win gold medals in consecutive Winter Olympics (in 1988 and 1992). Italy also has a successful record in the Olympics, particularly in track and field events, and the nation is among the five countries that have won the most gold medals.

In team sports, Italy has a successful record in men's volleyball, and the fastest-growing spectator sport in Italy is basketball, which has steadily grown since the 1960s, when U.S. players were first allowed to compete in Italian professional leagues. With a professional domestic league competition, Italy has a growing presence in international rugby, and the country competes in the Six Nations competition, alongside France, England, Scotland, Wales, and a combined team from Ireland and Northern Ireland.

J. PLOWRIGHT

The San Siro stadium in Milan, home to both Inter Milan and AC Milan soccer teams.

Food and Drink

Italians consider their cuisine the best in the world because of its great variety of recipes and the combination of fresh ingredients. In modern times, Italian restaurants serve customers in many countries, and words like pasta, spaghetti, pizza, and espresso are understood around the world.

Italian emigration in the late nineteenth and twentieth centuries, as well as mass tourism to Italy itself, spread Italian food, recipes, and restaurants across all continents. However, Italian dishes served in restaurants in other countries are often adaptations of Italian cuisine rather than the simpler, fresher, additive-free food that is characteristic of Italy itself. In a cuisine based on pasta, sauces, cheese, fish, meat, and fresh fruits and vegetables, there are many regional variations, and Italian cuisine is both diverse and innovative.

HISTORY OF ITALIAN FOOD

The Italian way of cooking and serving dishes has its roots in Imperial Rome. Wine, oil, figs, honey, and wheat were the most common agricultural products of the ancient era. Later, the introduction of new crops from western Asia, North Africa, and the New World, like lemons, oranges, sugar, tomatoes, corn, bell peppers, and potatoes, added more diversity and complexity to Italian cuisine.

For Italian people, eating together in a slow-paced atmosphere is an important element of friendship and trust, and mealtime conviviality plays an important role in family life. Generally, although fast-food restaurants are now widespread in Italy, there is a strong will to preserve traditional meals (what has come to be known as "slow food") and to acquaint young people with their culinary heritage. Restaurants, pizzerias, and traditional snack bars are often family-run, and some of them are more than two hundred years old.

Several products have attained what is called a DOC (Denominazione di Origine Controllata) denomination, which designates a particular standard of quality, to prevent imitations. These include Parma ham and Soave, Frascati, and Valpolicella wines. Culinary fairs and festivals, often dedicated to a single dish, are a popular tourist attraction year-round, and some food festivals have become international events.

A traditional outdoor pizza oven.

CULINARY HABITS AND TYPICAL DISHES

Breakfast in Italy is mainly based on coffee with milk (cappuccino), pastries, and cakes. The breakfast meal is often eaten rapidly and is relatively high in sugar content.

Dinner and lunch are more elaborate, and, in most cases, a precise order of courses is followed. A typical Italian meal starts with appetizers (*antipasti*), followed by a first course (*primo*) based on pasta or rice, and a second course (*secondo*) based on fish or meat. Fresh vegetables are ubiquitous and are also served as salads or side dishes (*contorni*). Cheeses, fresh fruits, and desserts are served as the final course, before a cup of espresso, a strong coffee often topped with milk, cream, cocoa, or liquors. A good meal in a restaurant always ends with an *ammazza-caffè* (literally, "coffee-killer"), which is generally liqueur, perhaps grappa or amaretto.

Cereals are usually the main ingredients of a first course. Cornmeal is used for polenta, a typical northern Italian dish, served with cooked meat and sauce. Pasta comes in a surprising variety of shapes, and there are numerous methods of preparation. Spaghetti, thin pasta cylinders, is the most common, but penne (pasta tubes), lasagne (sheets), and fusilli (corkscrews) are all popular. Risotto, a creamy rice dish often cooked with fresh mushrooms, vegetables, or seafood, is also a favorite.

Wheat flour is most commonly used for bread dough. Bread shapes and types vary from city to city. Bruschetta is finger-thick bread, toasted, rubbed with garlic, and drizzled with olive oil and salt. Focaccia is a yeast-based bread, which is flavored with herbs, sun-dried tomatoes (*pomodori secchi*), or cheese. Ciabatta, made with olive oil, is crunchy and is the favorite bread for a sandwich or snack.

A wheat flour dough is also the base of pizza, another world-famous dish, which is said to have originated in the city of Naples. The most famous version was called Margherita to celebrate an Italian queen; it consists of dough, tomatoes, mozzarella cheese, basil, and olive oil, and is cooked in a wood-fired oven.

Pork, lamb, beef, rabbit, and chicken are the most popular types of meat. Charcuterie products, such as hams and sausages, are produced in hundreds of different ways, from the northern Italian hams to southern Italian spicy sausages and salami. There are two types of prosciutto (cooked and raw ham), the uncooked variety (*prosciutto crudo*) being air cured and served in wafer-thin slices. Prosciutto becomes sweeter as it ages. Pancetta is a baconlike ham that is a key ingredient in many Italian recipes, such as *spaghetti alla carbonara*. Flavored with peppercorns (and sometimes with wine), it adds variety to dishes.

Seafood and fish are also widely used. Mediterranean species like squid (calamari), swordfish, tuna, and octopus are grilled, stuffed, and cooked in soups, or transformed into fine mousses. For variety and quality, Italian dairy products are not easily rivaled. Parmesan, produced in the Po Valley, is called the "king of cheese;" mozzarella, made of buffalo milk, is the most famous southern fresh cheese. Other cheeses include pecorino from Sardinia, provolone, and cheeses from the mountainous north, such as gorgonzola and fontina. Owing to the favorable climatic conditions, Italy is a major producer of fresh vegetables, mostly from the warm coastal zones of the south.

Desserts like tiramisú or *cassatella* (a ricotta cheese-based cake that is topped with marzipan and glacé fruits) are popular, and fruits may be accompanied by a rich sauce as in *arancia di salsa di Marsala* (oranges in Marsala sauce). Almonds are a favorite flavoring; *biscotti* (cookies), often flavored with almonds, are a frequent accompaniment to a dessert. *Cartellate* are pastry spirals drizzled in honey; *panettone* is a tall, round, fruit-filled, sweet bread that is eaten at the Christmas season. *Granita* is a favorite dessert made of coarse ice, sugar, and flavorings; one of the most popular desserts is ice cream (*gelato*), which comes in many different flavors. Fine pastries offer another tasty conclusion to a meal.

REGIONAL DIFFERENCES

Each region of Italy has developed its own culinary culture. Northern Italy was influenced mainly by central European, Austrian, and French cuisines, using butter instead of olive oil. Genoese cooking, and the recipes of coastal zones in general, has developed countless ways of cooking fish with fresh herbs, tomatoes, and olive oil. Bologna, homeland of lasagne and tortellini, is the center of a rich, elaborate cuisine, while Naples and Sicily have created pastries influenced by the different cultures in these regions at the central crossroads of the Mediterranean.

Southern Italian cuisine makes extensive use of fresh vegetables and generally tends to use stronger spices, like the famous Calabrian chili pepper. Puglia, situated in the far southeast, is the principal Italian producer of durum wheat and olive oil. Italian cuisine of the islands has some unique characteristics: Sicily, having been colonized by the Arabs for a brief period, shows influences of North African cuisine, while Sardinia makes much use of lamb and mutton meat in its recipes.

A vineyard in Tuscany, where Sangiovese wine is produced.

BEVERAGES

Wine is a typical Italian product, dating back more than 2,500 years. The southern part of the Italian Peninsula was called Enotria (literally, "the land of wine") by Greek settlers. Today, Italy is one of the biggest producers, exporters, and consumers of wine in the world. Italian wine comes in an impressive variety of types: sparkling, dry, sweet, or liquorlike (vermouth). While northern Italian wines (like Barbera, Barolo, Soave, and Prosecco) are believed to be finer and similar to French varieties, southern and island wines (such as Cirò, Primitivo, Falanghina, Zibibbo, Marsala, and Nero d'Avola) are usually stronger due to lesser precipitation. The wines of central Italy (like Chianti and Montepulciano) have their own character. Each course of a meal has its traditional accompaniment of a particular kind of wine.

Beer was traditionally produced only in some northern regions of Italy. However, the country imports a large quantity of beer from all over the world. Nonalcoholic beverages are widespread, and it is common to find in bars (especially in summer) bitter aperitifs, mint syrups, cold tea, freshly squeezed juices, and *latte di mandorla*, a Sicilian almond-based drink. Natural sparkling mineral water is also widely consumed, and Italy is the largest consumer of bottled mineral water in the world. The most famous Italian liquors are *grappa*, distilled from marc (which is made from grape skins); *limoncello*, a lemon liquor made in southern Italy, often in a creamy form; *sambuca*, made with aniseed; *mirto*, based on myrtle, which comes from Sardinia; and *amaro*, a bitter digestive liquor produced in many different ways. Throughout the day, the beverage of choice is coffee, commonly espresso in the afternoon and evening and cappuccino generally only in the morning.

S. BRUNO

DAILY LIFE

Religion

Italy is essentially a Roman Catholic country. Historically and culturally shaped by Roman Catholicism, Italy is one of the European countries where religion and the state have come into the closest association.

While Roman Catholicism is still the dominant religion in Italy, it can no longer be said that all Italians are Catholic. Early in the twenty-first century, 87 percent of Italians were Roman Catholic, with around 37-40 percent practicing. Some 12 percent of the population is now recorded as nonreligious, although most will have been baptized and raised as Catholics or in a Catholic culture. Sunni Islam and others account for more than 1 percent of the population, probably considerably more because of unrecorded illegal immigration.

For nearly two millennia, Italy has been the center of the Roman Catholic Church and, from the eighth century CE through the nineteenth century, the papacy ruled much of central Italy. Today, the Holy See is still sovereign, although the Vatican City State is now the world's smallest country.

THE CATHOLIC CHURCH AND THE ITALIAN STATE

The relationship between the Holy See and the Italian state is formally regulated by the Lateran Treaties signed in February 1929 by a representative of the pope, Cardinal Pietro Gasparri (1852–1934), and the prime minister of Italy, Benito Mussolini (1883–1945; in office 1922–1943). Until then, the saying "a free Church in a free state" had loosely defined the duties and the rights of the two powers—religious and secular; the Lateran Treaties ratified in detail the separation of, and the relationship between, these two entities.

Decades of disputes had followed the annexation of Rome by the new Italian kingdom in 1870, after which the pope retreated to the Vatican, where he regarded himself as a prisoner, refusing to recognize the loss of the Papal States. Various attempts were made to ease tension between the papacy and the Italian state, but it was not until the Lateran Treaties that the Holy See was accorded absolute and visible independence, allowing it to become, once more, a separate territory in which the pope could exert full sovereignty. Moreover, the treaties confirmed that Roman Catholicism was the only official state religion, as

already documented in the first article of the Italian constitution. The pact also granted the Church privileges concerning the citizens of the Vatican City State, the immovable property of the Holy See, and tax exemptions. Finally, the treaties included an assignment of shares to the Vatican as compensation for the annexation of Rome to the Italian state.

Part of the Lateran agreement, called the concordat, established the validity of religious marriages and of the power of the Rota (the supreme ecclesiastical tribunal that judges cases brought before the Holy See) to invalidate them. The concordat also guaranteed the teaching of Catholicism in Italian schools at every level of the educational system. As a result, the Lateran Treaties gave the Roman Catholic Church far-reaching authority and powers within the Italian state.

After the ousting of the monarchy in 1946, the provisions of the Lateran Treaties were included in Article 7 of the 1947 republican constitution. This action was promoted by the largest political party at the time, the Christian Democratic Party, and agreed by the

Pope Benedict XVI (born 1927) leads Mass in Saint Peter's Square in Vatican City.

second-largest party, the Communist Party, which was anxious to avoid conflict that could have weakened the new republic.

However, a long process of consultations between the Italian state and the Vatican for a revision of the Lateran Treaties took place, beginning in 1969 and leading, in 1985, to a new agreement that enshrined the citizens' right to freedom of religion and the independence of the Catholic Church, but also abolished the compulsory weekly hour of religion in the school curriculum and ended the state stipend to the clergy. Moreover, according to the *protocollo addizionale*, an appendix to the concordat of 1985, the constitutional provision according to which Catholicism is the only state religion was considered to be no longer in force.

The Shroud of Turin, revered as Christ's burial cloth, has been the subject of much research concerning its authenticity.

CATHOLICISM TODAY IN ITALY

Discussions on possible further revisions of the Lateran Treaties, promoted by some politicians, are ongoing and cause tension between the political establishment and the Church. The ethos of the Italian state is still Catholic, but the role of the Church has changed and its influence is greatly reduced.

The Church has always been involved in Italian politics. Traditionally, Catholics were politically represented by the Christian Democratic Party, which ruled the country (usually in coalition) from 1945 until its collapse in 1992, when a police investigation into corruption resulted in the disintegration of the party system in place at the time. Today, a Catholic component is present in both center-right (People of Freedom) and center-left (Democratic Party) parties. Despite the removal of the Church's privileges, church leaders still pronounce on political matters in which there is a moral dimension. As recently as 2003, Cardinal Joseph Ratzinger (born 1927; since 2005 Pope Benedict XVI) wrote a *vade mecum* (a handbook for personal use) in which he advised Italian members of parliament regarding which laws and measures discussed by the legislature were ethical and which were not.

Italy was historically divided into hundreds of dioceses, and every city (as well as most towns of any local importance) has a cathedral. Improved transportation in the nineteenth century and economic considerations concerning the expense of so many diocesan administrations, along with falling Mass attendances in the twentieth century, led to a drastic territorial reorganization of the Italian Church. Many small or sparsely populated dioceses were merged with their neighbors. As a result, modified diocesan names incorporating the names of several formerly separate sees, such as the archdiocese of Sant'Angelo dei Lombardi-Conza-Nusco-Bisaccia, are common. Rationalization has reduced the number of dioceses in Italy to 225, which is still far more than in any other European country and more than in the United States.

NON-CATHOLICS

The largest non-Catholic religion in Italy is Sunni Islam and, although there are fewer than 15,000 Muslim Italians, Muslim residents who are not Italian citizens account for more than 750,000 people. Many of these are illegal immigrants, and the true size of Italy's Muslim population is not known. Muslims resident in Italy come from Albania, Kosovo, Turkey, and North and sub-Saharan Africa. Because of the dominance of the Catholic Church and the role of Rome as the seat of the pope, there has always been strong resistance to the building of mosques in Italy, particularly in Rome because of its symbolism as the center of Catholic Christianity. When it was suggested in the 1930s that a mosque should be built in Rome for the citizens of Italy's colonies at the time (Somalia, Eritrea, and Libya), Mussolini prohibited construction, famously saying that there would be a mosque in Rome only when a Roman Catholic church was allowed in Mecca. The Vatican dropped its objections to a mosque in Rome in 1965 and has since been favorable toward the provision of facilities for Muslims in Italy. In 1989, the first large mosque was constructed in Rome. However, objections by local people still effectively delay, or restrict, the number of mosques in Italy.

Members of other religions form small minorities in Italy. Jehovah's Witnesses and Protestants each number a little over 330,000 adherents. There are also small communities of dissident Catholics, Orthodox Christians, and Mormons. There are around 90,000 Buddhists and nearly 30,000 Jews in Italy. Italy has never had a large Jewish population, compared with central and eastern European countries. Before World War II (1939–1945), Italy took in German Jewish refugees, despite the alliance between Nazi Germany and Fascist Italy, but under the northern Italian Nazi puppet state, the Italian Social Republic (1943–1945), often called the Republic of Salò, some 20 percent of Italy's Jews died in German concentration camps.

The Italian constitution states that religions different from the Catholic faith are equal in law and are free to organize themselves according to their statutes as long as these are compatible with Italian laws. Their relationship with the Italian state is regulated by single agreements between their respective representatives and the state. Such agreements are already in force with the Jewish, Waldensian, and Muslim communities.

E. GARAU

Family and Society

Italian family life and society changed dramatically during the last half of the twentieth century. Large-scale emigration, immigration in modern times, the declining influence of the Roman Catholic Church, the spread of women's rights and the decline of a patriarchal society, and the fall in the birthrate to one of the lowest in the world have all had a profound effect upon Italy and Italians.

Although the family is still the center of daily life in Italy, the family is no longer male-dominated as it was 50 years ago. The "economic miracle" of the 1950s and 1960s brought great economic change and, with it, social changes as families no longer lived within the same area. Economic migration dispersed family members and, as a result, the nuclear family (parents and their children) replaced the extended family as the main building block of Italian society. At the same time, the rise of liberal movements in the 1960s transformed society, and the nation has moved toward a modern postindustrial society. Previously an agricultural society, in modern times some 67 percent of Italians are urbanized.

EVOLUTION OF THE ITALIAN FAMILY AND THE ROLE OF WOMEN

Until the advent of industrialization and subsequent social changes, traditions were strongly observed, especially in rural communities and the regions of the south, the Mezzogiorno. Italy had a largely agricultural society, with a high population growth rate and a relatively low rate of urbanization. There was also a strong sense of kinship among relatives. Positions of authority within the family were based on age and gender; an older male was head of the family, and his decisions affected the education and careers of the young. The Catholic Church was the supreme moral authority, and the local priest was an important figure.

The role of women in society was greatly limited. However, at the end of the 1950s, an emerging Italian generation, influenced by American ideals and fashions, pressed hard for greater freedom of choice, fighting against moral conservatism. Representative of this situation was a debate, which split the whole country into two factions, over the judicial proceedings against cycling champion and popular hero Fausto Coppi (1919–1960), who while married was involved in an extramarital relationship with a married woman.

At the same time, Italy was politically polarized between right-of-center and left-wing parties. While this division was regional, the split was also, in part, generational. From 1965 through 1976, the country experienced deep changes, periods of social tensions and struggles, as liberal movements became a strong social force. The energy of the younger generations who grew to adulthood after World War II (1939–1945) transformed Italian society and family: the old, thrifty, slow, patriarchal Italy was left behind in favor of a society centered on new values, personal realization, and freedom, sometimes obtained at any cost.

Central to these changes was the spread of women's rights. Suffrage was granted to women in 1946; divorce and abortion were legalized in the 1970s and confirmed by referendums. However, the participation of women in senior management and national and regional government is still relatively low compared with general Western standards, even though more women (57.5 percent) are in tertiary education than men. Personal freedom and individualism are now seen as untouchable rights, and the sense of a united family has declined. The annual number of divorces was 11,796 in 1971, the year in which divorce finally became legal; this figure grew to 45,097 by 2001. At the same time, the number of couples having church weddings has fallen dramatically. As in most of Europe, only civil marriages are legal, and only 67.6 percent of Italian couples opt for an additional religious wedding, when, previously, a church wedding was the norm.

In modern times, gender equality is enshrined in law but, in practice, some differences remain. Pay differentials still exist, and some women earn less than their male counterparts. Women are also more likely to be in part-time employment than men. There are also regional differences. The old image of women as wives and mothers rather than employees persists in some rural areas, particularly in the Mezzogiorno.

Homosexual rights are fewer than in many western European countries. Same-sex civil partnerships are not allowed, and, in a country where young males have traditionally placed great emphasis on "manly" activities and images, male homosexuals face considerable prejudice.

POPULATION GROWTH

Italy's population growth rate has been stable since 1981. Italy is rapidly aging: in 2008, people above age 65 accounted for 20 percent of the population, one of the highest rates in the world.

Population Distribution in Italy

There are considerable regional variations in the distribution of population in Italy. The lowest population densities are in the Alps and the Dolomites in the north, in the Apennine mountain ridges of the center, through the Italian Peninsula into Calabria in the far south, and the inland regions of Sardinia.

The rural regions of eastern and northern Sicily, the fertile Campanian countryside surrounding Naples, the Arno Valley in Tuscany, the Venetian lowlands, and the Po Valley lowlands around Milan are all fertile farming or horticultural regions and have a much higher population density than other rural regions.

Italy's politically fragmented history up to the mid-nineteenth century worked against the emergence of a single large agglomeration. Instead, regional capitals developed; in the past, these were also the capitals of different countries. As a result of this historical and political state of affairs, Italy has four large metropolitan areas with populations of a roughly similar size: Rome, Milan, and Naples, each above two million inhabitants, and Turin with more than one million. Palermo, Genoa, and Florence are also former national capitals and important regional centers.

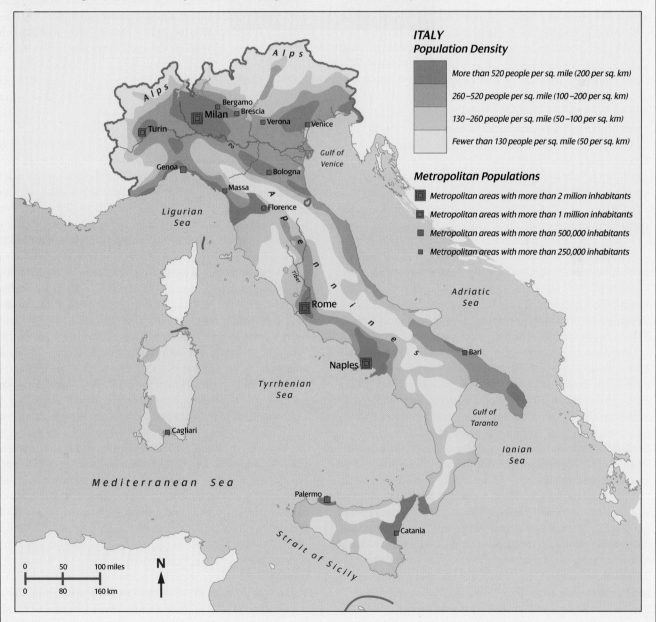

ITALY
Population Density

- More than 520 people per sq. mile (200 per sq. km)
- 260–520 people per sq. mile (100–200 per sq. km)
- 130–260 people per sq. mile (50–100 per sq. km)
- Fewer than 130 people per sq. mile (50 per sq. km)

Metropolitan Populations

- Metropolitan areas with more than 2 million inhabitants
- Metropolitan areas with more than 1 million inhabitants
- Metropolitan areas with more than 500,000 inhabitants
- Metropolitan areas with more than 250,000 inhabitants

The number of births is declining year after year (a general trend in Europe), and, in 2008, was 8.4 live births per 1,000, a figure that is below the replacement rate. Southern Italy continues to have a slightly higher birthrate than the north. The average age of Italian mothers at first childbirth is now over 30 years. The decline in the birthrate is due to women gaining control of their reproductive health (through the spread of contraception) and also to a general sense of economic and social insecurity among young couples. As a result, early in the twenty-first century, the Italian government offered incentives and tax reductions to encourage couples to have children.

The percentage of young men and women still living with their parents is high compared with other European countries. Marriage is increasingly delayed, as is the age at which young adults leave home. About one-half of the male population and one-quarter of females only leave home to live on their own between 30 and 39 years of age. Rising housing prices and job insecurity have made many young people opt for the safety of living with the family.

An apartment building in Naples, where there are great differences in the standards of living between the wealthy and the poor.

domestic service and health care) before the 1990s. Now, the majority of immigrants come from eastern Europe, and there is also a growing Chinese community, engaged in commerce. Clandestine immigration rates are high, with dozens of small ships landing every year from the African coast in southern Italy and its islands. The true figure for illegal immigration is not known, but the majority of illegal immigrants are Muslim men from North and sub-Saharan Africa.

The integration of immigrants is generally successful, although there are some difficulties, due to a perception that high crime rates are recorded among immigrants. Some 26 percent of the Italian prison population are foreigners. There is also prejudice against the non-Catholic religions of immigrants and, often, strong local resistance to the construction of mosques.

IMMIGRATION

Italy was traditionally a country of emigration and, through the second half of the nineteenth century and the first half of the twentieth century, many people, especially from the Mezzogiorno, emigrated to the United States, Argentina, Brazil, Australia, Germany, France, and Belgium. Remittances (money sent home) became an important source of income.

During the economic boom years from the 1950s through 1970s, the country's need for industrial workers was satisfied by millions of people from the Mezzogiorno and the northeast settling in Lombardy and Piedmont for employment. Emigration continued, on a lesser scale. Now, the country is coming to rely on adding to its workforce through immigration.

Italy still has an overwhelmingly European population, with 94 percent of the population being Italian speakers. The country also has linguistic minorities such as German speakers in South Tirol, French speakers in Valle d'Aosta, and Slovenes, Friulians, and Ladins in Friuli–Venezia Giulia. Smaller traditional minorities included Greeks and Albanians. In modern times, migration from other European countries, particularly Albania, Romania, and the countries of the former Yugoslavia, has increased, and there are around 3 million foreigners legally resident in Italy.

There was a migratory wave from Muslim North Africa (mainly men) and from the Philippines (mostly women in

THE ITALIAN WAY OF LIFE

Italians are known to be open, talkative, and convivial. They enjoy spending time outdoors, walking in city streets, eating with friends, drinking coffee, and watching passers-by. Leisure activities and sports are popular, although just one-fifth of Italians engage in sports regularly. Young Italians show interest in fashion and cars (the country has the largest number of cars per capita in Europe) and are generally concerned about grooming and appearance. Spending time with family is important, and religious and civil holidays are occasions for family celebrations. Even though the literary and scientific production of the country is high, and arts, music, and drama have a large following, Italy has a low percentage of habitual book readers compared with the European average. Watching television is a popular activity, and soccer arouses great passions. Political opinions are strongly held, but politicians are generally distrusted—82 percent of Italians, according to surveys in the early twenty-first century, do not trust politicians.

One of the characteristics of Italian society is a deep sense of individualism. Local pride is often exaggerated; Italians term this phenomenon *campanilismo*, originally a rivalry between two small villages as to which has the highest bell tower (*campanile*). Integration with the European Union (EU), as well as cultural exchanges with other countries, is gradually helping to dilute provincialism, although Italians still tend to be proud of their local cultural heritage. Each Italian region has strong characteristics in language, culture, traditions, and mentality, and there is still a certain sense of rivalry, and a reciprocal exchange of jibes and jokes, between northerners and southerners.

S. BRUNO

Health and Welfare

The Italian health care system is modern and free, funded by the state and a compulsory insurance system. Welfare is provided through a state network of social security.

The Italian welfare and health care system is funded by the state and employee contributions, but it is sometimes seen as expensive and in need of rationalization. The great majority of the citizens receive free services provided by the state, with some differentiation determined by factors such as age, income, occupation, and family circumstances.

THE WELFARE SYSTEM

The Italian welfare system has its roots in the historic strong presence in Italy of the Roman Catholic Church. The church was involved in countless charity and health care activities from before the birth of the Italian nation in 1861. The church and other charity organizations were largely supplanted in the twentieth century by the creation of a public welfare system.

In the 1970s, the current comprehensive welfare system came into place. The current model is, effectively, a mix of the two systems. A number of state agencies, including the main institute, INPS (Istituto Nazionale della Previdenza Sociale; the National Social Insurance Institute), provide a wide range of assistance services. The system has often been criticized for its excessive demands on public expenditure and its perceived disorganization. Reforms were carried out in the 1980s and the 1990s to correct some of the imbalances and rein in more expensive elements of the system. Further reforms are planned.

Under a contributory system, a percentage of each worker's salary is paid into a central retirement pension fund. A full state pension is paid after 40 years of contributions into the fund, but this figure may soon be changed because the aging population is placing ever-increasing demands upon the fund. As a result, Italian workers may have to work longer to qualify for a full pension. The amount of the pension depends upon a number of factors, such as the sector in which the individual was employed and the total amount of contributions made by a worker in her or his working life. There are also social pensions, which are paid from age 65 to people who have no income or insufficient contributions for a full contributory pension.

The state security system includes a number of other benefits, such as unemployment benefit, payments to large or poor families, widows' pensions, pensions for disabled people, and war veterans' pensions. Payments are made in the form of subsidies or monthly checks. Workers who are ill, unemployed, or on maternity leave receive a payment of between 30 percent and 80 percent of their previous salary, depending upon their individual circumstances. Inability to work must be certified by a doctor.

WELFARE REFORM

Because individual circumstances, levels of contributions, and some differences between economic sectors are taken into consideration when assessing health and welfare payments, there are some inequalities in benefits received between individuals, the different regions of Italy, and even between public- and private-sector employees. As a result, there are demands for a simpler, more uniform system.

The reform of the welfare system in Italy is an important issue that often generates strong conflicts between various social classes and interest groups. In 2008, public expenditure for pensions accounted for 15.2 percent of GDP (gross domestic product, the total value of all the goods and services produced in a country in a fixed term, usually one year). A rapidly aging population (some 20 percent of Italy's population is over age 65), a relatively high unemployment rate (6 percent of the workforce in 2007), and inefficient management of the pension system threaten to increase the already large public deficit. Reforms are periodically advocated by international institutions, like the European Commission (one of the two main executive bodies of the European Union or EU) and private economics research bodies. While the expensive welfare system is viewed as an economic burden by some, Italian politicians and the electorate generally claim that social security and free health care are basic rights in a modern state and should not be touched.

HEALTH CARE

The Italian public health care system—the Servizio Sanitario Nazionale, known as the SSN—is regarded as one of the most accessible by the World Health Organization (WHO), which regularly ranks the Italian state system among the five best in the world. However, some smaller regional hospitals, particularly in the south, are overcrowded and relatively underfunded, and many hospitals may appear somewhat stark and lacking in comforts by North American standards.

Venetian ambulances are adapted to the canal-based system of transportation.

The present SSN was founded in 1978 and aims to provide equal access to public health care services to all Italian citizens. The country is divided into regional and local health care districts to provide hospital management, clinics, and first aid services in their area. A large number of private organizations provide specific medical procedures. Access to public health care is available to all, and most expenses are met by the state and by revenue from the compulsory health insurance program to which all workers belong. Workers and their dependents receive free health care, as do pensioners and those receiving benefits. Hospitalization, treatments, visits to general practitioners, medication, and tests are all free. Partial payments must be made for drugs and dental care. Family doctors are responsible for primary care, and pharmacies treat some minor ailments.

According to a 2007 estimate, life expectancy in Italy is 80.1 years, 77.1 years for males and 83.2 years for females. The most common causes of death are cardiac diseases and cancers, followed by road accidents. Italy has a worse record in work-related accidents than any other EU member. Some illness is also related to pollution, particularly unsafe disposal of dangerous wastes. Smoking, drugs, and alcohol consumption are on average European levels, with some 22 percent of Italians being smokers early in the twenty-first century. Since December 2005, it has been against the law to smoke in the workplace or in any public place. As a result of these measures, around 5 percent of Italian smokers quit the habit; most of those giving up cigarettes were adult males.

The Italian public health care system is often criticized for its costs and sometimes for a general inattention to efficiency and economies, which tends to lead to overspending on health care budgets. Italians have high expectations of the system and have coined the word *malasanità* (literally, "health crime") to describe lack of care, accidents, public appointments in which nepotism have played a part, disorganized management, and the intrusion of political interests in health care. However, although such incidents do occur, the standard of health care is generally high.

S. BRUNO

Education

Italy, which has some of Europe's oldest universities, provides free primary and secondary education and affordable tertiary education to all of its citizens.

When the kingdom of Italy was formed in 1861, some 80 percent of Italians were illiterate. Consequently, primary education became compulsory in an attempt to eradicate mass illiteracy. However, before that time, Italy had many private schools and Catholic schools and universities, including some of the oldest in Europe, such as Bologna (founded 1088), Padua (1222), Naples (1224), Siena (1240), La Sapienza in Rome (1304), Perugia (1308), Florence (1321), and Pisa (1343). In modern times, these ancient universities and many others are prestigious centers of research and are still making important contributions in the sciences and humanities.

Because of economic constraints and the lack of existing basic educational infrastructure, the illiteracy rate in Italy remained high until World War I (1914–1918), when it was around 40 percent. A major educational program began when dictator Benito Mussolini (1883–1945; in office as prime minister 1922–1943) employed philosopher Giovanni Gentile (1875–1944) to design a new educational system for the nation. Under Gentile's recommendations, schooling became compulsory until age 14. The educational system, in addition to promoting Fascism, included instruction in Roman Catholicism in the curriculum. The results were rapid and encouraging, and, by 1940, the illiteracy rate in Italy had dropped to 13 percent. The political and religious subjects were removed from the curriculum after World War II (1939–1945).

PRIMARY AND SECONDARY EDUCATION

In modern times, the illiteracy rate in Italy is less than 2 percent. Gentile's system, although modified over time, still forms the basis of the Italian educational system. His system was based on five years of primary school, three years of middle school, and either three years of secondary school (which allowed students to continue studies toward university entrance) or three years in a professional training course. The vocational provision was abolished in 1962, but the division of the schools into primary (scuole elementari), middle (scuole medie inferiori), and secondary (scuole medie superiori) remains. Students may leave full-time education at age 16, although many continue in secondary education to age 18.

Public schools are free and available to everybody, but private, fee-based, usually Catholic, schools and academies still attract a considerable enrollment. The national educational system is based on six cycles: preschool education (optional nursery schooling), primary school (five years), middle school (three years), secondary school (five years), and postsecondary education and universities. At primary school, from age five and a half or six (depending on the season in which a student's birthday falls), students study Italian, English, math, science, geography, music, computer studies, social sciences, and religion (which is optional).

Middle school students study a national curriculum, but there are local differences and the option of additional lessons in subjects such as music, computing, sports, and foreign languages. At the end of middle school, students take a standard national written examination in Italian, math, science, and a foreign language, as well oral examinations in other subjects, for the diploma di licenza media (middle school diploma).

After obtaining the diploma, students have several options for secondary education, although in more remote or sparsely populated areas, not all these options may be locally available. Students may attend a liceo classico (which is oriented toward humanities, with compulsory Latin and Greek), a liceo scientifico (whose courses are based in sciences and humanities), an istituto tecnico (for industrial, technological, or economic studies), a liceo artistico (for the arts), a liceo linguistico (whose courses focus on foreign languages), or an istituto professionale (which offers many practical and technical subjects, intended for those who opt for a quick entrance to the labor market). Attendance at secondary school was around 93 percent in 2007, and the secondary school student-teacher ratio—which is 10.2:1—is one of the best in Europe.

A comprehensive final examination is scheduled at the end of the fifth year and allows access to any type of tertiary institute. Examination grades in the secondary school diploma are awarded, ranging from 60/100 to 100/100. Those not reaching the level required for a 60/100 grade do not earn the diploma.

TERTIARY EDUCATION

Education currently accounts for 4.8 percent of Italy's GDP (gross domestic product, the total value of all the goods and services produced in a country in a fixed term, usually one year); however, tertiary education accounts for only 0.9 percent, a relatively low percentage compared with other European countries. In 1999, minister of education and former Communist Party leader Luigi Berlinguer (born 1932) modified the university system to make it more oriented toward specialization, bringing average, and Rome's La Sapienza, with around 150,000 students, is the largest university in Europe in terms of student numbers. The most prestigious Italian universities include Bologna, La Sapienza, Pisa, Florence, Milan Polytechnic, Trieste, Pavia, and Siena. The largest departments in terms of student numbers are economics, political science, and law. There are also specialized higher education institutions, such as journalism schools, music conservatories, and design schools.

There are some 1.8 million university-level students in Italy, with nearly 320,000 new students enrolling each academic year. About 2.1 percent of students in tertiary education in Italy are foreigners. University fees are relatively low compared with other Western countries, and many forms of financial assistance and discounts are given according to factors such as merit, income, and family situation. European student exchange programs, like Erasmus-Socrates, welcome foreign students and give Italian students the opportunity to study in other European countries.

Graduate studies are focused on research and specialized training, leading to a doctorate (PhD), known in Italy as *dottorati di ricerca*. Italy has many prestigious research institutes, coordinated by the National Research Council (CNR), particularly in the fields of biotechnology, medicine and pharmacy, energy, engineering, and physics.

EDUCATIONAL ISSUES

Bologna university, founded in 1088, is one of the oldest in continuous operation in the world.

In modern times, the Italian educational system has attracted some internal criticism. The quality, standards, and rigor of Italian public schools are perceived to be below those of many other European countries, and Italy has fewer habitual readers than other European states—some 60 percent of the Italian population do not read a book in a year, and only 12.9 percent of Italians read more than 10 books in a year. The academic world in Italy is often portrayed as an oligarchy, in which a small elite shapes research in line with its particular interests. As a result, an increasing number of Italian researchers prefers to move abroad to study.

the sector more in line with European standards. Berlinguer's reforms introduced separate bachelor's (*triennale*) and master's (*specialistica*) degrees and switched from a system based on single examinations to a credit-based one. Each examination or parallel activity now accounts for a certain number of credits; an examination can be worth from four to eight credits, for example, and degree programs take five to six years to complete.

Italy has 66 universities and higher learning institutes of university status, including 41 state and 15 private universities. State universities tend to be larger than the western European

S.BRUNO

Housing

The rapid urbanization of Italy after World War II (1939-1945) greatly increased the urban housing stock. Home ownership is more common than in many European countries.

After World War II, Italy experienced large-scale reconstruction, and the once largely rural country became rapidly, and in many instances quite chaotically, urbanized. Some 67 percent of the Italian population lives in urban areas, and some built-up areas have a high population density. The region with the highest density is Campania, with 1,101 people per square mile (425 per sq. km). Portici, a suburb of Naples, has one of the highest population densities in the world: 38,140 people per square mile (14,726 per sq. km). The largest metropolitan areas—Rome, Milan, Naples, and Turin—have the greatest amount of modern housing and also the greatest housing demand.

HOUSING DEVELOPMENTS

With more than 750,000 houses damaged or destroyed during World War II—almost 20 percent of total dwellings—Italy had, in 1945, a large homeless population, and many people lived in inadequate accommodations. Government housing programs were started after the war, including public building as well as incentives to the private sector. From 1953 through 1961, 15 million new rooms in domestic dwellings were created, radically changing the country's landscape. Rental houses accounted for more than one-half of total dwellings.

Government incentives and a lack of town-planning programs allowed widespread speculation and an unplanned distribution of new residential areas, mostly large concrete apartment buildings. The urbanization that followed the economic boom of the 1950s through 1970s caused serious overcrowding in the peripheral urban areas of virtually every large city, and these new suburbs often lacked public services. After the economic slowdown of the 1970s and the housing emergency caused by the earthquake that hit the Irpinia region

Modern high-rise apartment buildings offer a contrast to the old buildings in Naples. Urban overcrowding is commonplace and housing costs account for over half of the average Italian family's budget.

near Naples in 1980 (leaving more than 300,000 people homeless), the building industry experienced significant growth again in the late 1990s. However, in the 1990s, more rigorous planning and zoning laws were also implemented, but not before some coastal areas had been blighted by unauthorized building.

CURRENT HOUSING ISSUES

In 2007, some 73 percent of Italians were owner-occupiers, a high figure compared with most other European countries. Real estate is for many Italians a preferred investment. Public housing accounts for 4.6 percent of the total dwellings and 23.1 percent of rented accommodation. In 2005, there were 28,328,000 dwellings for 22,835,000 households in Italy; this figure shows the extent of vacation-home or second-home ownership in Italy, although there are also many empty dwellings.

Housing has become a secondary issue in national policies: the responsibility for public building has been transferred to regional councils, while rental legislation was liberalized, which caused a boom in the real estate market. Between 250,000 and 300,000 new dwellings are constructed annually. The supply is lower than the demand: the numbers of low-income families, both immigrants and Italians, are constantly increasing, and every year more than 250,000 new families enter the housing market. However, at the start of the twenty-first century, the housing market, like that in many Western countries, is in recession. Many households have difficulty with rising rents, which increased by 65 percent (and by 85 percent in big cities) between 1996 and 2006. Monthly rental costs can amount to more than 50 percent of the household's income.

S. BRUNO

Rome

The national capital of Italy, Rome is known as the Eternal City. Once the seat of a mighty empire, Rome is Italy's largest city.

Rome's metropolitan area had a population of 3,402,000 in 2008 (Italian government estimate). In the same year, some 2,719,000 people lived within the city limits. Rome is located along the Tiber River in a relatively low-lying region some 15 miles (24 km) inland from the Tyrrhenian Sea. The downtown area is surrounded by seven hills, the highest of which rises to 394 feet (120 m), giving Rome its nickname, the City of the Seven Hills.

IMPERIAL ROME

By legend, Rome was founded in 753 BCE. While there is no evidence to support this date, archaeology proves that there was settlement on the Palatine Hill during the eighth century BCE. The date traditionally given for the foundation of the Roman Republic is 509 BCE, but the republic cannot have been founded until after 474 BCE, when the Etruscans withdrew. The city-state had many local enemies and, in 387 BCE, Rome was sacked by Celts.

By the third century BCE, Rome was the most powerful city on the Italian Peninsula, and public buildings, temples, baths, and the Forum, on Palatine Hill, were constructed. Migration to the city, in the second century BCE, boosted its population, and, by the end of the century, Rome controlled all of Italy, the Adriatic, Iberia, Greece, much of north Africa, and parts of Asia Minor (modern Turkey). In 27 BCE, the line of Roman emperors began, and the city was embellished with grand building projects. The Great Fire of Rome (64 CE) allowed much redevelopment, at a time when the population exceeded half a million. While there is no agreement among historians concerning how many people lived in Rome at its height, it is likely that the population was more than one million.

Ancient Rome had little industry, relying on subsidies of food and supplies from the provinces to survive. The population and the fortunes of the city began to decline toward the end of the second century CE. In 330 CE, Constantinople became the imperial capital, hastening Rome's decline. In the fifth century CE, with the empire divided into western and eastern parts, Rome was threatened by invasion by Vandals and Visigoths and, in 410 CE, the city was sacked.

THE SEAT OF THE PAPACY

The empire in the west was finally toppled in 476 CE but, by this time, Rome had gained another significance, as seat of the papacy and the center of the Christian Church. By the end of the fourth century CE, the pope lived in the Lateran Palace and the first Saint Peter's Basilica had been built.

The city's population fell after its sacking in 410 CE, and although much of the Mediterranean region of the Roman Empire was reunited under the Eastern Roman, or Byzantine, Empire in 480 CE, the Western Empire was ruled from Ravenna, not from Rome. In the Gothic Wars (546–552 CE), Ostrogoths twice captured Rome, which was greatly damaged, and much of the city lay in ruins.

By 570 CE, the Lombards had confined the Byzantine Empire to a few areas of coastal Italy, including Rome. The emperor in distant Constantinople had little influence in Rome, where the pope had become the leading public figure. In the eighth century CE, after the pope called upon the Franks for protection from the Lombards, the link with the east was effectively broken, and the pope became the ruler of Rome and central Italy, the Papal States.

By 1000, pilgrimages to Rome, the activities of traders and merchants in the city, and the emergence of a Roman nobility revived the fortunes of the city, which was, however, sacked by Normans in 1084. In 1143, Rome's citizens rebelled, founding a republic, the Commune of Rome. The revolt was put down in 1155. Recurring disputes between the papacy and the Holy Roman emperor, and between the pope and the city, brought periodic outbreaks of violence and damage to property.

Through the Middle Ages, powerful Roman families, such as the Orsini and Colonna, struggled for power and, toward the end of the thirteenth century, the pope transferred his residence from the Lateran, in the city, to the Vatican, along the opposite bank of the Tiber. In the early fourteenth century, while the pope was in Avignon—a virtual prisoner of the French king—a Roman politician, Cola di Rienzo (c. 1313–1354), attempted to refound an Italian state centered on Rome. His efforts were unsuccessful, and in 1377 the pope returned from Avignon.

RENAISSANCE AND REFORM

The return of the papacy to Rome marked the beginning of a new period of growth and prosperity, but it was another 70 years before the papacy was the unchallenged ruler in Rome. Pope Nicholas V (1397–1455; reigned 1447–1455) patronized artists, promoted pilgrimage, and gave impetus to the Renaissance. Subsequent popes constructed great monuments; for example, Sixtus IV (1414–1484; reigned 1471–1484) had the Sistine Chapel constructed, while Julius II (1443–1513; reigned 1503–1513), Leo X (1475–1521; reigned 1513–1521), and Clement VII (1487–1534; reigned 1523–1534) presided over the rebuilding of the Vatican and the construction of the present Saint Peter's Basilica. However, the invasion of the city by imperial forces in 1527 effectively brought this period of development to an end.

Pope Sixtus V (1520–1590; reigned 1585–1590) revived the city, enforced the law, had entire districts flattened for the construction of new broader streets, and reordered the administration of the church, the city, and the Papal States. Subsequently, the city developed, commerce grew, and Rome's princely families constructed great palaces, but Rome was not the leading city in Italy. Naples was larger, and the peninsula was divided into many polities.

A NATIONAL CAPITAL

Rome was capital of the Papal States until 1798, when—inspired by French revolutionary ideas—the Roman Republic was established. The state was short-lived and, in 1800, the pope's sovereignty was restored. In 1809, Rome and the surrounding region were annexed to France, but the Papal States were reestablished in 1814. At this time, the population of Rome was around 177,000, and Rome was just one of a number of Italian cities that were national capitals. However, the legacy of the Roman Empire endured and, to many Italians, Rome was regarded as the only choice for the capital of a united Italy. In 1849, a short-lived Roman Republic was declared. The tide of Italian nationalism eventually reached Rome in 1870, when French troops, which had been protecting the pope, withdrew. Subsequently, forces of the new kingdom of Italy (founded in 1861) invaded, and the pope, who refused the offer of retaining the Leonine City (the modern district of Borgo, surrounding the Vatican), withdrew to the Vatican, declaring that he considered himself a prisoner in the Vatican.

Rome became the capital of Italy. At the time, the city had a population of 245,000, but, with the national government transferred to Rome from Florence and the establishment of a national transportation network centered on Rome, the city rapidly grew, reaching a population of 440,000 in 1893, 542,000 in 1911, 689,000 in 1922, and 1,008,000 by 1931. In 1929, the Lateran Treaties created the State of the Vatican City, restoring papal sovereignty in a small area surrounding Saint Peter's Basilica. Under the dictatorship of Benito Mussolini (1883–1945; in office as prime minister 1922–1943), Rome was modernized; boulevards, such as the Via della Conciliazone, were created; and new districts, such as the EUR (Esposizione Universale Roma, but always referred to by its initials), Trullo, and Garbatella, were constructed. During World War II (1939–1945), Rome was exempted from Allied military actions and, as a result, remained unscathed.

THE MODERN CITY

Rome is a living museum of more than three thousand years of history. Its historic buildings attract many tourists as well as Catholic pilgrims to the Vatican. Remains from ancient Rome center on the Forum, the urban space around which the Roman city grew. The Forum contains pillars and other remnants of nine temples, as well three basilicas and four monumental arches. The most famous Roman building in the city is the Colosseum, the largest Roman amphitheater ever built. The domed Pantheon, the best-preserved of all Roman buildings, has been a Catholic church since the seventh century CE. Other outstanding reminders of Rome's imperial past include the Baths of Caracalla, the catacombs, the remains of the Appian Way (Roman road), and Castel Sant'Angelo, which was built as a mausoleum for Emperor Hadrian (76–138 CE; reigned 117–138 CE).

Medieval Rome is represented by churches, such as Santa Maria Maggiore, and defensive towers, such as Torre dei Conti. Many of the major public buildings in Rome are Renaissance and baroque, including Piazza del Campidoglio and the neighboring Palazzo Senatorio (the city hall). Rome has many palaces constructed for the city's princely families, including the Farnese, Barberini, and Chigi palaces—the latter is the official residence of the Italian prime minister—and papal residences, such as the Quirinale Palace, which from 1870 to 1946 was the royal palace and is now the residence of Italy's president. The Palazzo Madama now houses the Senate, while the Palazzo Montecitorio is home to the Chamber of Deputies. The most famous example of baroque art in Rome is the huge Trevi Fountain. Renaissance and baroque church architecture includes the Cathedral of Saint John Lateran and Saint Peter's Basilica.

The city's sights include Roman columns and statues; elegant parks, such as the landscaped grounds of the Villa Borghese and the Villa Ada; the Spanish Steps, a flight of 138 steps rising from the Piazza di Spagna; and upscale shopping streets, such as Via Condotti. Famous museums and galleries include the Borghese Gallery, the Capitoline Museums, the Museum of Roman Civilization, and the National Museum of Rome, as well as the great collections of the Vatican Museums.

Rome has two international airports (Fiumicino and Ciampino). The subway system is limited—construction has been constantly delayed by archaeological excavations. The city is the seat of the national government and headquarters of most of Italy's major corporations as well as being a media center, the home of one of Europe's largest film industries (at the Cinecittà studios), a major retail center, and an educational center, with many pontifical universities and institutes as well as La Sapienza—a fourteenth-century university that is the largest in Europe in terms of student numbers (around 150,000 students)—and two major public universities. Rome is characterized by the large number of Catholic seminarians and priests, nuns, and other members of religious orders studying or in administrative posts in the church.

Industries in Rome include food processing, banking, electronics and electrical engineering, aerospace industries, clothing and footwear, engineering, printing and publishing, and a wide variety of consumer goods. In modern times, the city's population has increased, in part, owing to an influx of immigrants from eastern Europe (particularly Romania and Poland) and from Africa.

C. CARPENTER

Florence

Florence (in Italian, Firenze) is the capital of the region of Tuscany. In 2008, the metropolitan area had a population of 429,000, while 365,000 people lived within the city limits.

The city of Florence is situated along the Arno River in a basin, surrounded by hills. The historic downtown area is a UNESCO World Heritage site, and the city, which is famous for its art collections and architecture, is often claimed to have been the birthplace of the Renaissance.

FLORENCE IN HISTORY

Florence was founded by the Romans as a military settlement in 59 BCE. The city was taken by the Ostrogoths as the Roman Empire collapsed in the fifth century CE. From the sixth century CE, it was part of the Lombard kingdom and, in the eighth century CE, it became part of Tuscany, whose capital was Lucca. Around 1000, the ruler of Tuscany moved his capital to Florence, and the city began to develop rapidly as a regional center and the base of a flourishing decorative art industries.

Florence became a republic in 1208, and the city-state became dominated by the de' Medici family, who were bankers to the pope, in the late fourteenth century. Cosimo de' Medici (1389–1464; leader of the Florentine Republic 1434–1464) made Florence into Europe's greatest banking center and was a patron of the arts. His grandson, Lorenzo I de' Medici (1449–1492; in office 1478–1492), was called the "ideal Renaissance prince" for his learning and patronage of artists Leonardo da Vinci (1452–1519), Sandro Botticelli (c.1445–1510), and Michelangelo (Michelangelo di Lodovico Buonarroti Simoni; 1475–1564).

In the late fifteenth century, Girolamo Savonarola (1452–1498; ruler of Florence 1494–1498), first vicar-general of the Dominicans, attempted to set up an ascetic Christian republic, but he was ousted by the Florentines, tried for heresy, and executed. The de' Medicis returned to power in Florence in 1512 and, in 1531, became hereditary dukes of Florence. In 1569, the de' Medicis became grand dukes of Tuscany and, under the dynasty, the city became the leading artistic and commercial center of central Italy. Until their extinction, they ruled Tuscany, filling palaces with great art collections (which now attract tourists).

Florence then became the seat of various branches of the Austrian Hapsburg dynasty, who ruled the grand duchy (except for 1801–1814, when French puppet states were established) until 1860, when Tuscany was annexed by Sardinia-Piedmont during the unification of Italy. From 1865 through 1870, Florence was the capital of Italy. During World War II (1939–1945), Florence was occupied by German forces from 1943 to 1944. In the fall of 1966, the Arno River burst its banks, severely damaging many of the city's art treasures.

THE MODERN CITY

Florence maintains many medieval and Renaissance churches and palaces. Florence's city hall, the Palazzo Vecchio, has a tall tower, built in 1299. The sixteenth-century Uffizi Palace is lined by great colonnades. The largest palace, the Pitti Palace, was largely created in the sixteenth century for the city's dukes. Behind the palace, the Boboli Gardens, famous for water features and statues, occupy a natural amphitheater. The vast Strozzi Palace is a fifteenth- and sixteenth-century structure; the Medici Palace is a fifteenth-century building. Ecclesiastical buildings include the large medieval Santa Maria Novella (Dominican) and Santa Croce (Franciscan) churches; the church of San Lorenzo; and the cathedral, the Duomo, whose dome is a symbol of the city.

The service sector dominates Florence's economy, and tourism is the city's main industry. The university, founded in 1321, has more than 60,000 students, making it one of the largest in Italy. Florence also caters to large numbers of foreign (including many U.S.) students. Industries include food processing, furniture, textiles, chemicals, and engineering (including steam turbines), with most of the industrial facilities located in the outer suburbs. The city has a clothing and footwear industry (with firms such as Gucci) and was, until the last quarter of the twentieth century, the center of the Italian fashion industry. Near the downtown area, many decorative artists produce leatherwork, ceramics, glass, and other craft items. Gold and silverware are sold in tiny shops along the Ponte Vecchio, a bridge that is lined by sixteenth-century buildings overhanging the Arno.

The city is a route hub, the focus of railroads and roads in northern central Italy. Privately owned cars are banned from the historic downtown area. Florence has an airport that handles domestic and European flights, but the greater part of international air traffic in the region uses Pisa airport. Florence hosts important music and arts festivals, including the annual May arts festival, and colorful medieval festivals, such as Saint John's Day in June.

C. CARPENTER

Milan

Milan (in Italian, Milano) had a population in the metropolitan area of 2,983,000 in 2008 (Italian government estimate). In the same year, some 1,300,000 people lived within the city limits.

The Milan area is Italy's largest industrial region. The city, which is the financial and commercial capital of Italy, is characterized by a high population density and has fewer open spaces and more high-rise buildings than other major Italian agglomerations.

The triumphal arch leading into the Galleria Vittorio Emanuele II.

THE DEVELOPMENT OF MILAN

Rome conquered the Milan area in 222 BCE, founding the city, which became an important regional center. In 313 CE in the Edict of Milan, Christians were given freedom to practice their religion in the Roman Empire. Huns overran Milan in 452 CE; in 539 CE, Ostrogoths captured and largely destroyed the city; and, in 569 CE, the Lombards took Milan.

When, in 774 CE, Franks conquered the area, Milan was incorporated into what became the Holy Roman Empire. The city flourished as a trading center, benefiting from the rich local agriculture and trade routes to the north through Alpine passes. Along with other cities in the region, Milan was a member of the Lombard League, which won independence from the Holy Roman Empire in 1183. Milan subsequently became a hereditary seigniory and, from 1395, a duchy, ruled by the Visconti dynasty from 1317 to 1447. The Viscontis and their eventual successors, the Sforzas (who reigned from 1450 to 1535), constructed public buildings, churches, and palaces and greatly extended the duchy across Lombardy.

The French occupied the city from 1499 to 1512 and 1515 to 1525 and, after the extinction of the Sforzas in 1535, the city and duchy passed to Spain (until 1714) and Austria (1714–1797). French forces occupied Milan in 1797, and the city was subsequently the capital of two French puppet states, the Cisalpine Republic and, after 1805, the kingdom of Italy. In 1814, the region returned to Austrian rule, against which it unsuccessfully rebelled in 1848. In 1859, Sardinian-Piedmontese and French forces wrested Lombardy from Austrian rule and, in 1861, Sardinia-Piedmont became the new kingdom of Italy.

As part of Italy, Milan benefited from the construction of the national railroad network, of which it became a hub, and the industrialization of the nation. Large numbers of rural poor left southern Italy to settle in Milan to work in new factories. As a result, the city's population grew from 178,000 in 1859 to 262,000 in 1871, 322,000 in 1881, 492,000 in 1901, 663,000 in 1913, and 992,000 in 1931. During World War II (1939–1945), Milan was occupied by German forces (1943–1944) and was severely damaged by Allied bombing.

THE MODERN CITY

Milan is the fashion capital of Italy, the stage of haute couture shows and the home of some of the world's most famous upscale fashion houses. The main retail districts of boutiques selling luxury goods, clothes, and footwear are Galleria Vittorio Emanuele (which is often claimed to be the world's oldest shopping mall) and Via Montenapoleone.

The city has a large service sector and is home to banks, insurance companies, commercial corporations, and the Italian stock exchange, the Borsa Italiana. Milan is a media center with publishing, newspaper, radio, and television companies, and it is the center of the Italian advertising industry. The city is also home to two of Europe's strongest soccer teams, Internazionale (known as Inter Milan) and AC Milan; the rivals share San Siro stadium.

At Rho in the outer suburbs, the largest trade fair and exhibition facility in the world has, since 2005, been home to the famous Feria Milano, the city's influential trade fair. Industries include electrical and electronic engineering, food processing, a wide range of consumer goods, textiles (including silk), aerospace industries, automobiles (including Alfa Romeo), chemicals, and engineering. In modern times, Milan has a flourishing tourist industry. Visitors are attracted to sights such as the Duomo, the cathedral—one of the largest in the world—which is characterized by many spires; Castello Sforzesco, the Sforza family's castle, now housing Milan's museum and art galleries; the famous opera house, La Scala; and the church of Santa Maria delle Grazie, with the *Last Supper* by Leonardo da Vinci (1452–1519).

Roads and railroads converge on the city, which has a subway system, suburban railroads (brought into the downtown area through the Passante, a railroad tunnel across the city), trolleys, tramways, and two international airports, Malpensa and Linate. The city is an educational center, with more than a dozen institutions of university status. The Biblioteca Ambrosiana, which houses Leonardo's drawings and notebooks, is a huge library collection and one of the greatest treasures of European culture.

C. CARPENTER

Naples

The largest city in southern Italy, Naples, the capital of the region of Campania, had a population in the metropolitan area of 2,229,000 in 2008 (Italian government estimate), when some 973,000 people lived within the city limits.

The beauty of the site of Naples, around the Bay of Naples between Posillipo headland and Sorrento Peninsula and at the foot of Mount Vesuvius, is famous. In modern times, the suburbs of Naples stretch toward the dormant volcano, and large districts in the eastern outer city are vulnerable to any future eruption.

from poor southern rural districts into the cities in search of employment boosted the population of Naples from 533,000 in 1893 to 678,000 in 1911 and 839,000 in 1931. Naples developed as an industrial city but suffered considerable damage as a result of Allied campaigns in 1943 during World War II.

NAPLES IN HISTORY

Naples was founded by Greeks in the seventh century BCE, and the city flourished as a center of Hellenistic culture. The name Naples derives from the Greek Neapolis, meaning "new city." In the fourth century BCE, it came under Roman rule, but the city maintained its Greek culture during the Roman Empire, and the area became a favorite resort of Roman emperors. In 79 CE, Vesuvius erupted, burying the towns of Pompeii and Herculaneum.

When the Roman Empire fell, the area was invaded by Ostrogoths but eventually became part of the Eastern Roman Empire (or Byzantine Empire) in the sixth century CE. By the ninth century CE, Naples was an independent duchy, but by the early twelfth century, Normans had taken control of most of the formerly independent principalities in the region. Naples was the last of these states to fall to the Normans in 1137. The Normans then joined Naples to their kingdom of Sicily. In 1266, when the Angevin dynasty was expelled from Sicily, the ousted king reestablished himself in Naples, founding the kingdom of Naples, which lasted in various forms for seven centuries.

In 1442, the crown of Naples passed to the kings of Aragón. Although the kingdom was ruled by Spanish viceroys, Naples became one of the leading cities and cultural centers of Europe. It became a center of trade, banking, and the Renaissance. Spain lost Naples in 1714, and a junior branch of the Spanish Bourbon dynasty succeeded to the throne of Naples.

Under its Bourbon kings, Naples was the second-largest city in Europe, and, by 1750, Naples had a population of 305,000. By 1820, Naples had 450,000 people but, for most of the rest of the nineteenth century, the city experienced a relative decline, particularly after 1861, when it lost its status as a national capital, a role Naples had enjoyed for centuries. By 1881, the population of Naples was 494,000. From the late nineteenth century, a wave of migration

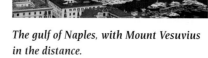

The gulf of Naples, with Mount Vesuvius in the distance.

MODERN NAPLES

Naples has a distinctive character reflected in its cuisine (famous for pizza, which was invented in the city), its strong local dialect, its musical heritage (particularly opera), and its somewhat faded yet elegant public buildings. The city has extensive poor districts, which contrast with the prosperity of some outer suburbs. It remains the leading port of southern Italy, but its trade is considerably diminished. Ferries from the port link Naples with Sicily, Sardinia, and other Italian islands. Naples has trolley and bus networks, cog railroads, a suburban railroad system, and a subway, as well as an international airport.

The city's industries include food processing, wine, textiles (which developed from the eighteenth-century silk industry), car assembly, electrical and electronic engineering, iron and steel, metalworking, and petroleum refining. Government encouragement after World War II broadened the range of industries in Naples, and many of the corporations that established operations in the city were state-owned. Naples has a range of service industries, including tourism. Visitors are attracted by the bay and by the city's medieval, Renaissance, and baroque architecture. The city centers around Piazza del Plebiscito, which is lined by the seventeenth-century royal palace and the classical domed church of San Francesco di Paola with its white colonnades. The San Carlo theater, one of the oldest opera houses in the world, adjoins the palace, and the famous Galleria Umberto shopping arcade is opposite the theater. Other public buildings include the thirteenth-century Castelo Nuovo; the Castel dell'Ovo, a Norman castle on a small island; and the medieval cathedral, which contains a vial of the blood of Saint Gennaro (believed to liquefy twice a year). Overlooking the city, the eighteenth-century Capodimonte Palace contains a major art collection, while the archaeological museum houses artifacts from Pompeii and Herculaneum.

C. CARPENTER

Palermo

The largest city and capital of the island of Sicily, Palermo had a population of 852,000 in the metropolitan area in 2007 (Italian government estimate), when some 663,000 people lived within the city limits.

Palermo lies along the northwest coast of Sicily, around the Gulf of Palermo, which forms a natural harbor on the Tyrrhenian Sea. To the south, a restricted fertile plain, the Conca d'Oro (literally, "shell of gold"), is lined by mountains, which protect Palermo on the landward sides.

PALERMO IN HISTORY

Palermo is more than 2,700 years old, having been founded by the Phoenicians in the eighth century BCE. The settlement eventually passed to the Carthaginians, Phoenicians who founded an empire centered in Carthage (in modern Tunisia), but the port was also contested by Greeks, who controlled eastern Sicily from Syracuse (modern Siracusa). The Greeks gave the city the name Panormus (meaning "all port"), from which Palermo derives. In 254 BCE, Palermo was captured by the Romans, and it remained part of the Roman Empire until 440 CE, when it was overrun by the Vandals. In 488 CE, the Ostrogoths ousted the Vandals.

In 535 CE, the Eastern Roman Empire (the Byzantine Empire) retook Palermo, which remained under Byzantine rule until 831 CE, when Arabs from North Africa captured the city and made it the capital of their emirate of Sicily. The city prospered, trading with Muslim Spain and North Africa, and it replaced Syracuse as the principal city of the island. In 1072, a Norman army invaded Sicily, ousting the Arabs, and established the kingdom of Sicily, with Palermo as its capital. Under Norman rule from 1072 through 1194, the city was embellished with royal, defensive, and ecclesiastical buildings, and Palermo was the capital of one of the richest kingdoms in Europe. The golden age of Palermo continued under the German Hohenstaufen dynasty, and Frederick II (1194–1250; reigned as Holy Roman emperor, 1212–1250 and as Frederick I, king of Sicily, 1197–1250) established his court in Palermo.

Under the succeeding French Angevin dynasty, Palermo lost much of its importance. The unpopular Angevins were deposed in Sicily in a revolt, the Sicilian Vespers (1282), which began at the Church of the Holy Spirit, near Palermo. Taking advantage of the rebellion, King Peter III of Aragón (1239–1285; reigned as Peter III of Aragón, 1276–1285 and Peter I of Sicily, 1282–1285) landed an

Palermo Cathedral, founded in 1185.

army and proclaimed himself king of Sicily. Palermo began a long period of decline under Spanish monarchs, particularly after 1412, when the crowns of Sicily and Aragón were merged and Sicily was ruled by absentee monarchs. Spanish rule continued until 1713, when the kingdoms of Naples and Sicily were united as the Two Sicilies. However, the capital of the kingdom was Naples, and Palermo lost status.

Along with the rest of the Two Sicilies, Palermo became part of the kingdom of Italy in 1861, when the city had a population of 195,000. By 1881, Palermo had 245,000 inhabitants, rising to 390,000 by 1931. During World War II (1939–1945), the city suffered much damage during the Allied invasion of Sicily (1943).

THE MODERN CITY

In modern times, Palermo has benefited from being the capital of Sicily, which gained autonomy within Italy in 1947. The city is a commercial, industrial, retail, and administrative center with food processing, chemical, engineering, consumer goods, ship repairing, machinery, glass, and cement industries. Most of the agricultural and mineral exports of Sicily pass through Palermo's port, which has regular passenger and commercial services to Naples and North Africa. Palermo has an international airport and receives many Italian and foreign tourists. However, the modern development of the city has been impeded by the perception that Mafia activity makes parts of the locality unsafe for business.

The principal sights of the city include the domed Norman cathedral, which incorporates additions of various periods up to the eighteenth century and is connected to the neighboring archbishop's palace by a spectacular arcade, and the former royal palace, Palazzo dei Normanni, which is largely Norman and includes the Palatine Chapel, famous for its twelfth-century mosaics. Other major buildings include Norman-Byzantine churches, such as the twelfth-century San Cataldo; the archaeological museum, which houses a major collection of ancient Greek and Etruscan artifacts; the early medieval Zisa and Cuba royal hunting lodges; the restored Teatro Massimo opera house; and the Capuchin Catacombs.

C. CARPENTER

Turin

The city of Turin, the capital of the region of Piedmont, had a population in the metropolitan area of 1,702,000 in 2008 (Italian government estimate), when some 908,000 people lived within the city limits.

Turin (in Italian, Torino) is a route hub, with river valleys converging on the site along the Po River. To the west and the north, the location is lined by the foothills of the Alps, while to the south the city is bordered by the Monferrato Hills.

THE DEVELOPMENT OF TURIN

A settlement on the site of Turin was destroyed by a Carthaginian invasion in 218 BCE. During the first century BCE, the Romans founded a military colony and, in modern times, parts of the walls as well as the imposing Palatine Towers (the best-preserved Roman remains in northern Italy) survive. After the fall of the Roman Empire in the fifth century CE, Turin was captured by the Lombards and was included in their kingdom until 773 CE, when the Franks overran the region.

In the eleventh century, a county was formed in Turin. Through much of the twelfth century, the local bishop ruled the county, which was eventually acquired by the Savoy dynasty in 1280. For the next six centuries, the fortunes of the city were linked with those of the Savoy family, and, in 1563, Turin became the capital of the duchy of Savoy. The dukes of Savoy gave the city public buildings, churches, and palaces, but Turin was vulnerable to invasion through Alpine passes from France. From 1536 through 1562, the city was occupied by the French, who again besieged the city in 1640 and 1706.

In 1718, the duke of Savoy gained the title of king of Sardinia—the kingdom was often referred to as Sardinia-Piedmont. The city fell to the French in 1798, and the king retreated to the island of Sardinia. The French occupation ended in 1814, and Turin was restored as a capital. Subsequently, it became the leading center of the *risorgimento* (the political movement that brought about Italian unification). In 1859–1860, Sardinia-Piedmont acquired Lombardy and then parts of central Italy; when the kingdom of Italy was proclaimed in March 1861, Turin was its first capital.

Turin grew from a population of 90,000 in 1820, to 137,000 in 1850, and 205,000 in 1858. However, after the loss of its status as a national capital in 1865, the city developed slowly, reaching a population of 253,000 by 1881. Rapid growth came in the early twentieth century, when Turin developed as an

Mole Antonelliana, a film museum and one of the city's major landmarks.

industrial center, and the population increased from 336,000 in 1901 to 427,000 in 1911, and 597,000 by 1931.

THE MODERN CITY

In modern times, the population of the city is decreasing while people and industry move into the outer suburbs and satellite towns. Consequently, the population of the overall metropolitan area is still growing. Turin is a major commercial, media, educational, industrial, transportation, retail, and administrative center with metallurgical, chemical, food processing (particularly chocolate), consumer goods, wine, paper, rubber, and electrical and electronic engineering industries, but the city is most famous for its automobile industry. Turin—home to Fiat, the largest Italian automobile corporation, and to Lancia—is responsible for the greater part of Italy's car production. Toward the end of the twentieth century, Turin diversified and encouraged high-tech industries, electronics, and computing. At the same time, the city's tourist industry grew, encouraged by staging the 2006 Winter Olympic Games.

Turin has a strong character, rooted in its own dialect, cuisine, and institutions. Its citizens are divided in their allegiance to the city's two famous soccer clubs, Juventus and Torino. The city has a major university (founded in the fifteenth century), a polytechnic, and a renowned business school. Major improvements in transportation early in the twenty-first century included the construction of a subway system, new downtown arteries, and a major crosstown boulevard that runs over a realigned main railroad and new station. The city also has an international airport. The tourist industry mainly caters to European visitors who are attracted to the city's many sights: its Roman ruins; the seventeenth-century former royal palace, the Palazzo Reale, and other former royal palaces and castles; the Museo Egizio, which houses the finest ancient Egyptian collection outside Egypt; the basilica of Superga, on a hilltop reached by cog railroad; and the fifteenth-century cathedral, which houses the Turin Shroud, a linen cloth regarded by many as the grave cloth of Jesus, although detailed research suggests a more recent origin.

C. CARPENTER

ECONOMY

Italy is one of the G8 countries, the nations with many of the largest economies in the world. Italy is the world's seventh-largest industrial power, the sixth-largest exporter, and the seventh-largest importer of manufactured goods.

Through the second half of the twentieth century, the Italian economy grew rapidly. However, Italy is now facing the consequences of some of the economic choices of the past: a stagnating economy, differential development between the north and south, and the burden of a large national debt.

When Italy was unified in 1861, there were considerable differences between the developing regions in the north (Piedmont, Lombardy, Tuscany, and Emilia-Romagna), the center, and the poor, overpopulated northeast and the southern regions (the Mezzogiorno). The relative isolation of the protectionist economy of the south and the center kept the *latifundia* (huge estates usually specializing in a single crop) system alive, and this practice represented a significant obstacle to modernization. Although there were a few industrial facilities in southern Italy (some heavy industries and textile plants, all concentrated in a few areas), most of the Mezzogiorno was still under a feudal agricultural system, protected by heavy customs duties. The unification of Italy inexorably led southern enterprises to lose their market shares, while agriculture remained managed by a few families. The subsequent southern economic crisis led to a massive emigration wave, mostly to the Americas.

Despite a lack of natural resources, northern Italy started to develop heavy industries and small enterprises, thanks to entrepreneurial dynamism and geographical proximity to more developed countries, like Germany and France. The south continued to export agricultural products, but it was still unable to develop a modern economy.

During the Fascist era (1922–1945), Italy moved toward a corporatist system, with strong intervention by the state in the economy. Italy enjoyed moderate economic and social growth, mainly due to a vast program of public works and social services. However, there was an economic price to pay for some unwise choices made by the regime: currency appreciation; economic sanctions by the League of Nations (after the 1936 Italian invasion of Ethiopia); a poorly organized attempt to achieve self-sufficiency; and, then, extensive damage to the economy caused by involvement in World War II (1939–1945). After the war, the government sought to reconstruct the devastated country and to reduce the gap between north and south.

Italy was a major beneficiary of the Marshall Plan (a program of U.S. economic aid for the reconstruction of Europe from 1948 through 1952). The country experienced an "economic miracle" driven by entrepreneurs in the 1950s and 1960s. Encouraged by membership in the European Economic Community (EEC, now the European Union or EU)—of which Italy was a founding member—the country built a modern manufacturing sector based mostly on steelworks and achieved a high quality of design and technology. The importance of agriculture was reduced, and industry surpassed agriculture in 1961.

As in the past, the north remained the center of industry and services, winning a valuable share of world markets for clothes, automobiles, chemicals, and engineering products, while the Mezzogiorno remained oriented toward farming. The south also provided the labor force for the northern industrial boom through large-scale internal migration.

ECONOMIC CHALLENGES

After a nationalization policy, introduced in 1963, strengthened the already conspicuous role of the state in the economy, the 1960s and 1970s saw an economic slowdown. In this period, social conflict, a high inflation rate, and the consequences of the 1973 oil crisis (when oil prices rose dramatically) all seriously risked undermining economic growth. Italy, however, experienced another economic boom in the 1980s, which saw the service sector becoming the dominant part of the economy. This growth, however, was achieved at a price: the uncontrolled growth of the national debt, which in 2008 amounted to 106.8 percent of GDP (gross domestic product, the total value of all the goods and services produced in a country in a fixed term, usually one year). This level of indebtedness is the second-highest rate in Europe, and addressing high levels of debt is just one of the challenges still facing the Italian economy.

Milan is known for its shopping and high fashion.

Curbing high rates of public expenditure is also a challenge. Through the 1970s and 1980s, there was a proliferation of lobbies and special interest groups, each promoting a particular region, city, or industry and lobbying for public funding for it. Because of the many parties and coalition governments that characterized public life before 1992, promising high public expenditure, in order to win electoral favor, was the norm.

From the 1990s, Italy implemented a tight fiscal policy and some privatizations of state-run industries in order to meet EU requirements. Previously, state-run industry and corporations formed a pyramid of state ownership, with the Istituto per la Ricostruzione Industrial (IRI; Institute for Industrial Reconstruction), a public holding company created in 1932 to counteract the effects of the Great Depression, at the top. Below the IRI were state-owned financial holding companies, each controlling state enterprises in a different sector. The lower layer of the pyramid comprised controlled corporations, such as Alitalia, the state airline; SIP, the state telecommunications company; and ENI, the national hydrocarbons agency, which is a world leader in the energy sector. The IRI was closed in 2000, and through the other layers of the pyramid, partial and full privatizations occurred, for example, Mediobanca SpA, the country's largest merchant bank, was partially privatized.

Through a tight monetary policy and privatization, inflation (previously high) was brought under control and interest rates were kept low. However, the adoption of the euro (the common currency of the EU) in 2002 removed some financial control from the Italian authorities. In 2008, Italy's GDP growth rate was 1.9 percent, after four years of stagnation. However, as an international slowdown in 2008 deepened, a contraction of the Italian economy was expected.

The country has faced a number of challenges associated with competition and wage demands. The private sector is characterized by small firms; around 98 percent of Italian companies employ fewer than 20 people, and, in the early twenty-first century, the number of larger firms decreased. As a result, Italy has fewer large corporations that are able to benefit from economies of scale than many other nations. Competition from manufacturers in East Asia, which benefit from lower labor costs, has affected Italian industry, and rising energy prices in a country that is heavily reliant upon energy imports have also tilted the balance of trade against Italy. Stronger competition from emergent economies led many enterprises—discouraged by bureaucracy, a heavy tax burden, and high labor costs in Italy—to outsource production to eastern Europe and eastern Asia, or to close down.

Some problems remain to be solved: the influence of lobbies and pressure groups, bureaucracy, corruption, public debt, a lack of innovation, and excessive reliance on state intervention. The taxation system is also not conducive to enterprise. Although there is a relatively small number of direct and indirect taxes, there is a large number of marginal and local taxes, often levied on a regional or municipal basis. Labor costs are generally lower than the western European average, but strikes and industrial action have been a constant feature.

In modern times, Italian workers are subject to the sixth highest level of taxation in the world. Incomes have declined in the

Gondolas are the traditional form of transportation in Venice.

early twenty-first century relative to the rest of Europe; for example, Spanish incomes have overtaken Italian ones. The introduction of new, more flexible contracts for workers has improved productivity but also generated much discontent among young people, who are often in a less secure employment situation. According to a 2006 survey, 15 percent of Italian families experience difficulties in balancing their monthly budget, and qualified people, especially in the south, are often forced to take low-paid and low-skilled jobs.

The relative underdevelopment of the Mezzogiorno remains. From 1950 through 1984, the state-funded Cassa per il Mezzogiorno (Southern Development Fund) initiated public works and fiscal subsidies for the region. However, these measures did not have the desired effect. New southern enterprises were unable to withstand competition when subject to a free-market environment, and many new businesses were short-lived or started simply for speculation purposes. In a few years, heavy industries introduced to the south became underutilized and expensive to run, and they were popularly nicknamed "cathedrals in the desert." There were some successes, however, such as the large modern steelworks erected at Taranto. At the same time, the public sector grew rapidly, making the Mezzogiorno dependent on state and civil service jobs and welfare. Moreover, organized crime, an inefficient transportation network, and bureaucracy discouraged foreign investments in the south. In the Mezzogiorno, the unemployment rate was approximately 20 percent in 2007, far above the national average of 6 percent in the same year. In the past, there were conspicuous population displacements from the rural areas of the south to the industrialized north and to Rome, which both needed a considerable workforce, but, in the twenty-first century, such movement from the south is minimal.

Today, the north contributes nearly 55 percent of Italy's GDP, more than double the contribution of the Mezzogiorno. Northern Italian politicians have highlighted the difference between the great contribution made by the north to the national economy and the far smaller receipt of government and EU funds by the region, when compared with the Mezzogiorno. As a result, some separatist and regionalist parties, such as the Northern League (Liga), now effectively part of the (center-right) People of Freedom (PdL) party, have emerged.

ITALY
Industry and Resources

- Principal gas fields
- ✈ Aerospace industries
- Agricultural industries
- 🚗 Auto construction
- Building materials/Cement
- Chemicals
- Clothing/Footwear
- Consumer goods
- Decorative arts
- Electronics
- Engineering
- Entertainment
- Fishing
- Food processing
- Glass
- Iron and steel
- Metalworking
- Petroleum refining
- Printing and publishing
- $ Services/Commerce
- Shipbuilding
- Textiles
- Timber
- Tourism

Alps

Bolzano-Bozen
Aosta (Fe)
Varese   Como
Monza   Trento   Udine
Novara   Bergamo   Vicenza
(As)   Milan   Brescia   Verona   Treviso
Turin   Piacenza   Venice   Trieste
Alessandria   Padua
Reggio nell'Emilia   Ferrara
Genoa   Modena   Bologna
San Remo   Parma   Ravenna
La Spezia (M)   Massa
Lucca   Prato   Rimini
Pisa   Florence   Pesaro
Livorno   Arezzo   Ancona
(Fe) (F)
Perugia
Tiber
Terni   Pescara
L'Aquila

Ligurian Sea

Adriatic Sea

ROME
Latina   Campobasso   Foggia
Caserta   Barletta
Naples   Andria   Bari
Salerno   Potenza (Bx)   Brindisi
Taranto   Lecce

Tyrrhenian Sea

Gulf of Taranto

Sassari
(F)
Cagliari
Sarroch

Mediterranean Sea

Catanzaro

Ionian Sea

Palermo   Messina (Pc)
Marsala   Reggio di Calabria
Catania
Augusta
Siracusa

Strait of Sicily

N

Transportation
- —— Major roads
- —— Minor roads
- —— Major railroads
- ✈ Major airports
- ⊗ Major ports

Mineral deposits
- (Fe) Iron ore
- (As) Asbestos
- (M) Marble
- (Bx) Bauxite
- (Pc) Pumice
- (F) Feldspar

0	50	100 miles
0	80	160 km

Italy has traditionally been a country of emigration, but, in modern times, it is no longer an exporter of labor, but an importer. Some 3 million foreigners live and work in the country, often taking low-paid jobs. Many of the most recent migrants have come from eastern Europe, especially Romania, Albania, and Kosovo, and they, along with the growing population of North and sub-Saharan Africans, have encountered some difficulties integrating into Italian society. Although migrants provide labor, there is a growing public expense catering to their needs and welfare.

Another economic challenge facing Italy is addressing the large unofficial economy. The unofficial economy is unrecorded, untaxed, and often associated with criminality. Small illegal enterprises are particularly characteristic of the Mezzogiorno. In this unrecorded sector, wages are low, and there are no benefits or public assistance for workers. Fiscal fraud and tax evasion are high, even in the recorded sector. Inquiries by public prosecutors in the early 1990s brought to light a pervasive system of corruption in politics, based on bribes, exchange of favors, and nepotism. Corruption in business is still perceived to exist in places.

Another serious issue is the role that organized crime plays in the economy. The crime families of the Mafia are active in the legal economy, both through money laundering and in setting up legal businesses. Early in the twenty-first century, it was estimated that the revenues of enterprises linked to, or owned by, organized crime in Italy accounted for 7 percent of GDP. Criminal organizations, besides preventing the freedom of enterprise through unfair competition, are responsible for acts of sabotage and racketeering, interception of EU funds, and infiltration in public works.

An olive grove; Italy is the world's largest exporter of olive oil.

Although the struggle against the Mafia and its network reported some successes early in the twenty-first century, *ecomafia* (environmental crime committed by Mafia gangs) was widely reported and is a worrying phenomenon; bribery in the waste disposal industry cost people heavily in terms of environmental pollution, especially in the area around Naples, which suffered a prolonged garbage collection strike as a result in 2008.

According to most international observers, the Italian economy needs serious structural reform in order not to be disadvantaged by global competition. Commentators highlight imbalances in regional development, organized crime, public indebtedness, a taxation system that discourages enterprise, and overdependence on imports as the principal challenges to be addressed.

NATURAL RESOURCES

Italy has natural resources (some oil, natural gas, marble, and minerals), but their quantity is inadequate for the needs of local industry. The paucity of its natural resources, in part, accounts for Italy's late industrialization. Consequently, Italy imports most of the raw materials it requires.

Iron ore is commercially exploited on the island of Elba, but only on a small scale. Other iron deposits at Cogne, in Valle d'Aosta, are no longer commercially viable. There are deposits of pyrites in Tuscany, asbestos in Piedmont, fluorite and sulfur in Sicily, and bauxite in Puglia. All these are mined, but because the most easily accessible deposits have been exploited, none is now of international significance, and Italy has to import additional minerals. However, Italy is a major producer of stone, including the famous white marble of Massa and Carrara, and is the world's largest producer of pumice and feldspar.

Small coal fields in Tuscany are no longer worked, and Italy is a major coal importer, shipping coal from Russia, the United States, and South Africa. The nation is an energy importer and, as a result, is extremely vulnerable to fluctuations in oil and natural gas prices. A small oil field off the coast of Sicily is exploited, as are gas fields in Lombardy, off the Sicilian coast, and (more importantly) under the Adriatic Sea. Natural gas production is now enough to allow exports. Hydroelectric power plants (mainly in the Alps) provide a fraction of Italy's energy needs, and nuclear energy was abandoned after a national referendum on nuclear power in 1987. Some 75 percent of the nation's energy must be imported, and the main supplier is Libya, a major oil exporter. Italy also imports electricity from neighboring countries.

AGRICULTURE

Until the rapid industrialization and land reform of the 1950s, Italy was a largely agricultural country. In modern times, on the other hand, agriculture supplies only 1.9 percent of the nation's GDP and, along with forestry and fishing, employs just 5 percent of the workforce. Arable land covers 26.4 percent of the national territory, and another 9.1 percent is permanent cropland.

farms have considerably higher yields than holdings in the south. Italy also grows rice on large, highly mechanized farms in the lowlands of Lombardy and Piedmont, where irrigation water is available. The crop has been grown in Italy since the late fifteenth century and, in modern times, Italy is the leading European producer of rice, exporting around 60 percent of the crop.

The country is one of the world's greatest producers of olive oil and wine. Olive groves cover large areas of Sicily, Puglia, and Calabria, where, in some areas, olives are grown to the exclusion of other crops. Nearly every region of Italy grows grapes for wine, and there is great regional variation in the types of wine produced. Light, white quality wines, such as Asti, Soave, and Valpolicella, are produced in the north, while heavier, full-bodied reds from the south make vermouth or marsala.

Tomatoes are a major crop in Emilia Romagna and Campania, and production greatly increased in the late twentieth century, with mechanization and improved cultivation methods. Much of the crop is exported. Italy is also an important exporter of citrus fruits, with most of the production coming from Sicily (which also grows almonds) and, to a lesser extent, Calabria and Campania. The north and central regions, especially Emilia Romagna, grow apples, peaches, pears, and plums, while Campania is famous for cherries. Horticulture produces a wide variety of vegetables for domestic use and export, and cut flowers for export.

Despite the pre–World War II policy of self-sufficiency, Italian farms cannot produce enough food to feed the nation. Production is high quality, and exports include fruits, rice, wine, olive oil and flowers. Italy imports large quantities of meat, cattle, wheat, and corn, with meat being the main food import. Around one-sixth of Italy is pastureland, with sheep being mainly kept in the south and cattle, pigs, and poultry in the north. Buffalo are raised in Tuscany and near Naples for their milk, which is made into mozzarella cheese. While Italy produces enough butter for the home market, much of the cows' milk production goes to the cheese industry, which produces gorgonzola and parmesan; meat production is relatively small and, in modern times, Italian farmers have difficulty competing with meat and dairy producers from other parts of the EU.

Italy's forests have been overexploited, particularly during the nineteenth century. Around 10 percent of the national territory is now wooded, and efforts have been made to reforest upland areas. More than four-fifths of the commercial woodland is broad-leafed, with coniferous forest largely confined to the north and the mountains, particularly in Trentino–Alto Adige. Chestnut forests in Calabria and the northern Apennines are commercially important. Sicily, Sardinia, Puglia, and the lowlands of Lombardy and Venetia have little woodland. Many areas are unsuitable for forestry because of seasonal drought.

The Italian fishing industry greatly increased its production through the second half of the twentieth century, but, in the early twenty-first century, there has been a significant contraction owing to overfishing in the Mediterranean Sea. The fleet comprises mainly small boats, many of which are family-owned and crewed, but, in modern times, some formerly productive small fishing ports have virtually ceased commercial activity. Italy, a major consumer of fish, now relies heavily upon imports.

STANDARD OF LIVING

Italy's 2007 per capita GDP—adjusted for purchasing power parity (PPP), a formula that allows a comparison of prices and living standards between countries—was $30,400. There are no recent official figures for the percentage of the Italian population living below the official poverty line.

EMPLOYMENT IN ITALY

Sector	Percentage of labor force
Agriculture, forestry, and fishing	5 percent
Industry	32.0 percent
Services	63.0 percent

Source: Italian Government 2001–2002

In 2007, 6 percent of the labor force was unemployed.

ITALY'S GDP

The gross domestic product (GDP) of Italy was $1.79 trillion in 2007. This figure is adjusted for purchasing power parity (PPP), an exchange rate at which goods in one country cost the same as goods in another. PPP allows a comparison between the living standards in different nations.

MAIN CONTRIBUTORS TO THE ITALIAN GDP

Agriculture	1.9 percent
Industry	28.9 percent
Services	69.2 percent

Source: European Union, 2007

Landholdings are typically small and family owned, and Italian farming is highly mechanized and specialized. In most of Italy, small farms are a relatively modern phenomenon. Until land reform in the 1950s, much of the land was organized in large estates owned by the aristocracy, and most farm workers were landless, working for poor wages, or were sharecroppers, renting land from an estate in return for a share of the crop. Reform redistributed land, and many workers gained small farms. The majority of these holdings—mostly in the Mezzogiorno and central Italy—are now regarded as being too small to be commercially viable and, without EU payments, many farmers would be unable to operate. Northern Italy, however, has traditionally had larger farms, particularly in the Po Valley, the nation's most fertile region.

In the 1920s and 1930s, a program to make Italy self-sufficient in food was implemented, and additional areas were planted with cereals. The lowlands of northern Italy grow soft wheat for bread and pizza, as well as corn and barley, while the south grows hard wheat, which makes pasta. Larger, more mechanized northern

INDUSTRY

Italian industry contributes 28.9 percent of the nation's GDP and employs 32 percent of the labor force. Traditionally, the state played an important role in the development of industry through a number of corporations, which are now either partly or fully privatized. However, large firms are greatly outnumbered by medium and small-scale enterprises.

Heavy metallurgical industries were the key to national industrial growth in the 1950s, and these enterprises are concentrated in Piedmont, Lombardy, and Liguria. The state-run steel industry was greatly expanded and, by the 1980s, Italy produced one-fifth of western Europe's steel. Reliant upon imports, state support, and unable to compete with foreign producers, the industry has since contracted, although Italy is still an important steel producer. Italian steel supplies many other industries including the automobile, domestic appliances, machine tools, and machinery (including textile machinery) industries.

The automobile industry is centered in and around Turin, the home of the Fiat corporation, which began production in 1899. Today, the company is still the largest car producer in Italy and also maintains facilities abroad, which produce versions of Fiat cars under license. Milan houses the Alfa Romeo and Lancia facilities, while other car factories are located in Brescia and Naples. Italian car production rapidly increased in the 1950s through 1970s, but since suffered from competition—except in the upscale end of the market—from Japanese producers. Ferrari cars, manufactured near Modena, symbolize the emphasis on elegance that has come to characterize so many luxury Italian goods.

Italian domestic appliance manufacturers include Zanussi, which makes refrigerators, freezers, and washing machines, and Olivetti, which was founded as a typewriter company in 1908 and now makes computing, telephone, and telecommunications equipment. Light manufacturing is more evenly spread across the national territory than engineering and heavy industry, which are largely centered in an industrial heartland that is bordered by Genoa, Milan, and Turin, in the north, although there are large industrial facilities, such as the steelworks at Taranto, in the Mezzogiorno, established by state funding.

One of the principal light industries is textiles, which first grew in medieval times when Tuscany was famous for silk and Lombardy specialized in woolen goods and textiles. The industry diversified into cottons and artificial fibers and the clothing industry. In modern times, Milan is one of the world's major fashion centers, producing upscale clothes as well as expensive

A hydroelectric power facility in the Italian Alps. Hydroelectric power provides a small portion of Italy's energy needs: the nation imports 75 percent of the energy it uses.

shoes and other leather goods. Design and style are part of the international appeal of Italian goods, including ceramics, glass, furnishings, and furniture. The chemical industry was originally centered in the production of dyes for the textile industry and fertilizer for agriculture. From the 1950s, a large petrochemical industry has developed, and Adriatic Sea natural gas boosted the industry and its diversification into artificial fibers and synthetic rubber.

Although the highest concentration of industrial facilities is in northern and central Italy, large industrial facilities are now also located in Puglia, Campania, and Sicily. Food processing is found in almost all urban areas and includes wine making, producing olive oil, making tomato paste, food packing, making cheese, and preserving fruits. Construction is also widespread and, in some years, employs more than 40 percent of the industrial workforce. As a result of globalization, the Italian manufacturing sector is facing serious challenges. Chinese imports have dramatically increased, and some Italian businesses cannot withstand competition from cheaper imported products, especially in the low-cost textile sector.

SERVICES

Italy has a long tradition in trading, due to its strategic geographical position and its financial institutions, some of which date back hundreds of years. More than 12 million Italians now work in the services sector, which contributes almost 70 percent of the GDP. The most developed sectors are commerce, finance, tourism, real estate, and information technology. The banking system includes large national banks as well as smaller regional or cooperative banks. Smaller banks were important in local development until modern times; in the 1990s, the country's financial sector underwent rationalization, and smaller banking and finance houses were absorbed by a few national banking groups. These groups own holdings and shares in nearly all the large industrial and tertiary corporations. Milan is the center of Italian finance and commerce and the seat of the country's principal stock exchange. The services sector also includes the activities of central, regional, and local governments, all of which—along with state-owned industries—are major employers.

Tourism almost surpasses manufacturing in revenues. Every corner of the country is visited by Italian and foreign tourists, from historical centers to mountain and beach vacation centers. The industry is a major source of foreign currency. Historic cities like

Venice, Florence, and Rome are visited by nearly 30 million people a year; vacation destinations include Alpine ski resorts, small Tuscan hill towns, and Adriatic beach resorts, and the country is the fifth-largest tourist center in the world.

TRADE

In 2007, Italy exported goods and services worth $501.4 billion and imported goods and services valued at $498.6 billion, giving the nation a small trading surplus. Italy is a net importer of energy, raw materials, and meat, and a net exporter of some foodstuffs, textiles and clothing, automobiles and machinery, and luxury goods. The principal exports are engineering products, textiles and clothing, machinery, automobiles and transportation equipment, chemicals, and food and wine. In 2006, the main recipients of exports from Italy were Germany (which took 13 percent of Italian exports), France (11 percent), Spain (7 percent), the United States (7 percent), Great Britain (6 percent), Switzerland, Belgium, Netherlands, Austria, and Japan.

In the same year, the main imports were engineering products, chemicals, transportation equipment, fuel and energy products (including electricity), minerals and nonferrous metals, and food. The principal sources of imports were Germany (17 percent), France (9 percent), China including Hong Kong (6 percent), the Netherlands (6 percent), Belgium (4 percent), Spain (4 percent), Great Britain, Belgium, the United States, Switzerland, Japan, and Libya. Membership in the EU greatly promoted Italian trade, which is overwhelmingly with other EU members. Competition from Greece, Spain, and Portugal was a challenge when those countries joined the common market, but, early in the twenty-first century, the expansion of the EU into central Europe and parts of the Balkans, regions in which living standards are rapidly rising, brought new trading opportunities.

TRANSPORTATION AND COMMUNICATION

The complex geography of Italy, its relatively long north-south extent, and extensive highlands have always caused difficulties in communications between the regions. After 1945, a huge

Chianina beef cattle, which come from the Val di Chiana, near Arezzo.

program of public works began, particularly in highway construction. Today, the country has 4,114 miles (6,621 km) of expressways in a national network, which is most extensive in the northern and central regions. There are 297,057 miles (478,067 km) of other paved roads in a highway system that covers 301,171 miles (484,792 km). Road transportation is the principal means of transit within Italy. Most goods are carried by trucks, and the reliance upon trucking fleets is regarded as excessive and environmentally damaging.

Italy's railroads are managed by a public company, Ferrovie dello Stato, which was partly privatized in 1992. There are 12,095 miles (19,460 km) of railroad track, of which lines between the major northern and central cities and commuter railroads in the agglomerations are the most used. The construction of high-speed railroads, the TAV (Treno Alta Velocita), has been slower than the development of similar networks in France, Spain, and Germany, in part because local opposition to some routes delayed the project. Those parts of the high-speed network connecting Rome with Florence and Florence with Bologna were open by the twenty-first century. The enlarged network running across northern Italy from Turin through Milan, Verona, and Padua to Venice and the north–south routes from both Milan and Padua to Bologna and on through Florence to Rome, and the Rome to Naples link are operational from 2009. As in Spain and France, the high-speed railroad is expected to compete successfully with domestic air services. The Italian railroad system operates at a loss, with rural tracks, particularly in the south, being subsidized by the state for social reasons. Milan, Turin, Genoa, Naples, Trieste, and Rome have tram, subway, and light railroad systems.

Italy has 24 international airports and 101 airports with paved runways. The national airline, Alitalia, is state-owned, but companies from all over Europe and other continents operate in the country, providing services to and from the leading airports: Fiumicino in Rome, and Malpensa and Linate in Milan. The principal general ports are Genoa, Livorno, Civitavecchia, Ravenna, Sarroch (Cagliari), Taranto, and Venice, while the main petroleum ports are Augusta, Bari, Savona, and Trieste. The largest port by far, in terms of cargo and number of containers handled, is Genoa, whose expansion is limited by local geography. Livorno and Piombino have absorbed some overflow from Genoa. Regular ferry services link Palermo, in Sicily, with Naples, and Cagliari, in Sardinia, with Genoa. There are also other ferry services to Sicily, Sardinia, and smaller islands. The busiest ferry route is the Messina Strait between Messina (Sicily) and Reggio di Calabria on the mainland. The strait is subject to storms and a natural whirlpool. For many years, the construction of a bridge across the strait, which is liable to earthquakes, was debated, but, in 2006, the project was abandoned.

The nation has a modern, fully automated telephone and telecommunications system, operating high-capacity cable and radio relay networks. In 2005, there were more than 25 million main telephone lines and more than 72 million mobile cellular phones in service. In 2007, nearly 30 million Italians had Internet access.

S. BRUNO

Malta

Malta is an archipelago of three main islands, strategically located in the center of the Mediterranean Sea, between the Italian island of Sicily and Tunisia, North Africa. Malta was inhabited from around 5200 BCE; it passed to the Phoenicians around 600 BCE and then the Carthaginians, before being captured by the Romans in 218 BCE. The island group formed part of the Roman and Byzantine empires before being invaded in 870 CE by Arabs, who held it until 1090, when Malta became part of the kingdom of Sicily. In 1530, Malta was ceded to the sovereign Catholic Order of Saint John (later known as the Knights of Malta), who held it until a French invasion in 1798. Captured by the British in 1800 and confirmed as a British colony in 1814, Malta remained under British rule until 1964. During World War II (1939–1945), Malta was heavily bombed by Italian and German forces and, because of the courage of the islanders, the British sovereign awarded Malta the George Cross (the highest British civilian medal for gallantry) on a collective basis. Since independence, Malta, which became a republic in 1974, has became a major transshipment center as well as a financial and tourist center. Malta joined the European Union (EU) in 2004.

GEOGRAPHY

Location	Islands in the Mediterranean Sea, south of Sicily (Italy)
Climate	Mediterranean climate with mild, wet winters and hot, dry summers
Area	122 sq. miles (316 sq. km)
Coastline	157 miles (253 km)
Highest point	Dingli 816 feet (249 m)
Lowest point	Mediterranean Sea 0 feet
Terrain	Low-lying, rocky plateaus; cliffs along the coast
Natural resources	Limestone
Land use	
Arable land	31.3 percent
Permanent crops	3.1 percent
Other	65.6 percent
Major rivers	None
Major lake	None
Natural hazards	Drought

METROPOLITAN AREAS, 2005 POPULATION

Urban population	91 percent
Valletta	203,000
Valletta city	6,000
Birkirkara	22,000
Qormi	17,000

The promenade and bay in Sliema.

Zabbar	15,000
Sliema	14,000
Fgura	11,000
Hamrun	10,000
Mosta	19,000
Saint Paul's Bay (San Pawl il-Bahar)	14,000
Naxxar	12,000
Zejtun	11,000
Rabat	11,000
Zebbug	11,000
Attard	11,000

Source: Maltese census authority, 2007

NEIGHBORS AND LENGTH OF BORDERS

No land borders

POPULATION

Population	410,000 (2007 government estimate)
Population density	3,361 per sq. mile (1,298 per sq. km)
Population growth	0.4 percent a year
Birthrate	10.3 births per 1,000 of the population
Death rate	8.3 deaths per 1,000 of the population
Population under age 15	16.4 percent
Population over age 65	13.9 percent
Sex ratio	106 males for 100 females
Fertility rate	1.5 children per woman
Infant mortality rate	3.8 deaths per 1,000 live births
Life expectancy at birth	
Total population	79.3 years
Female	81.6 years
Male	77.1 years

ECONOMY

Currency	Euro (EUR)
Exchange rate (2008)	$1 = EUR 0.68
Gross domestic product (2007)	$21.9 billion
GDP per capita (2007)	$53,400
Unemployment rate (2007)	6.3 percent
Population under poverty line (2007)	N/A
Exports	$3.28 billion (2007 CIA estimate)
Imports	$4.11 billion (2007 CIA estimate)

GOVERNMENT

Official country name	Republic of Malta
Conventional short form	Malta

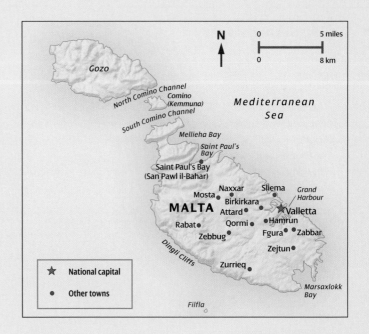

Nationality	
noun	Maltese
adjective	Maltese
Official languages	Maltese, English
Capital city	Valletta
Type of government	Republic; parliamentary democracy
Voting rights	18 years, universal
National anthem	"Innu Malti" (Hymn of Malta)
National day	Independence Day, September 21 (1964; independence from Great Britain)

FLAG

The flag of Malta comprises two vertical bands, from the hoist (the side next to the flagpole), white and red. These colors have been used for local flags since the eleventh century. An image of the George Cross—the highest British civilian medal for gallantry, which was collectively awarded to the Maltese people in 1942—appears in the canton (the upper quarter next to the hoist).

TRANSPORTATION

Railroads	None
Highways	1,384 miles (2,227 km)
Paved roads	1,251 miles (2,014 km)
Unpaved roads	133 miles (213 km)
Navigable waterways	None
Airports	
International airports	1
Paved runways	1

POPULATION PROFILE, 2007 ESTIMATES

Ethnic groups	
Europeans	more than 99 percent
Others	less than 1 percent
Religions	
Roman Catholic	98 percent; around two-thirds practicing
Others and nonreligious	2 percent
Languages	
Maltese	86 percent as a first language; understood by 98 percent
English	12 percent as a first language; understood by 76 percent
Italian	2 percent
Adult literacy	almost 93 percent

The Knights of Malta

The Sovereign Military Order of Malta—in full, the Sovereign Military Hospitaller Order of Saint John of Jerusalem, of Rhodes, and of Malta—is a Roman Catholic order that ruled Malta from 1530 through 1798. Previously, the knights had ruled the Greek island of Rhodes from 1310 through 1523, after they had been expelled from Palestine. The order was founded in 1050 to provide hospital care for poor and sick pilgrims in Jerusalem.

Despite losing its sovereign territory in 1798, when the French invaded Malta, the Knights of Malta are still recognized as a sovereign entity under international law and have diplomatic relations with more than 100 countries. The order has its own flag and passports and permanent observer status at the United Nations. The order still provides medical and emergency care for the poor, homeless, elderly, and others in many countries; it has some 12,500 members, around 80,000 volunteers, and employs about 13,000 medical personnel (doctors, nurses, and others).

A small minority of the 12,500 members are fully professed knights, who are members of a religious order, effectively monks. The Sovereign Council, the government of the order, is based in Rome, Italy, where its two main buildings have extraterritorial status (that is, they are not part of the Italian state). The Sovereign Council, along with other representatives of the fully professed knights, elect for life from their number the head of the order, who is known as the prince and grand master, with the title "most eminent highness." In 2008, Fra' Matthew Festing (born 1949), an English knight, was elected prince and grand master.

The megalithic temples of Hagar Qim.

CHRONOLOGY

c. 5200 BCE	Malta is inhabited by Neolithic (New Stone Age) people.
c. 3600–2300 BCE	Temples, now some of the oldest freestanding buildings in the world, are constructed in Malta.
c. 1000 BCE	Phoenicians from western Asia arrive in Malta.
c. 600–400 BCE	Greeks settle in Malta, founding a colony they call Melite (meaning "honeybee"). In 400 BCE, Malta becomes a Carthaginian possession.
218 BCE–440 CE	Malta is part of the Roman Empire. In 60 CE, Saint Paul is shipwrecked on Malta.
440–533 CE	The Vandals from North Africa occupy Malta.
533–870 CE	Malta is part of the Byzantine Empire and is incorporated into the Byzantine province of Sicily.
870 CE–1090	Arabs from North Africa occupy Malta.
1090	A Norman army from Sicily conquers Malta, which remains part of Sicily for four centuries. When Sicily becomes a Spanish possession in 1479, Malta also passes under Spanish rule.
1530	Malta is ceded to the sovereign Catholic Knights of Saint John (later known as the Knights of Malta), who had been ousted from Rhodes by the Ottoman Turks.
1565	The knights withstand a protracted siege by the Ottoman Turks.
1798–1800	The French invade the island, ousting the Knights of Malta. In 1800, British forces eject the French.
1814	British rule in Malta is confirmed by the Congress of Vienna. Under British rule, the natural harbor at Valletta attains importance along the seaward route to British India and Egypt.
1940–1942	The siege of Malta during World War II; Malta withstands a prolonged naval siege and aerial bombardment by Italian and German forces.
1955–1958	Proposals to integrate Malta into Great Britain gain majority support, but the project is abandoned in 1958.
1964	Malta gains independence from Great Britain as a dominion.
1974	Malta becomes a parliamentary republic.
2004	Malta becomes a member of the European Union (EU).
2008	Malta adopts the euro, the common currency of the EU.

GOVERNMENT

Malta has a parliamentary system of government, one in which power rests in the legislature rather than with the executive.

The chief of state of Malta is a president whose role is largely ceremonial. The president is elected for a nonrenewable five-year term by the Maltese legislature, the House of Representatives. The president represents Malta abroad, appoints and receives ambassadors, makes appointments to certain public offices (upon the recommendation of the prime minister), and invites the leader of the largest party in the legislature to form a government. The president may also, upon the advice of the prime minister, dissolve the legislature and call a legislative election.

THE GOVERNMENT AND THE LEGISLATURE

The respective powers of the different organs of government in Malta reflect the British system. The Maltese political system was originally based on the British model, evolving under the British colonial government before 1964. The government of Malta is run by a prime minister and other ministers, who are chosen by the premier to lead the eight ministerial departments. The government must enjoy a majority in the legislature, to which it is responsible.

The 65-member House of Representatives (Il-Kamra tar-Raprezentanti) is elected for five years by universal adult suffrage under the single transferable vote system of proportional representation. The voting age is 18 years and over. Members of the legislature are returned from 13 multiseat constituencies. When the relative representation in the legislature does not exactly reflect the percentage of first-preference votes cast—in part, owing to the percentage of votes cast for third and other parties—up to four additional members may be elected to more accurately reflect the percentage of the national vote achieved by the parties. At the legislative elections in 2008, four additional members were elected under this provision, which was introduced in 1987 to address the situation in legislative elections in 1981, when the party that gained an absolute majority of votes did not receive an absolute majority of seats.

POLITICAL PARTIES

Maltese politics is characterized by long-standing rivalry between two political parties, the (right-wing) Nationalist Party (Partit Nazzjonalista or PN) and the (left-wing) Labour Party (Partit Laburista or MLP). PN has been more in favor of membership in the European Union (EU) and has, traditionally, had close links with the Roman Catholic Church. MLP has a close relationship with organized labor. These two parties have dominated the political life of Malta since before independence; PN has won seven legislative elections since independence and MLP has won the other three. The divide between the two parties is deep, and newspapers and other media, organizations, and individual neighborhoods and families have strong political affiliations. In this environment, and because of the nature of the electoral system, it is difficult for a third party to flourish. The centrist (Green) Democratic Alternative (Alternattiva Demokratika) and the (far right) National Action (Azzjoni Nazzjonali), which opposes state intervention and immigration, contest elections but have not won a seat in the legislature.

LOCAL GOVERNMENT

Until modern times, Malta was generally considered to be too small to have a system of local government. Even in colonial times, before 1964, Malta had a centralized system of government, although a local council was established on the island of Gozo in the 1960s. In 1993, however, the country was divided into 68 local government areas (roughly the equivalent of municipalities in other countries), each with a directly elected council, headed by a mayor. Councillors and mayors serve for three years. There are 54 council areas on the main island of Malta; the other seven are on Gozo. In all, 11 communities traditionally have the status of cities—the other 57 localities are called either towns or villages—but all the councils have exactly the same powers. Malta is also divided into six districts, which have no administrative function other than being statistical and planning units.

C. CARPENTER

The Grandmaster's Palace in Valletta is the seat of the House of Representatives of Malta.

MODERN HISTORY

Malta came under British rule in 1800 and remained a British possession until 1964, when independence was obtained. The republic, established in 1974, has been characterized by a political divide between the nation's two main parties, the Nationalists and the Labour Party.

Malta's modern history may be said to start in 1798, when the (Catholic) Order of Saint John, often called the Knights of Malta, was ousted from Malta. The religious order had ruled Malta since 1530. Conscious of Malta's strategic value, with its centrally located, excellent, natural deepwater harbors, French general (later emperor) Napoléon Bonaparte (1769–1821) expelled the Knights of Malta and took the islands on his way to Egypt in June 1798.

BRITISH RULE

French rule introduced revolutionary ideas to a conservative society. In September 1798, the Maltese rose in a popular insurrection against the radical French regime, capturing the citadels of Malta (and the smaller island of Gozo), together with all the towns and villages. The French were subsequently confined to the fortified cities in and around the national capital, Valletta, along Grand Harbour. With the help of a British naval blockade, the Maltese forced the French to surrender in 1800. Great Britain, which the Maltese legislature (the Congresso Popolare) had called in as a protector, did not restore the Knights of Malta, as the Maltese had hoped. The Maltese insurgents were disarmed, and some were compensated for their losses. However, the British, unlike the French, maintained generally friendly relations with the influential Roman Catholic hierarchy in Malta. The Congress of Vienna (1814), the international conference after the Napoleonic Wars, confirmed Malta as a British colonial possession.

British colonial rule denied the Maltese any constitutional representation for some six decades. Great Britain's colonial presence furthered naval and maritime interests in Malta, neglecting agriculture and bringing about a population shift from the countryside to the towns. This move gradually concentrated population in the harbor area, especially in and around the growing naval dockyards, but, under British rule, development in Malta was uneven in the long term, leading to a widespread emigration.

In the 1870s and 1880s, after the unification of Italy (1859–1870), resentment and resistance to British rule increased, owing to the promotion of Anglicization as British public policy. This policy was intended to eradicate the Italian linguistic, literary, educational, legal, ecclesiastical, and even commercial heritage that had shaped Maltese life since the early Middle Ages. The Maltese response was the emergence of the Nationalist Party (PN), which advocated a Catholic, Latin, Mediterranean vision of Malta, rather than the Protestant, Anglo-Saxon one desired by the British. PN pressure gained representative government for Malta in 1887 and responsible government in 1921.

Nevertheless, Anglo-Maltese bonds eventually grew, especially during World War II (1939–1945), when Malta was bombed by the German and Italian air forces and its harbor cities were severely damaged. Allied naval convoys relieved Malta from starvation. In 1942, the Maltese were collectively awarded the George Cross, the highest British civilian order for gallantry. In postwar Malta, a second major political party, the secular, left-wing Malta Labour Party (MLP), had grown strong. In 1956, the MLP administration of Dominic Mintoff (born 1916; in office as prime minister of Malta 1955–1958 and 1971–1984) held a referendum, proposing Malta's integration with Great Britain. The proposal attracted much support, but the project fell apart on the opposition of PN, which preferred independence and opposed any measure that it believed would weaken Malta's Catholic identity. An impasse was reached, and the British imposed direct rule in 1958. With the option of integration removed, most Maltese favored independence.

INDEPENDENCE

Self-government was restored in 1962, and Malta proceeded to independence in 1964, under the PN government of George Borg Olivier (1911–1980; in office 1950–1955 and 1962–1971). Initially, Malta retained some defense and financial arrangements with the former colonial power. In 1971, Mintoff's MLP returned to power and sought to end the British military presence in Malta. He reached an agreement with the British for an annual payment for the base but, in 1979, the agreement was not renewed and relations with the British reached a low ebb. Mintoff established a republic in 1974 and fostered close relations with the radical governments of Libya and Algeria. When a maritime border dispute soured relations with Libya, Mintoff concluded a pact with Italy, guaranteeing Maltese neutrality.

Since then, power has transferred from the MLP to the PN and back again at various legislative elections. The two parties differed in their attitude toward the European Union (EU), but in May 2004, Malta became a member state of the EU, under PN leader Lawrence Gonzi (born 1953; in office since 2004). Malta subsequently adopted the euro (the EU common currency) in 2008.

H. FRENDO

CULTURAL EXPRESSION

Despite its small size and limited population, Malta has developed a distinctive cultural character rooted in its own language and literature, music and song, and art and design.

Maltese culture mixes elements of several different artistic and literary expressions. The island shares in the general Mediterranean culture of the region, blending Italian influences (Malta was part of the kingdom of Sicily from 1090 through 1530) with Arab culture (Arabs ruled Malta from 870 CE through 1090). A long period of rule by a (Catholic) religious order, the Order of Saint John (or the Knights of Malta), also left a strong cultural imprint, as did the British colonial period from 1800 through 1964.

In modern times, Maltese, one of the nation's two official languages, is the first language of 86 percent of Maltese and is understood by 98 percent. English, the other official language, is the first language of 12 percent of the population and is understood by 76 percent. Some 2 percent of the population are Italian speakers. The Maltese language is the only Semitic language written in the Latin or Roman script. The language derives from the Arab dialect that evolved in Sicily, when that island was under Arab rule from the ninth century CE through the eleventh century. This dialect is overlaid by Italian vocabulary, with the addition of English words in the nineteenth and twentieth centuries.

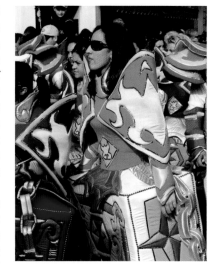

The Valetta Carnival is held annually in February.

LITERATURE

The Maltese sense of belonging has long inspired a creative expression among the islanders. Maltese geographer Giovanni Myriti (1536–c. 1590), wrote of Malta as "my dearest homeland." In 1647, Maltese noble Giovanni Francesco Abela (1582–1665) wrote a four-volume history of Malta, *Descrittione di Malta*, translated into Latin and revised in the eighteenth century. These and other writers worked in Italian or Latin, then the literary languages of Malta.

Maltese, the spoken vernacular, was unique to the islands and was not understood by outsiders. Pietro Caxaro (died 1485) wrote in Maltese, in 1475 composing the first known poem in the language, a love poem and lament, "Cantilena." By the second half of the eighteenth century, an erudite Maltese linguist, Michel-Antonio Vassalli (died 1829), realized the importance of the language and campaigned for its recognition. Vassalli compiled a grammar and lexicon of the language, which he believed should be taught. Now held to be the father of the Maltese language, he

promoted Maltese as a national language that was a reflection of the individuality of the Maltese people and a vehicle of their culture.

Slowly, a Maltese-language literature came into being, succeeding Italian as the main language of literary and cultural expression. This process was helped by the official British colonial policy in Malta in the nineteenth century of eradicating Italian cultural influences from the islands. The first literary novel in Maltese was *Inez Farrug* (1889) by Anton Manwel Caruana (1838–1937). Maltese became a vehicle for poetry, with the works of outstanding lyrical poets such as Ruzar Briffa (1906–1963), Karmenu Vassallo (1913–1987), and Dun Karm Psaila (1871–1961), who is considered to be the national poet and was the author of the poem that became the Maltese national anthem.

ART AND ARCHITECTURE

In the past, most aspiring Maltese painters and sculptors furthered their education in academies in Rome. Among them, baroque sculptor Melchiorre Cafà (1636–1667) left a number of outstanding statues and terra-cottas from his brief career in Rome. Cafà died at a young age from a work-related accident.

The greatest Maltese nineteenth-century artists were probably Giuseppe Calì (1846–1930), who painted mainly religious works, and Lazzaro Pisani (1854–1932), whose work included sacred art and portraiture. Other prominent Maltese artists include Edward Caruana Dingli (1876–1950), his brother Robert (1882–1940), and Gianni Vella (1885–1977). In sculpture, Antonio Sciortino (1879–1947), for many years director of the British Academy of Arts in Rome, excelled at art nouveau and futuristic representations, such as his famous *Wild Horses* and *Les Gavroches*. Other distinguished modern painters and sculptors have included Anton Inglott (1915–1945); Willie Apap (1918–1970); Emvin Cremona (1919–1987); his son Marco (born 1951), who combines painting and sculpture in his works; and Joseph Kalleya (1898–1998), an expressionist.

Independence in 1964 led to a cultural rebirth in all fields, not just in the visual arts but also in the writing of national history, and in folk and pop music. Bolder, inquisitive, experimental styles and media, collages, nudes, local characteristics, a less literal spirituality, and ceramics, were incorporated into the works of artists such as Antoine Camilleri (1922–2005), known for his innovative incised clay paintings; Esprit Barthet (1919–1999); and the abstract artist Alfred Chircop (born 1933). In modern times, decorative arts have also experienced a renaissance, particularly lace making and silver and gold filigree.

The sixteenth-century Fort San Angelo in Birgu was the first Maltese fortification built by the Knights of Malta.

In architecture, the first well-known Maltese architect was Girolamo Cassar (c. 1520–c. 1590), who was architect to the Order of Saint John (the Knights of Malta). He designed many of the baroque public buildings of the new city of Valletta, including churches and the grand master's palace. In the nineteenth century, the baroque style still influenced leading Maltese figures such as Nicola Zammit (1819–1899) and Emmanuele Luigi Galizia (1830–1906), who also experimented with Gothic styles. Like them, twentieth-century architects were much involved in church façades and decorations. Richard England (born 1937) blends vernacular Maltese styles with modernism. His innovative work includes Malta's national bank building and the twenty-first-century Saint James Centre for Creativity, both in Valletta, the Maltese national capital.

MUSIC AND PERFORMING ARTS

A popular folk theater (known as *teatrin*) emerged; by the twentieth century, it had evolved into a professional theater and dramatic art, playing to full houses at the eighteenth-century Manoel Theatre in Valletta. The best-known Maltese playwright is Francis Ebejer (1925–1993).

In music and composition, Malta had a long history from the *maestri di cappella* (chapel masters) in the Middle Ages to composer of operas Nicolò Isouard (1773–1818), who worked in Paris and Russia, and Paolino Vassallo (1856–1923), who was one of the first modern Maltese composers to move away from Italian influences. Malta has a tradition of musical families who have greatly contributed to the nation's art; the Nani and Bugeja families were much involved in philharmonic societies and parish church music.

Maltese singers have pursued international careers, for example the tenor Joseph Calleja (born 1978). Soprano Miriam Gauci (born 1958) has sung Italian opera in leading theaters around the world. Tenor Oreste Chircop (1923–1998) gained a reputation outside Malta, while singer and actor Joseph Calleia (1897–1975) acted on Broadway and in Hollywood movies. Composer Jesmond Grixti (born 1969), now based in Australia, writes chamber and orchestral music, while Charles Camilleri (1931–2009) wrote music based on Maltese traditions, including orchestrated folk songs and piano concertos.

Music groups in Malta, such as the Gukaturi and Etnika, have become more sophisticated, focusing on classical or folk genres. Impromptu repartee and storytelling song known as *ghana*, a symbolic, evocative variant of Mediterranean guitar-accompanied camaraderie, has survived, even in the Maltese diaspora (Maltese living abroad), especially in Australia. Maltese band clubs have their origin in the musicians who played in religious parades in the Middle Ages. This tradition broadened in the nineteenth century, when the example of British military bands—and the arrival of Italian musicians on the islands—boosted the popularity of bands in village festivities. Nearly every town and village now has a band club, and friendly rivalry between bands promotes competition.

FESTIVALS AND CEREMONIES

Most Maltese public holidays celebrate either religious festivals or events in the nation's history. Religious holidays include the feast of Saint Paul's shipwreck on Malta (February 10), Saint Joseph's Day (March 19), Good Friday, Saint Peter and Saint Paul's Day (June 29), Assumption Day (celebrated in Malta on August 14 instead of August 15), Our Lady of Victories (September 8), the Immaculate Conception (December 8), and Christmas Day. National Day, Independence Day, is September 21, marking independence in 1964, while Republic Day (December 13) commemorates the establishment of the republic ten years later. Sette Giurno (June 7) is the anniversary of a riot in 1919 when the British raised the price of bread and four Maltese were killed by British forces. Freedom Day (March 31) commemorates the final withdrawal of British troops from Malta in 1979. Labor Day (May 1) and New Year's Day are also public holidays.

FOOD AND DRINK

Initially, the presence of the British garrison—and subsequently the advent of tourism— motivated local production of beers, such as Blue Label, and the herb-based soft drink called Kinnie. In modern times, catering schools in Malta, encouraged by tourism, have given attention to typical Maltese dishes such as *imqarrun il-forn* (baked macaroni) or *soppa taí l-armla* (literally, "widow's soup") with the small Maltese goat cheese *gbejna* in it. Wine production by vintners such as Marsovin has shown great improvement in quality and choice; some wines are now exported. Maltese olive oil is judged to be of superior quality, and, in modern times, other local products, such as Maltese honey, syrups, and liqueurs, are used in local cuisine and are exported. Maltese bakers excel in the production of fresh crunchy loaves known as *hobz tal-Malt*. A rabbit stew, *fenkata*, is the national dish, perhaps challenged by spaghetti.

H. FRENDO

DAILY LIFE

Maltese life has been shaped by traditional Mediterranean patriarchal society, Roman Catholicism, and the influence of the British in colonial times.

Malta's remarkably homogenous society is nearly 100 percent European. The overwhelming majority of the population is Maltese, with small British expatriate and Italian and other communities. However, in the early twenty-first century, after Malta joined the European Union (EU) in 2004, illegal immigrants from sub-Saharan Africa, many of whom claim asylum on arrival, have come to Malta by small boats from North Africa, seeking to enter Europe.

RELIGION AND SOCIETY

Religion is not as all-important as it used to be, but various customs and habits linked to it continue to figure prominently in the calendar and daily life. Malta is still a largely Catholic country, where 98 percent of the population is Roman Catholic, with some two-thirds practicing—one of the highest rates in Europe. The modern illegal immigrants from Africa are mainly Muslims.

Maltese daily life is still somewhat traditional, with set norms of behavior more or less in conformity with an overarching Catholic morality. The work ethic is generally valued and, as practically everyone is Catholic, Maltese society is homogenous in spite of its rather mixed Mediterranean origins, even though there is a small Maltese nobility, with hereditary titles.

The family, nuclear and extended, remains a core value in daily life, although greater social mobility, work opportunities, and travel, not least among women, have seen more elderly people going to old-age homes instead of continuing to live with, or otherwise to be cared for by their children. Contacts with family members in the diaspora (Maltese living abroad), mainly in Australia and Great Britain, often remain close. Most Maltese couples marry in church; baptisms, engagements, and funerals continue to take a religious form. Burial rather than cremation is the norm. Divorce and abortion remain illegal, but the number of civil marriages has been increasing, as have separations, single parenthood, and children born out of wedlock.

The church and town or village are the center of social life, and the *festa* (saint's feast day), celebrated by a parade, band performances, races, and other events, is linked to a patron saint. A competitive spirit is part of Maltese life, between neighboring communities, band clubs, or the soccer teams of the

St. John's Cathedral in Valletta.

towns of the Valletta agglomeration and also between the supporters of the two main Maltese political parties.

Women's rights were relatively slow to be won in Malta. Women did not gain the vote until 1947 and subsequently did not play a major role in national politics, although Agatha Barbara (1923–2002) occupied the largely ceremonial presidency from 1982 to 1987. The National Council of Women of Malta monitors women's rights, and, although equality is enshrined in law, a gender pay differential is evident, and there are few women in higher executive roles in Malta.

HEALTH, WELFARE, AND EDUCATION

Health services are provided by the state and are generally free, funded by taxation and a compulsory national insurance system. However, except for emergency treatments, dentistry must be paid for, and there are charges for drugs, except for those on low incomes. Free health care has been a tradition in Malta since the time of the Knights of Malta or Knights Hospitallers, the religious order that ruled Malta from 1530 to 1798 and whose original (and modern) role was health care. A medical school was founded at the university in the eighteenth century, and the tradition in health care continues in the state-of-the-art general hospital, Mater Dei, completed in 2008.

Education is compulsory from age 5 to 16, and schooling is provided by state, private, and church sectors. Students attend primary schools from age 5 to 11, and secondary schools from 11 to 18. Education in Malta is based upon the British model, but public education, including the establishment of the University of Malta (founded 1769), predated British rule (1800–1964). The number of students at the university greatly increased from the 1980s, and tertiary courses are also offered by the Malta Polytechnic.

Pensions are mainly funded through the national insurance system. Benefits include old-age, widows', and orphans' pensions, and unemployment benefits. Malta suffers a housing shortage due to rising prices because of competition for accommodations from foreign expatriate residents. Consequently, Maltese banks increasingly loan money to younger couples for housing.

H. FRENDO

Valletta

Valletta, the national capital of Malta, occupies a peninsula beside Grand Harbour, the finest natural harbor in the central Mediterranean.

The city of Valletta occupies a restricted site, Mount Sceberras, on a narrow peninsula, with Grand Harbour to the east and the smaller Marsamxett Harbour to the west. It had a population, within the city limits, of only 6,000 in 2007. However, in the same year, the metropolitan area (comprising the statistical districts of Southern Harbour and Northern Harbour) had a population of 203,000 and included the virtually contiguous towns of Birkirkara (with a population of 22,000), Qormi (17,000), Zabbar (15,000), Sliema (14,000), Fgura (11,000), and Hamrun (10,000).

VALLETTA IN HISTORY

In historic times, the principal settlements on Malta were inland, on defensive sites away from the threats of invaders by sea. Following the Siege of Malta (1565), when the island was under a protracted blockade by the Ottoman Turks, a settlement was founded on Mount Scebarras in 1566 to create a strongly fortified site at the western entrance to Grand Harbour. At the time, the island was ruled by the sovereign Catholic Order of Saint John (later known as the Knights of Malta), who had been ceded Malta in 1530 by Holy Roman emperor Charles V (1500–1558; reigned as Charles I of Spain, 1516–1556, and Charles V, Holy Roman emperor, 1519–1555). The new city was named for the knights' prince and grand master, Jean Parisot de la Valette (c. 1494–1568; reigned as ruler of Malta 1557–1568). Valletta became capital of Malta in 1570.

Valletta was developed by the knights, who constructed fortifications and fine baroque churches and palaces. In 1798, a French invasion ousted the knights from Malta but, in 1800, a British invasion, following a revolt by the Maltese, drove the French from Valletta and the island. The city remained under British rule until 1964, when Malta became independent, and Valletta became the capital of a sovereign state. Through the nineteenth and early twentieth centuries, the British developed Valletta as a strategic location, and Grand Harbour was an important base for the British navy. Because of its strategic value, the city and harbor were repeatedly bombed by German and Italian forces in World War II (1939–1945), and the island was effectively besieged until the Italian fleet surrendered in the harbor in 1943.

MODERN VALLETTA

Despite damage during World War II, Valletta still has the outward appearance of a baroque city. Its skyline is dominated by the (modern) dome of baroque Saint Francis of Assisi Church, the towers of Saint John's cathedral, and fortifications, including Fort Saint Elmo. Saint John's, which was formerly the church of the Knights of Malta, is outwardly austere, but its rich interior has a painted ceiling, ornate chapels, and many art treasures. The palaces constructed by the knights survive and are now public buildings. The late sixteenth-century Palace of the Grand Masters is now the official residence of the president of Malta and also houses the national legislature as well as armory of the knights. Knights of different nationalities had their own palaces, called *auberges*. The Aragón and Bavarian *auberges* and three other palaces are government ministries, while the Castile and León Auberge houses the offices of the prime minister. The Provence Auberge is the National Museum. Sixteenth-century Fort Saint Elmo commands the entrance to the harbor. Other public buildings include the sixteenth-century University of Malta, the eighteenth-century National Library, the National Museum of Fine Arts (housed in a sixteenth-century palace), and Manoel Theatre. The entire baroque district and the fortifications have been designated a UNESCO World Heritage site. The city walls, which average 330 feet (100 m) high, are intact.

The city has few industries and is mainly a service center, catering to national government and tourists. It is also an important retail center. The harbor, which was a British naval dockyard in colonial times, is now a commercial dock that services and repairs ships. Valletta remains the commercial and administrative center of Malta, but people and industry have moved into other parts of the urban area, and the area within the Valletta city limits, which is congested and operates vehicular access restrictions, has a declining population. Within the agglomeration, Birkirkara is the largest commercial and residential center, and Sliema is a coastal resort.

C. CARPENTER

The Grand Harbour is a natural harbor that has been fortified and used for millennia.

ECONOMY

Malta is an example of a nation whose economic development owes more to location than resources. The small nation relies on foreign trade and services (including tourism) to pay for imports.

With a population of only 410,000 (2007 official estimate), Malta has too small an internal market to have greatly developed industrially. A dry climate and relatively poor soils have also impeded agriculture. Consequently, the country has used its climate and its strategic location, in the middle of the Mediterranean Sea, as the mainstays of its economy.

ECONOMIC CHALLENGES

Under British rule after 1800, Malta came to depend largely on British imperial trade, with Valletta and the towns around Grand Harbour attracting much entrepôt trade. The British navy used the berthing facilities offered by Malta, which became a refueling and service base; from the 1850s, naval dockyards serving the British Mediterranean fleet became the single largest employer. As a result, the population shifted from country to town. Harbor-related activities, supported by Malta's location along the sea route to British India as well as its proximity to both Europe and Africa, came to dominate the economy.

Malta had a dependent economy, which was subject to varying British needs. For example, the move of much of the British fleet to the North Sea in World War I (1914–1918) brought an economic slump to Malta. There was hardly any industrial or manufacturing base; even agricultural production declined. At the same time, the Maltese population increased, more than doubling—from 128,000 to 313,000—between 1851 and 1951. The country's economy was unable to provide enough employment for its people and, consequently, Maltese migrated around the Mediterranean basin, and, especially in the 1950s and 1960s, to Great Britain and Australia.

The Maltese economy began to assume a more structured form in the 1950s, when economic plans envisioned diversification from dependence on the dockyards and services for British forces. At the time, Great Britain was reducing its imperial commitments, as colonies gained independence. Consequently, a program was begun to make the dockyard a commercial enterprise rather than a naval one. Nevertheless, the activities of the dockyard decreased, resulting in considerable unemployment and more emigration.

The new goals of diversification were tourism, industry, and agriculture. Widespread opposition to independence from Great Britain in the early 1960s was largely generated by a fear that Malta would be unable to survive on its own. However, defense and financial agreements accompanied independence in 1964, and the creation of new jobs, through the development of tourism and industry, led to a building boom at the same time that British forces finally withdrew in 1979.

Modern economic growth has been promoted by the Central Bank, the Ministry for Tourism and Culture, and the Malta Development Corporation. The government introduced five- and seven-year plans, made loans and grants available to establish industrial facilities, and encouraged foreign investment. These

STANDARD OF LIVING

In 2007, GDP per capita in Malta was $53,400, adjusted for purchasing power parity (PPP), a formula that allows comparison between living standards in different countries. This GDP figure is one of the highest in the Mediterranean region. No figure is published for the number of people living below the poverty line, although poverty is limited.

EMPLOYMENT IN MALTA

Sector	Percentage of labor force
Agriculture and forestry	3 percent
Industry	22 percent
Services	75 percent

Source: Maltese Government 2005

In 2007, 6.3 percent of the labor force was unemployed.

MALTA'S GDP

The gross domestic product (GDP) of Malta was $21.9 billion in 2007. This figure is adjusted for purchasing power parity (PPP), an exchange rate at which goods in one country cost the same as goods in another.

MAIN CONTRIBUTORS TO THE MALTESE GDP

Agriculture	2.7 percent
Industry	22.3 percent
Services	75 percent

Source: Maltese Government 2003

new enterprises, initially mainly textile factories, were not always successful. After 1971, under the Labour Party government, some facilities were nationalized, and the least successful were eventually closed.

The emphasis changed with time and, from 1984–1987, under the National Party government, the manufacture of components was promoted, and value-added manufacture, computer parts, and pharmaceuticals became priorities. Malta benefited from its English-speaking workforce and its good sea and air transportation links with locations around the Mediterranean and in western Europe.

Tourism grew from the 1960s, as cheap air travel developed. Malta initially attracted mainly British visitors, and tourism soon became the nation's largest industry. Membership in the European Union (EU) from 2004 bolstered the economy and, in 2008, Malta adopted the euro, the EU common currency. The nation has successfully adapted to changing economic circumstances and, in 2008, had an economic growth rate of around 4 percent, higher than the EU average. One consequence of EU membership has been an influx of illegal immigrants from sub-Saharan Africa, coming to Malta on small boats from the North African coast. Wanting to enter the EU through Malta, many immigrants seek asylum upon arrival but find themselves unable to move on because of the EU's Dublin Convention, under which illegal immigrants may only seek asylum in the first EU nation they enter and may not move on or be moved on.

NATURAL RESOURCES AND AGRICULTURE

Malta has few natural resources except its climate and its location. Limestone, used in the building industry, is still quarried and, historically, was used in the construction of the nation's churches, public buildings, and defenses.

Agriculture in Malta is restricted by lack of surface water and poor soils, and, under British rule, farming was neglected. Consequently, around 80 percent of Malta's food has to be imported. Most farms are small and family-run, often by older or female family members and frequently on a part-time basis. Fields are small, often terraces on slopes; this feature, along with the small-scale nature of Maltese farming, deters mechanization. In modern times, investment in horticulture—producing cut flowers, seeds, and plants for export—has led to some diversification, but the main crops remain wheat, vegetables, and citrus fruits as well as fodder crops for cattle. Pigs, goats, sheep, and poultry are also raised. Fishing is largely small-scale, and development is held back by the relatively unproductive waters surrounding Malta. Family-run boats are typical, and the industry is partly seasonal.

INDUSTRY AND SERVICES

The dockyards, upon which the Maltese economy once depended, now provide commercial services, repair, and refurbishment, as well as some shipbuilding. Government encouragement since the 1960s

and 1970s led to the widening of Malta's industrial base. The first wave of investment by multinationals brought limited success, mainly with textile firms. An emphasis on valued-added manufacture from the late 1980s has brought more lasting results, and the principal industrial interests are now pharmaceuticals, computer parts (such as microchips), information technology–related industries, cosmetics, detergents, toys, and other consumer goods. Finished products or components tend to be light or small, allowing export by air as well as by sea. Traditional industries, such as food processing, have expanded, and decorative arts, such as lace, ceramics, silverwork, and glass, flourish.

The service sector is dominated by tourism. Malta caters to northern European visitors who enjoy the warm climate, particularly in winter, when many seniors come to Malta for extended stays. Many British tourists are attracted by a Mediterranean way of life that has been modified by (familiar) British influences, including the use of the English language. A number of English-language schools have been established on Malta, catering to students from the central Mediterranean region. Malta currently receives around 1.2 million foreign tourists a year, and it is thought that the industry may not be able to sustain much more expansion, as most of the best coastal locations have been developed and it would be difficult for the infrastructure to cater to larger numbers. Other service industries include administration and retail as well as commerce, the transshipment of goods, and the provision of facilities for oil corporations.

TRADE AND TRANSPORTATION

Malta has a substantial balance of trade deficit, importing goods and services worth $4.11 billion (2007 figure) while exporting goods and services worth $3.28 billion. Value-added goods and machinery are the main exports. In 2006, the main customers of Maltese exports were France (which took 15 percent of Malta's exports), Singapore (13 percent), the United States (13 percent), Germany (13 percent), Great Britain (10 percent), Japan, and China including Hong Kong. The main imports into Malta are machinery and transportation equipment, semi-manufactured goods, and food. In 2006, the principal suppliers of goods and services to Malta were Italy (28 percent), Great Britain (11 percent), France (9 percent), Germany (8 percent), Singapore, and the United States.

The Maltese road network covers 1,384 miles (2,227 km) of highways, of which 1,251 miles (2,014 km) are paved. Bus routes radiate across Malta from Valletta, and most households have a car. The limited railroad system closed in 1931. Ferries connect Malta with its smaller island, Gozo, and with Sicily. There is one airport, Luqa, which is the base of the national airline, Air Malta. Air services connect Malta with many European destinations as well as with North Africa and western Asia. In 2006, there were more than 202,000 main telephone lines in Malta. In the same year, 347,000 Maltese had mobile cellular phones and more than 127,000 Maltese had Internet access.

H. FRENDO

851

San Marino

The small state of San Marino is the world's oldest-surviving republic, claiming to have been founded in 301 CE. Saint Marinus (dates unknown) is recognized as the founder of the state, which kept its independence owing to its defensive site and inaccessibility. The constitution adopted in 1600 is still in force, and the papacy recognized San Marino's independence in 1631. When, in the mid-nineteenth century, Italy achieved unity through the acquisition of the other states of the peninsula by Sardinia-Piedmont, San Marino opted to remain separate. The republic was neutral through World War II (1939–1945), although both Axis and Allied forces entered its territory. From 1945 through 1957, San Marino had the world's first democratically elected Communist government. Much of the country is rugged, and its national capital, San Marino, is built around the triple peaks of Monte Titano, the state's highest point, but the majority of the population lives on lower ground in the north. The republic is not a member of the European Union (EU) but uses the euro, the EU currency. The economy depends upon tourism.

GEOGRAPHY

Location	Southern Europe, an enclave in central Italy
Climate	Mediterranean climate with mild winters and warm, dry summers
Area	24 sq. miles (61 sq. km)
Coastline	Landlocked
Highest point	Monte Titano 2,424 feet (739 m)
Lowest point	Torrente Ausa 180 feet (55 m)
Terrain	Rugged mountains; lower hills in the north
Natural resources	Building stone
Land use	
Arable land	16.7 percent
Permanent crops	0 percent
Other	83.3 percent

A traditional street scene in San Marino, the world's oldest republic.

Major rivers	Marano, San Marino
Major lake	None
Natural hazards	None

METROPOLITAN AREAS, 2006 POPULATION

Urban population	89 percent
Serravalle-Dogana	10,000
Borgo Maggiore	6,200
San Marino	4,400
Domagnano	3,000

Source: San Marino government estimates, 2007

NEIGHBORS AND LENGTH OF BORDERS

Italy	24 miles (39 km)

POPULATION

Population	30,800 (2007 government estimate)
Population density	1,283 per sq. mile (505 per sq. km)
Population growth	1.2 percent a year
Birthrate	9.7 births per 1,000 of the population
Death rate	8.4 deaths per 1,000 of the population
Population under age 15	16.8 percent
Population over age 65	17.2 percent
Sex ratio	109 males for 100 females
Fertility rate	1.4 children per woman
Infant mortality rate	5.4 deaths per 1,000 live births

Life expectancy at birth
Total population	81.9 years
Female	85.6 years
Male	78.4 years

ECONOMY

Currency	Euro (EUR)
Exchange rate (2008)	$1 = EUR 0.68
Gross domestic product (2004)	$850 million
GDP per capita (2004)	$34,100
Unemployment rate (2004)	3.8 percent
Population under poverty line (2001)	N/A
Exports	$1.3 billion (2004 CIA estimate)
Imports	$2.0 billion (2007 CIA estimate)

GOVERNMENT

Official country name	Most Serene Republic of San Marino
Conventional short form	San Marino
Nationality	
noun	Sammarinese
adjective	Sammarinese
Official language	Italian
Capital city	San Marino
Type of government	Republic; parliamentary democracy
Voting rights	18 years, universal
National anthem	"Inno Nazionale" (National hymn)
National day	Founding of the Republic Day, September 3 (the supposed anniversary of the foundation of San Marino in 301 CE)

TRANSPORTATION

Railroads	None
Highways	65 miles (104 km)
Airports	None

POPULATION PROFILE, 2007 ESTIMATES

Ethnic groups	
Europeans	Virtually 100 percent (96 percent Sammarinese; most of the rest are Italian)
Religions	
Roman Catholic	89 percent; up to one-half practicing
Nonreligious	9 percent
Others	2 percent
Languages	
Italian	Virtually 100 percent
Adult literacy	96 percent

FLAG

The flag of San Marino comprises two horizontal bands, from the top, white and pale blue. The state arms appear at the center, displaying a crown (to represent sovereignty) and three towers each topped by a castle, representing the castles on Monte Titano. The arms date from at least the fourteenth century.

Castello della Guaita on Monte Titano, with its panoramic view over San Marino.

MODERN HISTORY

Through the era of Italian unification in the mid-nineteenth century, San Marino—alone among the small states that had occupied much of central Italy—remained independent and did not join the new Italian kingdom. In modern times, the country has adopted a more visible role through membership in international organizations.

When the map of Europe was redrawn in 1815 by the Congress of Vienna, following the Napoleonic Wars, the independence and separate identity of San Marino was recognized. In the 1840s and 1850s, the tide of Italian nationalism and the demand for the unification of Italy grew. San Marino stood apart from this trend but gave safe refuge to a number of nationalists from other parts of Italy. As a result, when the new kingdom of Italy was formed in 1859–1861, San Marino's wish to be excluded was respected.

Government

The constitution adopted by San Marino in 1600 is still in force, the only surviving Renaissance city-republic constitution. Few major constitutional changes have since been made, apart from the extension of the vote—women were enfranchised in 1960—and the gradual evolution of a more modern executive.

The republic has a parliamentary system of government, in which power is vested in the legislature rather than the executive. The 60-member Great and General Council is elected by universal adult suffrage for five years under a system of proportional representation. The voting age is 18 years and over. The Council elects two of its members to be captains-regent, who jointly hold office as chiefs of state for a term of six months. It is usual for regents to be chosen from opposing political parties. The chiefs of state, whose role in modern times is largely ceremonial, may not serve two consecutive terms. The regents preside over a 10-member Congress of State (the equivalent of a cabinet), which is elected by the Council for five years. In modern times, the de facto head of government is the secretary of state for foreign and political affairs.

Five main political parties are represented in the Council: the (center-right) Christian Democratic Party (PDCS), the (social democratic) Party of Socialists and Democrats (PSD), the (centrist) Popular Alliance of Sammarinese Democrats (APDS), the (socialist) United Left (SU) including the Communists, and the New Socialist Party (PNS). Because no single party normally achieves a legislative majority, Sammarinese governments are always coalitions.

The country is divided into nine *castelli* (literally, "castles"), which are the equivalent of municipalities. Each has an elected council, headed by a *capitano di castello* (meaning "captain of the castle"), who is effectively the mayor of the *castello*.

Three members of the Guard of the Rock protecting an entrance to the Palazzo Pubblico, wearing their distinctive uniform.

A SEPARATE IDENTITY

Italy recognized San Marino's independence in a treaty in 1872. In the late nineteenth and early twentieth centuries, the republic was underdeveloped and, consequently, experienced high rates of emigration. San Marino declared neutrality in World War II (1939–1945), but, in 1944, retreating German forces entered San Marino, followed by Allied forces, which occupied the country for a few weeks.

After legislative elections in 1945, the Sammarinese Communist and Socialist parties formed a government, and the country became the first to have a democratically elected administration with Communist members. The two parties remained in government until 1957. In 1960, the franchise was extended to women.

In modern times, the country has enjoyed greater prosperity, largely as a result of tourism but also through the development of banking and the country's role as a tax haven. The population has considerably increased, particularly in Dogana and Serravalle, the settlements along the main road into San Marino from Italy. San Marino joined the Council of Europe in 1988 and the United Nations in 1992. In 2002, the republic concluded an agreement with the OECD (Organisation of Economic Co-operation and Development) to reform banking and taxation laws and practices to combat tax evasion by noncitizens.

C. CARPENTER

CULTURAL EXPRESSION

San Marino is Italian in language and culture, and a separate Sammarinese culture is difficult to identify.

The Sammarinese speak Italian, but, in everyday speech, words and phrases from a local dialect are still used. The population of the country is so small that a separate literary tradition has not emerged. In modern times, there are no significant Sammarinese published authors.

ARCHITECTURE

The republic does not have its own artistic styles, but local stone and tile roofs characterize many buildings. A tradition of stone carving is reflected by the relatively large number of statues in public places, and there is also a traditional ceramics industry. The towers that top the three peaks of Monte Titano, the highest point in the country, have become a national symbol. The Three Towers of San Marino are shown on the national flag. Rather than conventional castles with curtain (outer) walls lined by towers and courtyards, the Three Towers are literally single, central towers, constructed of local sandstone, with lower adjoining structures and no other prominent turrets. The oldest is eleventh-century La Guaita. Thirteenth-century La Cesta, located on the highest of Monte Titano's three summits, is the largest and most prominent of the towers, while Il Montale, on the lowest of the summits, was constructed in the fourteenth century.

MUSIC AND FESTIVALS

San Marino shares Italy's popular music but also has its own annual popular music festival, from which a number of local groups have emerged to play to a wider audience in Italy. They include Love Orchestra, described as a New Age group, and Miodio. The republic has a state-owned television station and a state-owned radio station but also receives Italian television broadcasts. The Sammarinese television station caters not only to the republic's small population but also to a much greater number of viewers in the surrounding regions of Italy.

San Marino celebrates 18 public holidays, more than most European countries. Religious holidays include Epiphany (January 6), Corpus Christi (a Catholic feast in early summer in honor of the Eucharist), Assumption Day (August 15), All Saints' Day (November 1), All Souls' Day (November 2), the Immaculate Conception (December 8), and three days at Christmas. New Year's Day and Labor Day (May 1) are also public holidays, as are April 1 and October 1, the days on which the captains-regent, the joint chiefs of state of San Marino, are installed for their term of office of six months. The National Day is September 3, Founding of the Republic Day, the traditional anniversary of the foundation of San Marino in 301 CE—there is, however, no historical evidence to confirm this date. Other holidays mark events in the history of San Marino. March 25 celebrates the establishment of the present democracy; February 5 marks the anniversary of the end of the Alberoni Occupation (1739–1740), when San Marino was occupied by forces of the Papal States. July 28 commemorates the end of Fascist rule in neighboring Italy in 1943.

SPORTS

The country competes in the Olympic Games and in international soccer in Europe. Soccer is the most popular sport, and the republic has a 15-team national league. However, those soccer players who become professionals compete in foreign leagues. Staging home games at the Stadio Olimpico in Serravalle, San Marino has one of the least successful records of any national soccer team. As of mid-2008, the national team, which first competed internationally in 1986, had won only one game, tied two, and suffered more than 70 defeats.

From 1981 through 2006, San Marino gave its name to a Formula One motor racing grand prix, but the race was held in Imola, in Italy, and not in the republic. Motor sports are popular in San Marino, and the Sammarinese motorcyclist Manuel Poggiali (born 1983) won the 125cc world championship in 2001 and the 250cc world championship in 2003.

FOOD AND DRINK

Although Sammarinese cuisine is basically the same as that of Italy, there are several local specialties. *La torta di tre monti* (cake of the three mountains) is a layered wafer cake that is covered in chocolate and shaped to represent the Three Towers of Monte Titano. *Bustrengo* is a local cake with raisins. Stewed cherries, cooked in red wine and served on bread, is a favorite dish. Other local dishes include *fagioli con le cotiche*, a soup of bacon and beans that is traditionally served at Christmas, and *nidi di rondine*, a baked pasta dish with beef and smoked ham, covered with cheese and tomatoes.

C. CARPENTER

DAILY LIFE

San Marino has a welfare state providing free health care and contributory pensions and other benefits, but the costs of provision are rapidly rising as the population ages.

The population of San Marino is remarkably homogenous. Almost 100 percent of the population are European, and 98 percent are Sammarinese. Most of the remaining 2 percent are Italian. However, nonresidents play a major role in the country: some 45 percent of the workforce commutes daily into San Marino from Italy.

RELIGION AND FAMILY

There is no official religion in San Marino, but some 89 percent of the population is recorded as Roman Catholic, with up to one-half practicing. Major services are held in the basilica in the city of San Marino, but the country does not have its own bishop and is included in the Italian diocese of San Marino and Montefeltro, which is centered in the Italian town of Pennabilli.

Social divisions in San Marino are fewer than in most larger European countries. Class is not a major factor. The family is the center of social interaction but, in modern times, Sammarinese families tend to be small: the fertility rate is 1.4 children per woman. Nuclear families (parents and their children) are now more significant in family relationships than extended families, but links with cousins and wider families are maintained, including with the 16,000 or more Sammarinese who work and live abroad. In modern times, the law ensures equal rights for women, but a woman did not become captain-regent, one of the two joint chiefs of state of San Marino, until 1981.

HEALTH AND WELFARE

San Marino has a comprehensive welfare and public health system funded through employer and employee contributions and by the state. These services are run by the Institute for Health and Social Security (ISS). Health care is provided by the state hospital, pharmacies, and general practitioners, where consultations, treatments, and medicines are free. Sammarinese must go to hospitals in Italy for certain specialized treatments, but the general standard of health care in San Marino is consistently measured by international surveys to be among the highest in Europe.

The ISS provides a generous state pension, and employee contributions are less than one-fifth of those from employers. Until 2002, when the retirement age was raised to 65, workers could draw a pension from age 60. However, the problem of a rising pension deficit, as life expectancy increased, led to reforms. The ISS also provides maternity, workers' injury, survivors', disability, unemployment, and other payments.

The City of San Marino

The city of San Marino, the national capital of San Marino, had a population of 4,400 in 2007, making it the third-largest city in the republic. San Marino clusters around the triple peaks of Monte Titano, the country's highest peak, which rises to 2,424 feet (739 m). Legend tells that the city was founded in 301 CE by Saint Marinus (dates unknown) and other Christian refugees fleeing persecution. The republic was initially limited to the city but, gradually, eight other towns and villages were included in San Marino.

In modern times, tourism dominates the economy of the city, and many shops cater to tourists. Some 3 million visitors, the overwhelming majority Italian, visit the city each year to see the famous Three Towers of Monte Titano, three medieval castles that top the peaks of the mountain. Extensive views across the republic and toward the Italian coast can be enjoyed from the capital, which also has historic public buildings, including the basilica, the Palazzo dei Capitano (the official residence of the captains-regent, the joint chiefs of state), public squares, and the Palazzo Pubblico, the late-nineteenth-century, castellated government building, which overlooks much of the city.

EDUCATION

Schooling is compulsory from age 5 through 16. Free day care and nursery education are provided for children under the age of 5. The educational system closely follows that of Italy. After primary education, students opt for one of two secondary (high school) routes, either academic or broadly vocational. Two years of additional education from age 16 through 18 are optional. A high school diploma, obtained at age 18 on successful completion of secondary education, gives access to Italian universities. All students who wished to follow a higher education course previously had to go to Italy but, in 1988, a small university opened in San Marino, although it offers only a limited range of courses.

C. CARPENTER

ECONOMY

The republic of San Marino has a high standard of living, based on tourism and other services. The country once experienced emigration but now has near full employment.

San Marino once relied upon stone quarrying and agriculture and, until the second half of the twentieth century, the economy was underdeveloped. As a result, emigration was common, and many Sammarinese settled in northern Italy, eastern France, and Argentina. In modern times, the country has a developed economy, a high standard of living, and a large service sector, which requires a greater workforce than the republic can supply. Consequently, around 45 percent of the labor force commutes daily into San Marino from Italy. Providing opportunities for the most highly qualified Sammarinese is also a challenge. In the past, all Sammarinese entering higher education had to go abroad to study, and many never returned, pursuing academic and other careers, mainly in Italy. The establishment of the university in 1988 has begun to provide some similar opportunities at home.

RESOURCES, AGRICULTURE, AND INDUSTRY

San Marino has few natural resources except building stone and lime. Sandstone quarries were once extensive, but most have been worked out and now only small quantities of stone are extracted, mainly for sculpture and decorative purposes.

Until the second half of the twentieth century, agriculture was a major industry. However, as service and other industries developed, farming greatly declined in importance. Grapes are grown for wine and liqueurs. Other crops include corn, wheat, olives, and vegetables, and cattle, pigs, and poultry are raised. San Marino can no longer produce enough food for its needs, and most of the nation's food is imported from Italy. Agricultural products are used in industry, including the production of baked foods, wine, cheese, and hides. Other industries include electronic goods, clothing, ceramics, synthetic rubber, and telecommunications equipment.

SERVICES, TRADE, AND TRANSPORTATION

The service sector dominates the economy, with a growing banking sector. The state is a popular offshore banking center but, since 2002, it has enacted reforms to introduce greater transparency in banking to reduce the problem of tax avoidance by non-nationals. More than 3 million foreign visitors, mostly Italians, come to San Marino each year. Most are vacationers on day trips. Restaurants, offices selling the republic's postage stamps (a major source of revenue), and souvenir shops catering to tourists are important employers. Dogana, along the main road into San Marino from Italy, has shopping malls that sell luxury and consumer goods to visitors. Tourism now supplies 50 percent of San Marino's GDP (gross domestic product, the total value of all the goods and services produced in a country in a fixed term, usually one year).

San Marino's international trade is overwhelmingly with Italy, which supplies foodstuffs and a wide range of consumer goods (some for re-export). San Marino also imports fuels and clothing. The country's main exports are consumer goods, building stone, postage stamps, lime, wheat, wine, and ceramics.

The republic has a road network of 65 miles (104 km), all paved. San Marino has neither railroads nor, because of the terrain and lack of space, an airport. The nearest international airport is at Rimini, 10 miles (17 km) away. In 2006, 21,000 main telephone lines were in use and, in the same year, 17,500 people had mobile cellular phones, and 15,500 people had Internet access.

C. CARPENTER

STANDARD OF LIVING

In 2004, GDP per capita in San Marino was $34,100, adjusted for purchasing power parity (PPP), a formula that allows comparison between living standards in different countries. No figure is published for the number of people living below the poverty line, although poverty is virtually absent.

EMPLOYMENT IN SAN MARINO

Sector	Percentage of labor force
Agriculture and forestry	0.2 percent
Industry	40.1 percent
Services	59.7 percent

Source: Sammarinese Government 2005

In 2004, 4.1 percent of the labor force was unemployed.

SAN MARINO'S GDP

The gross domestic product (GDP) of San Marino was $850 million in 2004. This figure is adjusted for purchasing power parity (PPP). No figures are published for the contribution to GDP of the different sectors of the economy, but service industries provide the biggest share.

Vatican City

The Vatican City, or Holy See, is a sovereign enclave entirely surrounded by Rome. The seat of the papacy and of the administration of the Roman Catholic Church, the Vatican City is the successor to the Papal States, which ruled central Italy from the eighth century CE through the mid-nineteenth century. From 1274 through 1791, the Papal States also included Avignon, in southern France, where the popes resided from 1309 through 1377. Under Pope Julius II (1443–1513; reigned 1503–1513), the papal territories in Italy included Lazio, Umbria, Marche, Emilia Romagna, Benevento, and Pontecorvo, and they retained this extent until 1860, when the northern Papal States rebelled during the unification of Italy under the kingdom of Sardinia-Piedmont. In late 1860, the papal territories except Lazio (the region surrounding Rome) were annexed to the new kingdom of Italy. A French garrison remained in Rome, protecting the pope, but was withdrawn in 1870. Italian forces then entered Rome, which became the capital of Italy, and the pope retreated to the Vatican, where he considered himself to be a prisoner. Italy and the papacy did not reach an agreement until 1929, when, under the Lateran Treaties, the territorial sovereignty of the Vatican City was recognized.

GEOGRAPHY

Location	Southern Europe, an enclave within the city of Rome (Italy)
Climate	Mediterranean with mild winters and warmer dry summers
Area	0.17 sq. miles (0.44 sq. km); the Holy See also possesses extraterritorial rights to a number of churches in Rome (including the Cathedral of Saint John Lateran), the papal villa at Castelgandolfo, and the Vatican radio station at Santa Maria di Galeria, but these sites are not part of the sovereign state
Coastline	Landlocked
Highest point	Unnamed location 246 feet (75 m)
Lowest point	Unnamed location 62 feet (19 m)
Terrain	Low hill; urbanized
Natural resources	None
Land use	
Arable land	0 percent
Permanent crops	0 percent
Other	100 percent

METROPOLITAN AREAS, 2005 POPULATION

Urban population	100 percent
Vatican City	560

Source: Vatican official estimate, 2005

NEIGHBORS AND LENGTH OF BORDERS

Italy	2 miles (3.2 km)

The Sistine Chapel in Vatican City was painted by Michelangelo for Pope Julius II (1443–1513; reigned 1503–1513).

FLAG

The flag of the Vatican City has two vertical bars, gold next to the hoist (the part nearest the flagpole) and white in the fly (the part farthest from the flagpole). The papal arms, which show the papal tiara and crossed keys (silver and gold), appear in the white stripe.

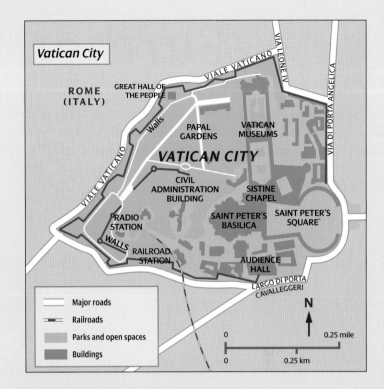

POPULATION

Population	560 (2005 official estimate); the Vatican has around 1,500 citizens of whom 560 live in Vatican territory
Population density	3,733 per sq. mile (1,273 per sq. km)

ECONOMY

Currency	Euro (EUR)
Exchange rate (2008)	$1 = EUR 0.68

GOVERNMENT

Official name	The Holy See or State of the Vatican City
Conventional short form	The Holy See or Vatican City
Nationality adjective	Vatican
Official languages	Latin and Italian
Capital city	Vatican City
Type of government	Ecclesiastical; the pope is elected in secret by a conclave of those cardinals of the Catholic Church under 80 years of age; the Vatican City is administered by a Pontifical Commission appointed by the pope and headed by the secretary of state
National anthem	"Inno e Marcia Pontificale" (Hymn and pontifical march)
National day	Coronation Day, April 24, 2005, anniversary of the coronation of Pope Benedict XVI (Joseph Ratzinger; born 1927; reigned since 2005)

Saint Peter's Square, the focal point of Vatican City.

Further Research

WORLD GEOGRAPHY

Agnew, John, Katharyne Mitchell, and Gerard Toal, eds. *A Companion to Political Geography*. Hoboken, NJ: Wiley-Blackwell, 2007.

Aguado, Edward, and James E. Burt. *Understanding Weather and Climate*. Upper Saddle River, NJ: Prentice Hall, 2009.

Clark, Audrey, ed. *Longman Dictionary of Geography: Human and Physical*. New York: Longman, 1985.

Duncan, James, Nuala Johnson, and Richard Schein. *A Companion to Cultural Geography*. Hoboken, NJ: Wiley-Blackwell, 2007.

Lomolino, Mark V., Brett R. Riddle, and James H. Brown. *Biogeography*. Sunderland, MA: Sinauer Associates, 2005.

Lutgens, Frederick K., Edward J. Tarbuck, and Dennis Tasa. *Essentials of Geology*. Upper Saddle River, NJ: Prentice Hall, 2008.

McKnight, Tom L., and Darrel Hess. *Physical Geography: A Landscape Appreciation*. Upper Saddle River, NJ: Prentice Hall, 2007.

National Geographic Family Reference Atlas. Washington, DC: National Geographic Society, 2006.

Strahler, Alan H., and Arthur Strahler. *Modern Physical Geography*. Hoboken, NJ: John Wiley and Sons, 1992.

Times Comprehensive Atlas of the World. London: HarperCollins Publishers, 2008.

REGIONAL GEOGRAPHY, HISTORY, AND CULTURAL EXPRESSION

Arnold, E. Nicholas. *Reptiles and Amphibians of Europe*. Princeton, NJ: Princeton University Press, 2003.

Blanning, T. C. W. *The Oxford Illustrated History of Modern Europe*. New York: Oxford University Press, 2001.

Blanning, T. C. W. *The Nineteenth Century: Europe, 1789–1914*. New York: Oxford University Press, 2000.

Blouet, Brian W. *The EU and Neighbors: A Geography of Europe in the Modern World*. Hoboken, NJ: John Wiley and Sons, 2007.

Bonney, Richard. *The European Dynastic States, 1494–1660*. New York: Oxford University Press, 1992.

Coldstream, Nicola. *Medieval Architecture*. New York: Oxford University Press, 2002.

Craske, Matthew. *Art in Europe, 1700–1830*. New York: Oxford University Press, 1997.

Crompton, Rosemary, Suzan Lewis, and Clare Lyonette. *Women, Men, Work, and Family in Europe*. New York: Palgrave Macmillan, 2007.

Cunliffe, Barry. *Europe between the Oceans: 9000 BC–AD 1000*. New Haven, CT: Yale University Press, 2008.

Cunliffe, Barry. *The Penguin Illustrated History of Britain and Ireland*. New York: Penguin, 2006.

Cunliffe, Barry. *The Oxford Illustrated History of Prehistoric Europe*. New York: Oxford University Press, 2001.

Favell, Adrian. *Eurostars and Eurocities: Free Movement and Mobility in Integrating Europe*. Hoboken, NJ: Wiley-Blackwell, 2008.

Gilbert, Jean. *European Festivals: Songs, Dances, and Customs from around Europe*. New York: Oxford University Press, 2000.

Goldstein, Darra, and Kathrin Merkle. *Culinary Cultures of Europe: Identity, Diversity and Dialogue*. Strasbourg: Council of Europe Publications, 2005.

Hefferman, Michael. *The Meaning of Europe: Geography and Geopolitics*. London: Hodder Arnold, 1998.

Hollister, C. Warren, and Judith Bennett. *Medieval Europe: A Short History*. Columbus, OH: McGraw-Hill, 2005.

Judt, Tony. *Postwar: A History of Europe since 1945*. New York: Penguin Books, 2006.

Kidner, Frank L., Maria Bucur, Ralph Mathisen, and Sally McKee. *Making Europe: People, Politics, and Culture*. Florence, KY: Wadsworth Publishing, 2007.

Koster, Eduard A. *The Physical Geography of Western Europe*. New York: Oxford University Press, 2005.

Macdonald, David W. *Mammals of Europe*. Princeton, NJ: Princeton University Press, 2001.

Merriman, John. *A History of Modern Europe: From the Renaissance to the Present*. New York: W. W. Norton, 2004.

Mullarney, Killian, Lars Svensson, Dan Zetterstrom, and Peter J. Grant. *Birds of Europe*. Princeton, NJ: Princeton University Press, 2000.

Parker, David. *Revolutions: The Revolutionary Tradition in the West, 1560–1991*. New York: Routledge, 2000.

Pinder, David, ed. *The New Europe: Economy, Society and Environment*. Hoboken, NJ: Wiley, 1998.

Pounds, Norman J. G. *An Historical Geography of Europe, 1500–1840*. New York: Cambridge University Press, 2009.

Rapport, Michael. *Nineteenth Century Europe*. New York: Palgrave Macmillan, 2005.

Roberts, J. M. *Europe, 1880–1945 (General History of Europe)*. Harlow: Longman Publishing Group, 2001.

Spicer, Dorothy Gladys. *Festivals of Western Europe*. Charleston, SC: BiblioBazaar, 2008.

Tutin, T. G., V. H. Heywood, N. A. Burges, and D. H. Valentine. *Flora Europaea*. New York: Cambridge University Press, 2001.

Unwin, Tim, ed. *A European Geography*. Upper Saddle River, NJ: Prentice Hall, 1998.

Wilkinson, James D. *Contemporary Europe: A History*. Upper Saddle River, NJ: Prentice Hall, 2003.

TRAVEL LITERATURE

Fodor's Italy 2009. New York: Fodor's, 2008.

Gilbert, Jonathan P. *Michelin Green Guide: Italy.* Greenville, SC: Michelin Travel Publications, 2007.

Moretti, John. *Frommer's Northern Italy: Including Venice, Milan, and the Lakes.* Hoboken, NJ: Frommers, 2008.

Renzulli, Melanie Mize. *The Unofficial Guide to Central Italy: Florence, Rome, Tuscany, and Umbria.* Hoboken, NJ: Wiley, 2008.

Steves, Rick. *Rick Steves' Italy 2009.* New York: Avalon Travel Publishing, 2008.

ITALY

Abulafia, David, ed. *Italy in the Central Middle Ages: 1000–1300.* New York: Oxford University Press, 2004.

Boatwright, Mary T., Daniel J. Gargola, and Richard J. A. Talbert. *A Brief History of the Romans.* New York: Oxford University Press, 2006.

Capatti, Alberto, Massimo Montanari, and Aine O'Healy. *Italian Cuisine: A Cultural History.* New York: Columbia University Press, 2003.

Davis, John A., ed. *Italy in the Nineteenth Century: 1796–1900.* Oxford: Oxford University Press, 2000.

Dixon, Susan M., ed. *Italian Baroque Art.* Hoboken, NJ: Wiley-Blackwell, 2008.

Duggan, Christopher. *The Force of Destiny: A History of Italy since 1796.* Boston, MA: Houghton Mifflin, 2008.

Hearder, Harry, and Jonathan Morris. *Italy: A Short History.* New York: Cambridge University Press, 2002.

Holmes, George. *The Oxford Illustrated History of Italy.* New York: Oxford University Press, 2001.

La Rocca, Cristina, ed. *Italy in the Early Middle Ages: 476–1000.* New York: Oxford University Press, 2002.

Lyttelton, Adrian, ed. *Liberal and Fascist Italy: 1900–1945.* New York: Oxford University Press, 2002.

Marino, John A., ed. *Early Modern Italy: 1550–1796.* New York: Oxford University Press, 2002.

Moliterno, Gino. *Encyclopedia of Contemporary Italian Culture.* New York: Routledge, 2003.

Najemy John M., ed. *Italy in the Age of the Renaissance: 1300–1550:* New York: Oxford University Press, 2005.

Paoletti, John T., and Gary M. Radke. *Art in Renaissance Italy.* Upper Saddle River, NJ: Prentice Hall, 2005.

MALTA

Badger, George Percy. *Historical Guide to Malta and Gozo.* Boston, MA: Adamant Media, 2005.

Bain, Carolyn. *Malta and Gozo.* London: Lonely Planet, 2007.

Crowley, Roger. *Empires of the Sea: The Siege of Malta, the Battle of Lepanto, and the Contest for the Center of the World.* London: Random House, 2008.

Holland, James. *Fortress Malta: An Island under Siege, 1940–43.* New York: Miramax, 2003.

Johnston, Shirley. *Splendor of Malta.* New York: Rizzoli, 2001.

Stephenson, Charles. *The Fortifications of Malta, 1530–1945.* New York: Osprey Publishing, 2004.

SAN MARINO

Bent, James Theodore. *A Freak of Freedom: Or the Republic of San Marino (1879).* Whitefish, MT: Kessinger Publishing, 2008.

International Business Publications. *San Marino Country Study Guide.* Washington, DC: International Business Publications, 2008.

Tucker, W. W., and Charles de Bruc. *The Republic of San Marino.* Charleston, SC: BiblioBazaar, 2008.

VATICAN CITY

Collins, Michael. *The Vatican.* New York: DK Publishing, 2008.

Duffy, Eamon. *Saints and Sinners: A History of the Popes.* New Haven, CT: Yale University Press, 2006.

Hintzen-Bohlen, Brigitte. *Rome and the Vatican City: Art and Architecture.* Madrid: H. F. Ullmann, 2008.

Vecchi, Pierluigi De, and Gianluigi Colalucci. *Michelangelo: The Vatican Frescoes.* New York: Abbeville Press, 1997.

Williams, Paul L. *The Vatican Exposed: Money, Murder, and the Mafia.* New York: Prometheus Books, 2003.

PERIODICALS AND OTHER MEDIA

California Italian Studies.
http://repositories.cdlib.org/ismrg/cisj/
Forum Italicum.
www.italianstudies.org/forum/
Journal of Modern Italian Studies.
www.tandf.co.uk/journals/routledge/1354571X.html

ELECTRONIC SOURCES

Euromonitor International: Italy.
http://www.euromonitor.com/Italy (country, market, and lifestyle information on Italy).
OECD Italy.
www.oecd.org/italy (a link for OECD reports and statistics on Italy).
Tourism in Italy.
http://www.italiantourism.com/ (Web site of the Italian Government Tourist Board).
Tourism in Malta.
http://www.visitmalta.com/main (the official Web site for tourism in Malta, Gozo, and Comino).
The World Factbook. CIA.
www.cia.gov/library/publications/the-world-factbook/index.html (for facts about Italy, Malta, and San Marino).
WWW History Central Catalogue: European History.
http://vlib.iue.it/hist-italy/Index.html (provides links to numerous topics on Italian history).

Index

WORLD AND ITS PEOPLES

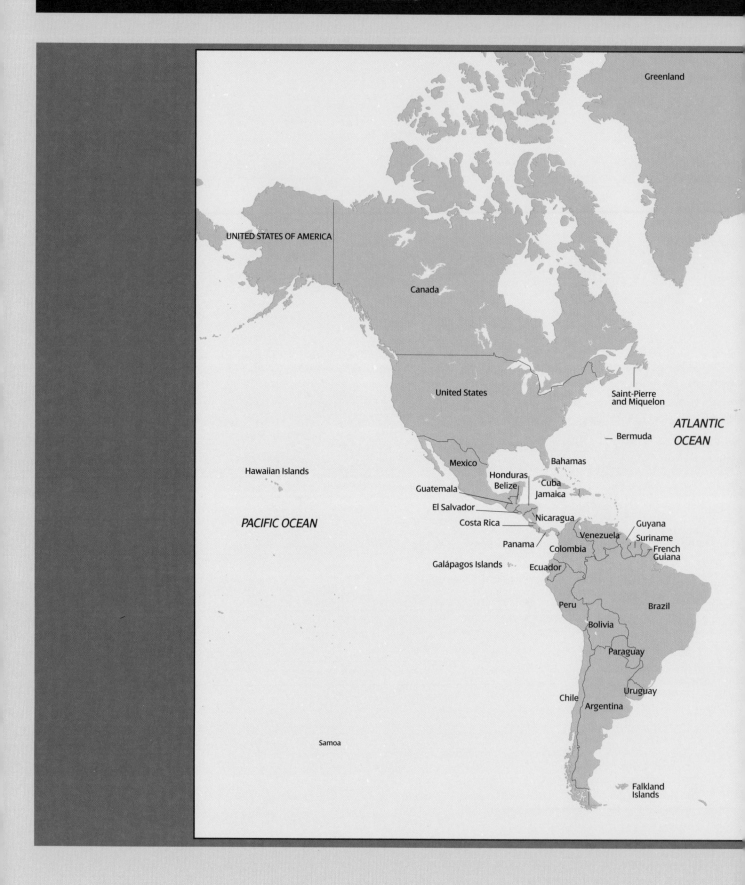

Greenland

UNITED STATES OF AMERICA

Canada

United States

Saint-Pierre and Miquelon

ATLANTIC OCEAN

Bermuda

Hawaiian Islands

Mexico

Bahamas

Honduras
Belize

Cuba
Jamaica

Guatemala

El Salvador

Costa Rica

Nicaragua

PACIFIC OCEAN

Panama

Venezuela

Guyana
Suriname
French
Guiana

Colombia

Galápagos Islands

Ecuador

Peru

Brazil

Bolivia

Paraguay

Uruguay

Chile

Argentina

Samoa

Falkland
Islands